People and Life on the Chars of South Asia

People and Life on the Chars of South Asia

Dancing with the River

Kuntala Lahiri-Dutt | Gopa Samanta

YALE UNIVERSITY PRESS NEW HAVEN & LONDON

FOUNDATION® BOOKS

FOUNDATION®
BOOKS

Foundation Books is an imprint of Cambridge University Press India Pvt. Ltd.

Cambridge House, 4381/4 Ansari Road, Daryaganj, New Delhi 110 002

www.cambridgeindia.org

This edition was published by arrangement with Yale University Press.

First South Asia edition 2014

Printed in India at Bhavish Graphics, Chennai

ISBN 978-93-82993-78-0 Hardback

This book is dedicated to our two much-beloved mothers.

From Kuntala to her mother, a third-generation tertiary-educated working woman, a beautiful, honest, and fun-loving person. I wish she had lived a few more months so she could have read this book.

From Gopa to her mother, who fought with the village headmen to send her daughters to secondary school, and who from the very beginning has supported each of her daughters' endeavors.

We want you both to know that our journey continues.

Contents

Preface

> Interposed between the sea and the plains of Bengal lies an immense archipelago of islands. . . . There are no borders here to divide fresh water from salt, river from sea. The tides reach as far as three hundred kilometers inland and every day thousands of acres of forest disappear underwater only to reemerge hours later. . . . The currents are so powerful as to reshape the islands almost daily—some days the water tears away entire promontories and peninsulas, at other times it throws up new shelter and sandbanks where there were none before.—AMITAV GHOSH (2004: 7)

By showing how human lives, land, and waters are intertwined, Amitav Ghosh draws international attention to the fascinating "borderland" landscapes of the Bengal delta. The mangroves, or the Sundarbans, literally "beautiful forest," are where land ends and sea begins, yet where the borders of land and water are imperceptible and merged. *Dancing with the River* offers glimpses into the microcosmic worlds of similar hybrid environments in South Asia. These are the *chars*—part land and part water, but neither fully land nor fully water—that rise from the shallow riverbeds in the lower Gangetic plains of deltaic Bengal. These sandy masses do not just constitute a movable feast of land and water in a certain proportion, but offer a different way of thinking about the environment. Chars exist in the real world, but they are also a metaphor for an ungovernable and borderless state of the environment. For chars, the very idea of border—environmentally, between the land and the water, and politically, between two administrative units—loses its usefulness. And as if to emphasize this point, borderless people inhabit this environment and make a living every day. This is why the existence of chars is never entirely "real" and why most of the *choruas*, the river-gypsies who live on the chars, are citizens of neither one country nor another. The nomadic chars and their wandering peoples inhabit a nonlegal, illegible, ungoverned, and ungovernable space, like many other peoples in Asia who have been, in James C. Scott's concise phrase, "extruded by coercive state-making."

A clarification is needed before we proceed any further. Throughout this book, we have been mindful of the physical unity of the Bengal delta, which was partitioned in 1947 between two political units, India and East Pakistan (now Bangladesh). Unless specifically mentioned as West Bengal, the eastern Indian state, "Bengal" in this book stands for this single geographical entity. Based on a similar reasoning, we have also held on to the older place-nomenclature (such as Calcutta, now Kolkata, and Burdwan, now Barddhaman).

Char environments are hybrid not only because human communities live on them and make a complex and diverse livelihood. They are hybrid also because this environment is neither fully land nor entirely water; it represents the fluid and complex worlds that lie within the rivers. Hybrid landscapes are thought, by D. Demeritt, among others, to provide "new metaphorical terrain" in which environmental historians and cultural geographers make more sense to one another and use metaphoric tools that "make it possible to imagine nature as both a real actor *and* a socially constructed object without reducing it to a single pole of nature/culture dualism." This book pushes the frontier of this strand of thought further to show that the commonly understood boundary between land and water is as artificial as that between nature and culture.

No strict or conventional geographical theorization can be applied to explain the diverse livelihoods of people living on the chars. The chars exist within the riverbanks as part of real rivers, coexisting with and lying next to the richest farming lands in South Asia, while remaining remote and unknown, physically difficult to access, and unencountered in the everyday lives of mainlanders. The question arises: How does one understand, explain, and interpret these lands, their environment, and resources, the people on these lands and their livelihoods? The answer is not straightforward, because of the ecological and cultural complexities of nature-human interactions in these chars. Although they are micro-scale geographical phenomena, chars pose big social-environmental challenges that defy definitions. They are part of the "vague, diffuse or unspecific, slippery, ephemeral, elusive or indistinct" world, as J. Law describes it: a world that "changes like a kaleidoscope, or doesn't really have much of a pattern at all." Chars cannot be disciplined and clarified through "methodological moralizing" that makes things clear. They inspire a transdisciplinary imagination that provides the framework for inquiry. They do not have a monolithic interpretation. The language of "context" and "contextualization" is important in explaining chars that provide the locale, the central points of reference where the river is much more than a physical entity, a presence, and a source of livelihood. Bestowed with multiple and symbolic meanings, chars help to build a sense of place and identity for the people who live on them. It is crucial to bear in mind that chars cannot be reduced to a fixed set of rules, and people's lives on chars may be different from one location to another. Hence, a transdisciplinary epistemology may provide a sufficiently robust and coherent interpretation across widely diverse situations.

A related question might be: What new insights can our modest empirical inquiry offer to the growing interdisciplinary field of cultural ecology, which has extensively debated human interactions with nature? Conventionally, many scholars had considered the physical environment as the "basis" or the "foundation" on which all human activities take place. Such a view of nature gave rise to the human-physical dichotomy in geography and created a positivist legacy that continues to divide the geographical understanding of place and space. More recently, the nature-culture dichotomy has been challenged by environmentalists, making way for our study, which takes us beyond the well-established categories of land and water. Because chars are not easily amenable to the rigid ways that land and water are treated as categories, we treat chars as hybrid landscapes where water, land, and people and their lives are intimately enmeshed.

If no such separation is assumed, then our ecological thinking needs to relocate the inquiry *down on the ground* where knowledge is made, negotiated, and circulated, and where, according to L. Code, the nature and conditions of the particular "ground," situations, and circumstances of the specific knowers, their interdependence, and their negotiations have claims to critical epistemic scrutiny equivalent to those of allegedly isolated, discrete propositional knowledge claims. Consequently, the project we undertook was practice-dependent. The ecological subjects of choruas, or char dwellers, who are the protagonists of this tale, are a distant relative of the abstract, interchangeable, and autonomous individuals, but are cognizant of being part of and specifically located in a social-physical world that enables as well as constrains livelihood practices. Chars are specific, unique locations with their particular ecosystems, communities, and resources; in such places, the "local place" matters to those who live on them and allows us to know the everyday geography of ordinary actions of ordinary people in their commonplace lives. (J. Rigg discusses this point usefully.) Finally, it must be mentioned that as our knowledge moved across the hybrid landscapes of chars, following the trajectories of diverse constitutive or obstructive lines of evidence, mapping their paths and surrounds, and shaping possibilities of living, the process of research was also emancipating in a way. To know the chars in a holistic manner required us to move away from the research methodologies rooted in positivist and reductionist philosophical genres that were handed down to us.

Our exploration in treading the hybrid environment where land and water are mixed to produce a new and fluid environment allowed us to think differently about land/water, people, and their ways of life. Our research is not primarily about theory, and although it is concerned with geographical themes of space, place, and scale, we see theory as useful only in helping us to structure and explain the patterns we view during fieldwork. This is why we explored the details of the tiniest aspects of the diverse and complex means of livelihoods on chars. A secret desire, of course, is to expand the conversation with the scholars residing in the Anglophone world, those who have so far theorized vociferously on environmental hybridity, and contribute a more grounded and holistic way of thinking about and looking at such environments. Such a dialog has been initiated by environmental historians working on South Asia (see R. D'Souza's interpretation of the simultaneous transformation of agrarian society and nature by colonizers of India), but less so by geographers working on hybrid environments. Hybridity, as envisaged by social researchers, however, implies "neither this nor that" but new formations that are best described as "sometimes this, sometimes that, and sometimes neither." Chars, as real-life examples and as metaphors of such hybrid environments, overlap the conservative categories of land and water. Choruas, like the chars on which they live, straddle the borders of legitimacy and illegitimacy. They also disregard the conventional meanings of security and insecurity in building their livelihoods on chars. For scholars of the South Asian environment, this has been an area of intense contestation as they have strived to find the answer to problems within a livelihood versus environment framework in this densely populated region. Chars show that it does not necessarily have to be "one way or the other," that either way, or even a mixed and complex way, is possible, and that such examples exist. Lastly, the themes dealt with in the chapters—land, water, migration, and vulnerability/security—have for some time been the core subject matters in environmental and geographical studies. Char people see these differently, and their lives, livelihoods, and worldviews illuminate these different meanings of commonly used words like "security" and "vulnerability." Ideally, the examples of "living with risk" that this book offers will encourage a rethinking of the manner in which scholars tend to use these ideas. Studying the hybrid environments of chars and the hybrid livelihoods of peoples on them might open new paths of inquiry in which geographers and historians will join hands once again. We hope to initiate the discussion; the far-reaching ecological impacts of land revenue administration of Bengal such as the Permanent Settlement and Bengal Alluvion and Diluvion Act (BADA) that were begun during the colonial period would be one line of inquiry for historians to take up. Similarly, other areas of future research would be to deepen the understanding of the daily and tiny amendments that people make to live in constantly changing environments like the chars. Livelihoods in such a dynamic offer new insights into how people adjust rather than adapt or change. This is an important and emerging area of concern among environmental scholars, and we hope that our book will contribute to this growing field of research.

Acknowledgments

We are indebted to many people, among whom only a few can be mentioned in this limited space. Before we name others, first of all we express our gratitude to those women and men who generously shared their time, gave us food and shelter when needed, and encouraged us to write their stories about their hopes and desires, their challenges and everyday struggles. This book attempts to bring into the public domain chars and the livelihoods of char dwellers, and we acknowledge the kindness with which they shared their time with us. Academically, we have benefited from scholarly insights of many friends and colleagues. But more importantly, the ideas expressed in this book were developed over time through extensive fieldwork; this is what allowed us to see what many others live with but do not see. For a better understanding of the nature of floods and river flows in the Himalayan foothills, we are grateful to Mr. Dinesh Kumar Mishra of Barh Mukti Abhijan, Dipak Gyawali and Ajaya Dixit of Nepal Water Conservation Foundation, and the Panos Institute for organizing the "Flood Trip" in the Kosi plains in August 1999. Academic colleagues everywhere have been supportive of the project. For constructive comments and ideas for further reading, we thank Dr. Rohan D'Souza of Jawaharlal Nehru University, New Delhi; Professor Ranjan Chakraborty of Jadavpur University, Kolkata; Mr. Ramaswamy Iyer of the Centre for Policy Research, New Delhi; Dr. Anjal Prakash of SaciWATERs; and Ms. Seema Kulkarni of SOPPECOM in India. In

Australia and elsewhere, we are grateful to Professors Willem van Schendel of the University of Amsterdam; Lesley Head of Wollongong University; Philip Hirsch of the University of Sydney; Richie Howitt and Debbie Rose of Macquarie University; Heather Goodall of University Technology Sydney; Avijit Gupta of the National University of Singapore; Dr. Douglas Hill of the University of Otago, New Zealand; Dr. Duncan McDuie-Ra of the University of New South Wales; Dr. McComas Taylor of ANU's College of Asia and the Pacific; and Dr. Deepa Joshi of Wageningen University, The Netherlands. Comments on parts of the draft from Professors Tim Scrase and Ruchira Ganguly-Scrase of Australian Catholic University; Dr. Margreet Zwarteveen of Wageningen University, The Netherlands; and Dr. Kalpana Ram of Macquarie University were useful. Last but not the least, Professor Richard Grove—when he was at the Australian National University (ANU)—always lent a patient ear and his insightful comments were invaluable in rethinking our subject. We also thank the ANU for providing the facilities to carry out the larger part of the research and writing, colleagues (particularly Professor James Fox) who read and commented on earlier drafts, and a publication subsidy.

The esteemed participants at the Tenth International River Symposium in Perth, 2010, where this work was presented as a keynote address, as well as the audiences at the Centre for Studies in Social Sciences, Kolkata; the Institute of France, Pondicherry, India; the Centre for Asia Pacific Social Transformation Studies at the University of Wollongong, Australia; and the Institute of Australian Geographers have received the ideas and the research enthusiastically.

Others to whom we are most grateful are Ms. Kay Dancey and Ms. Jennifer Sheehan of the cartography unit of the College of Asia and the Pacific at the ANU, who prepared the excellent maps and diagrams that add clarity to the text. We cannot thank Dr. David Williams enough for helping us with organizing the manuscript. For their inspiration to write up this research, we also thank our motley group of "local intellectuals" at the Barddhaman Avijan Gosthi, the University of Burdwan, where we started this work, and colleagues like Dr. Basudeb De and Burdwan Deepan Yuba Gosthi for providing a deeper understanding of the Damodar river. Mr. Shyamal Baran Saha did the watercolor of the chars presented in this book, Mr. Jayanta Biswas assisted us with financial diaries, and Mr. Ajoy Konar photographically recorded these exceptional pieces of land and the daily lives of their peoples. A key person who kept us on schedule was

Ms. Madhula Banerji, an editor whose professionalism in editing the manuscript has been amazing. Finally, we thank Jean Thomson Black, Executive Editor at Yale University Press, for her enthusiasm and support throughout. We express our sincere thanks to these talented friends and colleagues. The responsibility for all errors is ours.

Abbreviations

ADRI	Asian Development Research Institute
ANU	The Australian National University
BADA	Bengal Alluvion and Diluvion Act
BDO	Block Development Office(r)
BJP	Bharatiya Janata Party
BLRO	Block Land Revenue Officer
BNP	Bangladesh Nationalist Party
BTA	Bengal Tenancy Act
CDSP	Char Development and Settlement Project
CEC	Continuing Education Center
CP	Communist Party
CPI	Communist Party of India
CPI(M)	Communist Party of India (Marxist)
DFID	Department for International Development
DRDA	District Rural Development Agency
DVC	Damodar Valley Corporation
EBSATA	East Bengal State Acquisition and Tenancy Act
EGIS	Environment and GIS Support Project for Water Sector Planning
HYV	High Yielding Variety
IADP	Integrated Agricultural District Programme
IDS	Institute of Development Studies
ILO	International Labor Organization

IPCC	Intergovernmental Panel on Climate Change
IRDP	Integrated Rural Development Programme
ISDR	International Strategy for Disaster Reduction
ISPAN	Irrigation Support Project for Asia and the Near East
JLRO	Junior Land Reforms Officer
NGO	Nongovernmental Organization
NREGS	National Rural Employment Guarantee Scheme
OBC	Other Backward Castes
PRIO	International Peace Research Institute
Rs.	Rupees (Indian currency)
SC	Scheduled Caste
SHG	Self Help Group
ST	Scheduled Tribe
TVA	Tennessee Valley Authority
UNDP	United Nations Development Programme
UNEP	United Nations Environment Programme
UNESCO	United Nations Educational, Scientific and Cultural Organization
UNFCCC	United Nations Framework Convention on Climate Change
USCSP	United States Country Study Program

Dancing with the River

CHAPTER 1

Introducing Chars

Where Lands Float on Water

The river exists, so does the jungle, and also does the mouza. Nothing disappears for good.—DEBESH ROY (1988: 63), *Teestaparer Britanta*

This book is about people living on chars. The Bengali term *char*, or *charbhumi*,[1] denotes a piece of land that rises from the bed of a river. In this book, we present the chars as *hybrid environments*, not just a mixture of land and water, but a uniquely fluid environment where the demarcation between land and water is neither well defined nor permanent. The use of a contested and much-maligned term like "hybrid" requires some explanation. Many years ago, art historian Paul Zucker (1961) interpreted ruins as "aesthetic hybrids" because one could not be sure if they belonged to the realm of nature or the realm of art. Since the conceptual use of hybridity by Bhabha (1994) and other postcolonial theorists, the term has come to be closely associated with dense and opaque postcolonial theories and texts. But, at the same time, the biological source of the term "hybridity" is often conceptualized by postcolonial theorists in absolute terms: linguistic, cultural, or even racial. More abstract uses of the term are not uncommon; Canclini (1995) uses the term to show that traditional and modern cultures in Latin America are mixed, that instead of moving from one culture to another in a linear fashion, people move in and out of modernity. In recent years, individual disciplines have tended to interpret the term quite widely. For example, an urban community landscape has been interpreted as hybrid by architects Quayle and van der Lieck (1997) because it is generated by both top-down and bottom-up place-making processes. Karvonen and Yocom (2011), also urban planners, developing a relational ontology of urban nature, highlight the hybrid connections between humans and nonhumans. Archaeologist Qvistrom (2007) interprets the inner urban fringe as hybrid because it is a landscape that is out of order. Terrell et al. (2003) think of hybridity as presenting itself in the form of an interactive matrix in which people adjust and adapt their actions to circumstances to produce a hybrid domesticated landspace. By foregrounding indigenous oral histories and the politics of conservation, the historian of forests Skaria (1999) re-creates a hybrid history that primarily speaks from below. These uses of the term emphasize adulteration, contamination, and impurity and reveal how far its meaning has traveled from Bhabha's third space of hybridity, which is not an identity but an identification implying a process of identifying with and through another object (Bhabha 1990: 211). Closer to this meaning is a growing body of literature on traditional/aboriginal/indigenous societies showing that customary practices, state regulations, and market exchanges give rise to a "hybrid economy" (Altman 2009a, 2009b), a concept that finds its equivalence in Gibson-Graham's (2006) conceptualization of diverse economy. Geographers generally use the term in order to demolish the dichotomous division between nature and culture, and to highlight the coupling of nature and society (Swyngedouw 1999). One of the most influential scholars to oppose the view of nature as *the* cause and determining factor was Bruno Latour; in tracing the philosophical roots of Latour's various works, Blok and Jensen (2011) point out that his use of the term "hybrid networks" refers to the integrity of nature and society. Inglis and Bone (2006) suggest that this boundary-crossing has been marked by an increasing interest of social scientists in issues relating to the human manipulation of both biological life and so-called natural environmental forces and phenomena. These developments have fundamentally shaken the ways we think about nature, natural landscapes, and the natural world. Scholars have been increasingly concerned to challenge and alter what they take to be unsound, politically tendentious, and outmoded means of drawing boundaries between autonomous nature, on the one hand, and dependent human culture and society, on the other.

Philosophically, efforts to look at nature and society as a complex whole are rooted in postpositivist disillusionment with normative binary divisions and dualisms. Binaries in positivist philosophy became irreducible and absolute, and were attributed with characteristics that placed the two categories opposite to each other. Such dualistic epistemologies coexisted in tension; being mutually exclusive, one had to have the attributes of one or the other, but could never be a bit of both. The binary categories also implicitly attributed agency and autonomy more to one category than "the other," invoking hierarchies within the categories. As symbols, binaries involved organizational hierarchies that also invoked regulative norms and measures of control or disallowed the imagination of possibilities that could destabilize these categories. In recent years, geographers and environmental historians have challenged the binary of nature and human culture; one strand of the critiques argues that the "nature/culture divide" is not static, and that one side is now increasingly indistinguishable from the other. The dominant approaches in these influential writings question both the "production of nature" and the "social construction of nature" and invoke materiality and hybridity to create new resource geographies (Bakker 2006; Barnes 2008; Weir 2009). Head and Muir (2007) show that nature and culture are "together" in Australian backyards, but that "culture" there is increasingly turning into the dominant partner in the relationship (Head 2007). These scholars not only claim a social construction of nature and culture, but also emphasize that the two are intimately intermingled in landscapes.[2] Those following this paradigm shift have also challenged and, in some cases, rejected the once-abiding belief in the steady-state balance of nature. Instead, a large number of cornerstone ecological processes are now being described as nonequilibrium dynamics, long-term shifts, and historical conditionalities such as path dependencies and trajectories (Zimmerer 2000, 2007). Accordingly, the renewed emphasis on flux represents nature-society hybrids and is in bold contrast to environmental principles rooted in the belief of nature-tending-toward-equilibrium. The discipline of geography and related fields claims a territorial right over this complex domain of nature, society, territory, and scale. Geographers have contributed significantly to the ongoing debate on what is commonly described as "socionature." Drawing together notions of relational dialectics and hybridity, they have offered a rethinking of the nature-culture divide, the chasm that has most ailed the discipline and created a bipolar identity for geographers. Recently, such an effort has marked the study of the essential relations between water and society, analyzing both the history of water and how the idea of water articulates with its material and representative forms to produce this history (Linton 2010: 41).

The hybrid environments of chars offer real-life examples that challenge a number of naturalized concepts and categories, not just the nature/culture divide, but also the land/water dichotomy, one of the more foundational binaries in environmental studies.[3] These categories continue to pervade, in spite of interventions in more recent years from a number of geographers, a wide range of subfields within geography. Similar to the traditional concepts offered by political geographers—frontiers, boundaries and borders, rim lands and peripheries—land and water are so well established as two separate entities that it is difficult to challenge them. Chars point to the uncertainty of existence of these two well-established categories by their very physical presence at the border of land and water as ambiguous/uncertain/borderline/fringe zones. The tiny chars and their hybrid environments have the power to destabilize the land/water dichotomy, which has remained one of the foundational pillars of our environmental understanding.

Before we present the chars as offering a challenge to the conventional land/water binary, it will be useful to offer a *tour d'horizon*, a synoptic view of the principal arguments in understanding hybrid environments and landscapes. Reece Jones (2009) begins his essay on the "paradox of categories" by quoting Newman's lament over the lack of a "solid theoretical base" that would allow one to understand boundary phenomena that take place within different social and spatial dimensions: "[a] theory which will enable us to understand the processes of 'bounding' and 'bordering' rather than simply the compartmentalised outcome of the various social and political processes" (Newman 2003: 134). On the other hand, in dealing with the liminal and multidimensional challenges posed by the frontiers, borders, and edges, Howitt feels that the challenges are "on the ground," that the challenge is to understand that edges are not necessarily boundaries and that the distinction between "land" and "water" is not an ontological given (2001: 239).[4] Theory and empirical evidence are not mutually isolated. While environmentalists are rethinking the ways certain categories, borders, and boundaries are used as definite, watertight, and foolproof, a similar need arises to ensure that in critiquing "empty concepts," we do not resort to empty rhetoric. Cleary (1993) defines frontiers as unexplored areas or undeveloped spaces that get integrated into the national or global economy—from this perspective, chars, as metaphors, are frontiers in environment and resource studies. Moodie (1947: 73–74) is famous for his statement that "[f]rontiers are areal, boundaries are linear," and the idea that the frontier is "natural" and the boundaries are artificial or human-inspired is attributed largely to him. Borders have a political connotation acquired as a result of historical specificities that necessitated their formation—frontiers are zones at the periphery of a political division (Prescott 1987). This marginal zone in the last two centuries has been replaced by boundaries or lines of political control (for details of this discussion, see Banerjee 2010: xxiii–xxix). Moodie's views are not supported by Mikesell (1960: 62), who characterizes a frontier as "the outer edge of a settlement within a given area." In settlement expansion, "free land" is just one manifestation of a frontier, other aspects being social and economic fluidity (Agergard et al. 2010).

Central to the politics of nature and waters is the question of environmental knowledge, not only that of the subjective position of the knowledge producer, but also that of how this knowledge is produced, contested, legitimated, and hybridized. South Asian environmental scholars have emphasized the interdependence of biophysical and sociocultural domains, and highlighted the importance of thinking of the poor people's livelihoods as entrenched in local ecology (Gadgil and Guha 1992; Guha 1994). Agrawal (1994) has pointed out that any form of knowledge is embedded within a specific social context, a context that influences the process by which information is generated, processed, and disseminated. Such attention to specific social contexts, environmental historians Saberwal and Rangarajan (2003) comment, allows avoidance of the rhetorical stances on the value of scientific knowledge versus indigenous knowledge. Geographers have contributed to appreciating socially embedded knowledge, ideology, and institutions that mediate between people and nature to fill a gap in resource management and livelihoods and in rethinking the environment. They have pointed out that a "pure nature" or a "physical environment" as conceived earlier hardly exists. What we see as "the environment" is a product of human interaction and modification over many years. Bakker (2006) has shown that environmental discourses are embedded within institutional configurations of power, knowledge, and accepted authority, producing the effects of power within the self as a form of discipline. In understanding chars, one might want to use the lens of environmental history. If we take it that the environmental historians' conceptualization of nature is best expressed in William Cronon's idea of nature as a historical actor, "exist[ing] apart from our understanding of it" (1992: 40), then we are forced to return to the dualism that has had serious impact on the academic identity and integrity of geography as a discipline and that has been questioned by recent geographers. By viewing nature as a historical actor, they distinguish themselves from other historians, who typically treat nature as an object of human contemplation and controversy or as the physical stage for what are quintessentially human social, political, or situational developments. In making statements to the effect that "no landscape is completely cultural, all landscapes are the result of interactions between nature and culture" (Worster 1990: 1144), environmental historians seize upon the work done by cultural geographers.

The foremost among them is Carl Sauer, who led the Berkeley School of Cultural Geography, and whose work during the 1920s laid more emphasis on human civilization in modifying nature. This "cultural landscape" school took the dualism within geography (of physical and human, or nature and culture) for granted, and wrote primarily about human impacts on the natural landscape as a product of cultural preferences and potentials and many generations of human effort. Their efforts did not challenge the binary, but accepted it, thus resulting in an overall schizophrenia in geography that took nature either as an "immaculate linguistic conception" (a mental or social construction) or as knowable only through an absolutist knowledge of the real world entities and processes (pure physical geography) that are separate from human intervention (Whatmore 2002: 2). Grove and Damodaran (2006) have drawn attention to the early contributions made by geographers in developing the understanding of human interactions with environmental elements that shaped the branch of knowledge called environmental history today. They quote Gordon East (1938) to show how contemporary colonial anxieties were expressed in the work of academic geographers, who had begun to understand the extent and consequences of human interventions on nature, that is, "man's role in changing the face of the Earth." East, a geographer belonging to the old school, was noted for his concern over sudden and disastrous natural events like earthquakes: "If only by its more dramatic interventions, a relentless nature makes us painfully aware of the uneasy terms on which human groups occupy and utilise the earth" (1938: 11). This anxiety was rooted in the realization that dramatic and disastrous natural events have remained unpredictable, yet they repeat themselves in different contexts. Indeed, such views led to the rise of what is known as "neodeterminism" in geography, fully represented in the Russian geographer V. A. Anuchin's (1977 [1957]: 52) conceptualization of nature as more flexible but still an "advisor" to humans,[5] and his statement that determinism is "one of the most indispensable facets of dialectical thought."[6] Environmental determinism had split the discipline of geography and led to a set of essential dualisms of which the "physical" versus "human" had been the most contested.

Generations of geographers were trained to treat the physical environment as the *core* of geography, the very foundation on which the rest of the elements of geographical interest are placed. Although some of these geographical ideas about nature and the natural landscape have significantly contributed to the overall understanding of the environment, in recent years, many geographers have challenged the views that have created an unbridgeable chasm within the discipline. Two factors—a "cultural turn" within geography and a "spatial turn" in other social sciences (such as anthropology and history)—have enabled a wider and more continuous conversation among a number of disciplinary borders. At the same time, some recent geographical contributions have attempted to challenge such binaries and boundaries, particularly that of nature and culture. These recent contributions of geographers highlight the complex relationships of nature and culture and show that hybrid landscapes are not always in full agreement with the ways environmental historians conceptualize nature. The critique of the dangers posed by neoenvironmental determinism in methodological discussions has two major strands. One emerges from the postmodernists, who equate nature with a text whose meaning depends on the reading of it. This perspective has proven valuable in denaturalizing hegemonic ways of seeing the environment. But environmental historians have been dissatisfied with this strand of thinking because to them the world is not "denatured" and too sharp of a focus on human ways of seeing makes nature seem illusory (Demeritt 1994: 164). The other strand of critique has come from cultural ecologists, who have contested this nature-culture binary and highlight the coupling of nature and society. Inglis and Bone (2006) suggest that this boundary-crossing has been marked by the increasing interest of social scientists in issues relating to the human manipulation of both biological life and environmental forces and phenomena.

This book presents the hybrid environments of chars as lived-in landscapes. They are ecological elements of floodplains, but are also the products of colonial and postcolonial interventions into the lands and waters of Bengal, and thus are also the results of human intervention. As pieces of accumulated sand and silt, floating on and rising above the water of the riverbeds, they are literally embedded in water, enmeshed into the riverine environments. Thus, chars are also quintessentially hybrid because the distinction between the boundaries of land and water is not clear. The modernist view of environment that created a divide between land and water as two different elements belonging purely within the physical domain robbed the chars of their histories, extracted them from their social contexts of human experience, and essentialized them. Thus, waters and rivers came to be treated as just lines on maps devoid of the social and political dimensions of the nature-culture nexus. In this book, we bring back these dimensions by historically contextualizing waters and lands that lie within the rivers, and place the material practices of people on par with them. This makes the chars a fluid and problematic category as much of politics and history as of the environment; both of these social and natural elements are products of control—just as chars are also in part products of river control. Although a historical perspective is central to the argument, the discussion of the past in this book is neither chronological nor comprehensive. The chars under study also represent a borderless world, where borders are no longer fixed lines on the ground demarcating a territory, but are negotiated spaces or zones. On solid earth, borderlands contain zones that contain worlds that are inhabited by people with multiple identities. Furthermore, the location of chars on the border of land and water makes them "hybrid environments"; neither are they fully land nor can they be described as water, and the fusion of land and water in chars would not concede to be expressed in strict percentages of ingredient combination. Above all, neither are they the product of human imagination nor are they unreal entities and processes in the material world separate from social interventions.

Land and Water: Two Discrete Elements?

In riverine Bengal, the colonial British reinvented land and bounded the rivers to separate them from the land. The terrain was, and still is to some extent, characterized by the presence of innumerable rivers that criss-cross one another. Some of these rivers carry enormous amounts of silt and flow sluggishly over nearly perfectly flat plains for most of the year, only to rise during the monsoons to metamorphose into devastating torrents. In the Ganga-Brahmaputra-Meghna plains of the Indian subcontinent, chars form as the roaring rivers, descending from the Himalayas during the monsoons, almost choke with the enormous body of sand and other sediments carried in their waters.[7] The coarser sands create the *diaras* (as chars are called in the northern Bihar and eastern Uttar Pradesh flats), and the finer alluvium builds more expansive chars farther down the plain in the

Bengal delta. Within a few years of their emergence above the water, the warm and humid climate leads to the growth of coarse catkin grass and reeds, starting a slow process of organic breakdown that facilitates the fertilization of these lands.[8] In Indus plains, these lands are described as *kuchha* (wet and fragile)[9] and *baet* (rising like mounds between the two branches of rivers) and are also densely inhabited.

Within the Gangetic plains, the focus in this book is on the Bengal delta, about the *bagri*, or the western part of the delta. Under the microscope of examination are the chars rising out of the bed of the Damodar river in its lower basin where its flow marks the changing border between the Burdwan and Bankura districts. Scale, as in all geographical studies, is the key here; while land and water are intermingled in the entire Bengal basin, and particularly so closer to the mouth of the delta that houses the mangrove forests, or the Sundarbans,[10] the chars are microcosms of worlds where it is difficult to simply separate land and water.

Among the various ecological factors that contribute to the enormous amounts of sand and silt brought down by the rivers in the Gangetic plains, two are worth mentioning: the geological youthfulness of the Himalayan rocks and their brittle nature due to tectonic disturbances, and the heavy monsoonal rainfall which increases both stream discharge and velocity. Other contributing factors include the absence of lakes and reservoirs at higher elevations to trap sediments and deforestation in the hills. The key reason for the formation of chars in the Gangetic plains, however, is the sudden change in slope of the land; after rushing down the steep Himalayan slopes, the rivers suddenly lose their velocity on reaching the plains, spreading their sediments and choking on their own silt. This sudden loss of momentum, for example, caused the river courses to shift in this part of the world and has been the prime cause of the formation of the diaras on the Kosi river.

Kumar et al. (2011: 1) consider the British Empire as marking an exceptional global ecological moment in world history: "[I]ntegral to assembling the British empire was the relentless transformation of environments and landscapes." The unprecedented demands upon the natural world were imposed by the appetite of the empire for raw materials, resources, and commodities through a set of writings originating out of the "traveling gaze" of peripatetic colonialists, and finally through a range of policy initiatives listed under sobriquets such as conservation, scientific forestry, soil management, botanical networks and gardens, and so on. In his *Green*

Imperialism, Grove (1995) uncovers this dense flow of environmental ideas, views, and opinions that placed "the metropole and the periphery within the same analytical frame" (Thompson 2007: 456). British colonial rulers, encountering the Indian subcontinent, were astounded by the ferocity and utter strangeness of the tropics. The capricious rivers of Bengal, flowing only seasonally and shifting their courses at their whim, seemed quite different from what "nature" appeared to them and what they thought it should be. Environmental historians have written widely on the colonial transformation of the earth, where lands were underutilized or being laid waste, in need of being put to better use. Historian of early English settlement in America Cole Harris (2004) has shown how this led to more intensive cultivation to raise agricultural productivity and increased trade, but also led to the transformation of the "new world" and dispossession of the indigenous people by the Europeans. In dealing with the awe-inspiring lands and waters of the Indian subcontinent, the foundational binary in the British mind was that of a "state of nature" and a "state of culture," which in turn underpinned "the savage" and "the civilized." It has been suggested that the origin of such binary thinking lay in British philosopher John Locke's *Two Treatises*, especially its labor theory of property and its chapter on conquest. In England, the theory underpinned the doctrine of enclosure of the commons, which dispossessed thousands of English and Scottish peasants. In colonies like India, the conceptual equation of the state of nature with nonsettled cultivation and "wilde wastelands" formed "the *doxa* of land-use and ownership policies taken up by the British" (Whitehead 2010: 84). The application of English property law was not only to establish permanent zamindari[11] settlement of land tenure in South Asia, but also to debate what constitutes productive and unproductive uses of land. This was the basis of the creation of a category of "wasteland" as the oppositional binary of settled agriculture, which Whitehead describes as being not only a "constructed different landscape of value," but also loaded with the social subjectivities of groups inhabiting these specific territories. These wastelands, Whitehead shows, became subliminal "others" to private land or state-appropriated property to provide a pragmatic buttress to Locke's theory of property. But, for the sake of political liberalism to retain practical validity, some "common, good land" had to be left for others and, hence, a large mass of "wasteland" had to be found somewhere.[12] Iqbal (2010: 18–19) suggests that during the intense debates on the modalities of the Permanent Settlement (for more on this subject, see chapter 3), its framers, including

John Shore, attached importance to the wastelands in two different ways. First, the zamindars were incentivized to cultivate wastelands that fell within their permanently settled estates, and second, it was agreed that those wastelands that were not included in the Permanent Settlement in 1793 be reserved as Crown land and "as a source of income in the future." The boundary of estates was so vague in 1793 that the East India Company could very quickly decide to reassess and resettle what they saw as wastelands. As will be seen in this book, the chars in the Gangetic floodplains provided an answer to the search for wastelands. The chars are hybrid environments also because of this complex history of governance, shaped largely by colonial land- and water-management policies, and reflecting the environmental consequences of legal instruments such as the Permanent Settlement Act, the Bengal Tenancy Act, and the Bengal Alluvion and Diluvion Act, or BADA. An important point made in this book is that the colonial land revenue system, by seeing "the land" as more productive (in terms of yielding revenue) and useful, began the long historical process of the definition of rivers as destructive in riverine Bengal and in need of control. As the lands were in need of protection from the volatile rivers that change their courses without notice, they were walled-in by embankments and dikes, encouraging the rivers to stay within fixed courses to make the lands more permanent. The dominant narrative was adopted by positivist Bengal, as postcolonial history of land and water management shows. The Damodar, walled-in and bound by embankments, was further controlled by the construction of dams and barrages upstream. In the process, the fluid worlds of chars lying within the riverbeds were turned invisible.

This historical legacy makes the chars unique. Neither marsh, fen, peat land, nor water, they are remarkably different from other wetlands. The closest equivalents to char environments are the delta mouths where mangrove forests grow; the *haor* basins, which are saucer-shaped, interfluvial areas of Sylhet, Bangladesh, that are under water for a part of the year (Duyne-Barenstein 2008); and Everglades National Park in Florida (Grunwald 2007). Yet, for those who have been to both the chars and one of the other wetlands, none of these wetlands are actually quite like the chars. Chars are not covered by the Ramsar Convention, the intergovernmental Convention on Wetlands of International Importance, which provides the framework for national action and international cooperation for the conservation and use of wetlands and their resources, in spite of their use of a "broad framework" in the definition.[13]

Chars are currently not within the mainstream debates on environment and resource management. When environmentalists offer examples of ecological transition, problematize environmental degradation, and think of "nature into culture," they generally depend upon invoking behavioral analysis to make strategic policy decisions.[14] This analysis hinges upon discursive structures that condition how the environment is "read." An example of the different readings of landscapes is provided by the "forest islands" as described by Fairhead and Leach (1996: 20). These are dense semideciduous rain-forest patches within an open woodland savannah in the Republic of Guinea in Africa. The presence of such a vegetation mosaic has intrigued observers and invited considerable ecological debate. In their study, they have challenged existing environmental histories and ecological explanations. Most of these explanations were developed by "outside observers" from colonial to present times—from the late 1800s till the late 1900s. One explanation was that the patches were relics of an original and formerly much more extensive, dense, and humid forest cover. This "derived savannah" argument was incompatible with a second view that suggested that the stability of the forest-savannah mosaic was principally reflecting locally favorable edaphic (variations in soil, but also drainage and water table) conditions. Both views agree that the vegetation mosaic is purely natural in origin. Fairhead and Leach (1996: 15–16) also show that certain local agricultural practices encourage and enhance the regeneration of secondary forests in savannah lands; inhabitants themselves say that "where one cultivates, the forest advances." Indeed, they met with village elders who described how their ancestors encouraged forest patch formation around settlements. Local villagers also noted that the thickness and extent of such patches have grown over the years and not declined, as has been thought. Everyday resource use practices tended to assist these transitions; they "enhance[d] forest regeneration [which] may be of more general significance in accounting for the long-term evolution of the forest-savanna mosaic" (Fairhead and Leach 1996: 30). Even archival descriptions confirm the presence of distinct islands of humid forest in the almost-treeless tall-grass savannah. That the experiences and practices of local people tell a different story than the widely popular one of forest loss suggests that the outsiders' observations of vegetation and its local management practices were preconditioned by theories of "original" or "natural" vegetation—a climatic climax—in which all vegetation change constituted divergence from an undisturbed optimum, which in this case was dense semideciduous forest. Again, this climax vegetation was presented as "better" than the anthropogenic vegetation, and local practices were seen as invariably leading to the apocalypse of degradation. The fashioning of a forest history produces analytical dichotomies, which put the state and village in a confronting position, and privilege scientific and local knowledges by occluding the local environmental histories (Leach and Fairhead 2000).

One might stop here and ask: Why did the ecologists get it wrong? The biologists tend not to incorporate things like local knowledges, local histories, and local ways of seeing things into their explanations of the natural world. When encountered with hybridity of nature and culture, they tend to fall further back into positivist subdivisions or categories. This has resulted in a suite of numerical methods that is now available for the classification of geographical areas by "biotic similarity and difference" (Rensburg et al. 2004: 844). Long- or short-term temporal shifts, described as "rising variance" or regime shifts involving reorganizations of complex systems, also pose a problem to them (Carpenter and Brock 2006). The difficulty with such classificatory schemes is that every element of the universe has to be part of one or the other category. Yet, although the biologists are trained to see clear-cut and, more importantly, homogeneous categories, they have been interested in edges. As Rensburg et al. suggest, "sharp discontinuities . . . have long fascinated biologists because they are regions of considerable species turnover," but "[a]t larger scales, they have been used to define the spatial boundaries of biogeographical regions, which in turn have formed and continue to form a significant, though often contentious, basis for understanding the evolutionary history of life on earth" (2004: 843). Interestingly, edges have been long recognized by ecologists (see Odum 1971) as zones of transition from one ecosystem to another, where two different types of habitat or successful stages meet and intergrade (Turner et al. 2003: 440). But, when encountering such "sharp discontinuities" at smaller spatial scales, biologists have substituted for the explanation either historical data or the cultural ecology of local practices, the interpretation of which they were poorly trained to make. Some ecologists have in recent years increasingly appreciated "edge effects" in terms of "species richness," where species overlap with one another in their range margins between neighboring assemblages (Araújo and Williams 2001; Gaston et al. 2001). These effects, if located in areas of ecological transition, are seen by ecologists (Araújo 2002: 162) as effects where replacement between biomes or with local patterns of turnover can be associated with a specific determinant (such as a gradual rise in elevation). Harper et al. (2005) define the "edge" as the *interface between different ecosystem types* and consider it to be distinct as well as linear, that is, high contrast, such as between an open canopy young forest and a mature forest, or more soft, that is, low contrast, such as between two mature forest types. McKay (2000), after analyzing the diverse nature of edges, proposes that the "edge effect" may be used as a metaphor for the bringing together of people, ideas, and institutions. Turner et al. (2003) have used the concept to show that ecological edges are not just sources of biodiversity, but also cultural edges where different knowledge systems intergrade to produce a richness of knowledge and ecological practices that enhances the resilience of local communities. Thus, it is only recently that biologists have begun to explore the possibilities contained in ecological edges (Turner et al. 2003). Chars are literally and figuratively the "edges": Physically they straddle an ill-defined boundary between land, water, and the air; all their characteristics are always changing; and as spaces of human habitation, they support the most transient of communities.

The ecology of char formation makes them one of the most fragile environments; this physical vulnerability makes them risky, unstable, and dangerous places to inhabit. Speaking from a geographical perspective, Howitt remarks that such "liminal spaces" of edges make them "not [only] lines of separation but zones of interaction, . . . transformation, transgression and possibility." He asks: "Are we, as geographers, to interpret this image of vegetation sequences as . . . a metaphor for the creation of new spaces through co-existence and reconciliation?" (2001: 240). A conversation between biologists and ecologists has been absent so far, and our conceptualization of hybrid environments might fill this gap. One does not need to struggle to see the similarities in the ways the river islands of South Asia and the forest islands of Africa have been dealt with so far. Not only are the chars an edge, they are also spaces where nature and culture, land and water are enmeshed to give rise to hybrid environments. Use of an analytical framework that is based on the dichotomy of land and water ecologies makes the uniqueness of the chars invisible to both social and environmental scientists.

The analytical approach of ecology brings us to the other value of explaining chars as hybrid environments—the redefinition of widely used conceptualizations of security and insecurity as well as risk and vulnerability in both social and physical systems by ecological scientists. Again, mutual comprehension of each other's languages and reciprocal conversation between social and environmental experts remain lacking in this diverse field. Indeed, those experts trained in pure ecology are increasingly more comfortable with the idea that human action and social structures are integral to nature and that, hence, any distinction between society and nature is arbitrary. Adger has argued that the insights emerging from social nature, described by him as "social-ecological systems," complement and can "significantly add to a converging research agenda on the challenge faced by human environment interactions under stress caused by global environmental and social change" (2006: 268). Yet experts have struggled to find a "universally accepted way of formulating the linkages between human and natural systems" (Berkes and Folke 1998: 9). Adger (2006: 269) feels that our different formulations of research needs and methods and normative implications of resilience and vulnerability are responsible for this mutual lack of dialog; each tradition seeks to elaborate "the problem" as they see it, using theories that have the explanatory power only for particular dimensions of human-environment interactions.

The view of the environment as "a hostile power" is a strand of thought in contemporary environmental thinking. This view envisions a future rife with conflicts and anarchy resulting from the overcrowding of the poorer parts of the world, such as Bangladesh, where the poor are degrading the environment and spreading diseases, inciting mass migrations and group conflicts. This view is best expressed in the works of Homer-Dixon (1991, 1994) and Kaplan (1998). Kaplan's neo-Malthusian idea of the violent and conflict-ridden environment is connected with concerns over security: "It is time to understand 'the environment' for what it is: the national security issue of the early twenty-first century" (1998: 190). Such "securitising" of central environmental concerns, Levy (1995: 44) thinks, helped to attract the attention of policymakers within a void of security policy at the end of the Cold War (Gleditsch 2001: 259). The theory of "securitization" developed by the Copenhagen School, and sometimes portrayed as a distinctively "European" contribution to the debates over the social construction of security, has developed a broad and powerful research agenda of significance across the field of security studies. Williams gives an overview of the critiques of securitization theory, branded as "sociologically untenable," as "encapsulating several questionable assumptions" (2003: 512), and as at best morally ambivalent, and at worst verging on politically irresponsible. Barnett (2000) agrees that such securitization was both a product and a legitimation of the security agenda of Global North, and believes that the conflation of resources with environment was behind such theorizations. Urdal (2005: 418) believes that many aspects of this genre of thought were based on poor evidence, such as single case studies that in turn were also criticized for lack of methodological rigor. A number of research projects have since discredited the thesis that environmental insecurity is related to resource scarcity. The strongest thrust came from a heterogeneous group of scholars associated with the International Peace Research Institute, Oslo (PRIO), which used statistical methods and conducted large cross-national studies to disprove the connection; the group used causalities and correlations between environmental variables and conflicts, but did not pay adequate attention to studying those cases where environmental scarcity does not lead to conflict. The use of such purely objectivist theories in treating environment-induced insecurities pulls us away from the intentions, meanings, and logic for action by local groups and reaffirms the nature/culture binary that we set out to destabilize with our empirical example of chars as hybrid environments. A powerful effort to destabilize the environment-conflict thesis has been presented by the social theorist Ulrich Beck (1991, 1996), who has shown the ways in which the heightened sense of risk is central to our global society and how this sense of risk has begun to pervade every aspect of our lives, not just nature and ecology. Beck thinks that modernity introduces global risk parameters that previous generations have not had to face:[15] "[T]he historically unprecedented possibility, brought about by our own decisions, of the destruction of all life on this planet . . . distinguishes our epoch not only from the early phase of industrial revolution but also from all other cultures and social forms, no matter how diverse and contradictory" (1991: 22).

Another strand of literature in risk studies has increasingly put more attention on risk perception and risk as feelings (Slovic 2000, 2010), emphasizing the cognitive processes in which people look to their positive and negative feelings as a guide to their evaluation of an activity's risks to be meaningful. Psychological contributions to rebuilding the "theory of decision-making" put greater focus on the decision-maker. In thinking about this individual, studies have increasingly questioned the rational, profit-maximizing "economic man" who was seen as completely informed of his choices and was infinitely sensitive, and have moved into mental strategies called "heuristics" to explain judgments of probability and risk-taking decisions. The developing understanding is that resilience to vulnerabilities operates at micro-geographical scales; even from a systems analytical approach, this would mean adjustments in behavior to enhance the ability to cope with external stress (Brooks 2003: 8). In the context of climate change, following Pielke (1998: 159), Smit et al. (2000: 225) refer to adaptation as the adjustments in individual groups and institutional behavior in order to reduce society's vulnerability.

Adaptation to changes in the environment is a process, action, or outcome at household, community, group, sector, region, or country levels to better cope with, manage, or adjust to some changing conditions (Smit and Wandel 2006: 282). In tracing the history of the use of the term "adaptation," Head (2010) has suggested that although it has become a global catchword in recent years, it can potentially enhance the nature/culture binary by reinforcing or conflicting with the top-down prescriptions of mitigation. She suggests retrofitting the concept for the contemporary world by, among other things, paying attention to everyday practices and scale in space and time. In this book, both of these are done; what is also pointed out is that a semantic turnaround might be in the cards—while changes take place at the macro level, people make small, everyday adjustments to accommodate these changes. We show that although their cumulative effect is an intimate knowledge of and adjustment to the changing moods of the river, these adjustments often take place at a micro-geographical scale and at the level of the individual. To explain, we look into the classical studies in psychology (such as that conducted by Lehner et al. 1955) that illuminate the dynamics of personal adjustment to complex and challenging situations.

The ecological fragility of chars leads to environmental uncertainties and fluidities that make them true representatives of "environmental borderlands" (see, for example, Roche 2005, for a definition of such contexts). Chars not only constitute environmental borderlands, but also inhabit the poorly lit, gray area of legitimacy because they are not political units and their existence may often cut across such fixed categories. From that perspective, chars can be explained as ungovernable borderlands in the sense that Scott (2009) envisages in *The Art of Not Being Governed*. He describes the history of highland Southeast Asia as "anarchist," because these lands and peoples have escaped and stayed beyond state control, and laments that he could not do justice to the *orang lauts*,[16] the sea nomads or sea gypsies, in insular Southeast Asia, who are the seagoing, archipelago-hopping variant of swiddeners, by including them in that book. *Dancing with the River* in a small way fills the gap by focusing instead on the microscopic worlds of chars as one of the "watery regions of refuge" (Scott 2009: xiv). As chars emerge within the riverbed, they have no definite legal existence as legitimate and officially recognized pieces of land. The nonpermanent and ill-defined reality of the existence of chars raises questions of environmental and resource management and makes any effort to support human livelihoods difficult. Lying outside or at the margins of the land revenue system, the complex and fluid environment of chars presents opportunities to some people.

Being trained as geographers, we focus in this book on the interconnectedness of humans and nature. The age-old "interface of humans and nature" is explored, and how women and men make a living in this unique environment is outlined. Although some historically informed insights into the formation of the chars is provided, rather than studying the hydro-geomorphological mechanics of char formation, we treat the chars as special and distinctive places, as hybrid places, as places of a volatile nature, as places lived in by people who live with a changing and uncertain river on the strength of knowledges that develop from the experience of living.[17] The human-environment interactions—based on a livelihoods framework[18] developed by Robert Chambers—on chars located in a small area of the lower Damodar valley in the Indian part of the Bengal delta illuminate how people, immigrants, and other transient groups build livelihoods that are beyond our conventional conceptualizations; their home and livelihoods are well beyond the state. Interestingly, like the chars themselves, the livelihoods of people on them also present the complexities that can arise when people live at the border of land and water. Indeed, "livelihoods" is also a "boundary" term that brings disparate perspectives together, and allows conversations over disciplinary and professional divides (Scoones 2009). To put it simply, a livelihoods perspective starts with how different people in different places live: the means of gaining a living or a combination of the resources used and the activities undertaken in order to live. In explaining this complex *bricolage* or portfolio of activities, artificial categories are cut across to show how people make a living from minimal resources, in face of great uncertainties, and tap into their traditional knowledges as well as develop new skills to cope with adversities on a day-to-day basis. To live in the unpredictable and uncertain environment of chars, people are obliged to take risks and have to develop their livelihoods in such ways so as to be able to cope with the river's moods, which we call "dancing with the rivers."[19] To dance with the river means to be able to intimately know the riverine environment of chars, and to make constant and small adjustments to cope with the changing moods of the river with its changing movements. We note that while this coping is strategic, it is also purely contingent and temporary and, hence, should not be conflated with broadly ecological terms such as "adaptation." Neither do chars become a permanent "home" for immigrants, nor do the *chorua*s continually strive to leave the chars and settle elsewhere. An attempt has been made to reproduce aspects of char life in this book, in the hope that it would help redefine some of the rigid ways the environment has been conventionally categorized into "land" and "water," and rethink the way human well-being has been categorized into the binary opposites of "vulnerable" and "secure."

In the richer countries, wetlands and river islands provide areas of unique and rare plants and wildlife and are ideal locations for environmental protection and public recreational activities such as boating, fishing, and game hunting. Awareness of river islands from a human habitation perspective has so far been restricted; they are generally equated with swamplands of the floodplains. Yet the Pantanal of Brazil or the Okavango delta of Africa are ecologically different from chars; culturally too they do not offer such complex material for a researcher. Some of the swamplands, such as the Tajik chars in the Pjang river island of Khalton oblast, provided shelter to the "lost people," the stranded Afghan refugees who were "rediscovered" by the wider humanitarian and media world.[20] A large number of people live on the chars or similar habitats in the deltaic flats all over Asia, with the greatest concentration of habitation in eastern India and in Bangladesh.[21] Due to the weight of sheer numbers of inhabitants and their sociocultural complexities, and the unique ecology, the Bengal chars provide a unique ground for investigation. Bengal is one of the most densely settled parts of the world, and here millions of people live on and make livelihoods from the chars. Place and territoriality are central to this study; also central are the human uses of a unique place, their placelessness, and making home or regrounding, and above all forming a sense of place. Intensive investigations have been made on a limited number of chars, with the hope of revealing yet another contested world (and a world of contestations) to the growing understanding of waters and lands, and peoples and their livelihoods, and contributing to the geographical imagination by showing how spatial associations with people and particular territorial complexes are transgressed by those communities who build a place attachment or a sense of place.

Although chars are not as extensively studied in West Bengal, India, as they are in Bangladesh, we were able to tap into a rich literature on the history of control of the Damodar from colonial times: the construction of embankments on the river, and the sociopolitical context that gave rise to the development of Damodar Valley Corporation (DVC) dams and canals, and the later-day evaluations of DVC. McLane's (1993) rich historical work on the Burdwan Maharajas, *Land and Local Kingship in Eighteenth Century Bengal*, which shifted scholarly attention from the highest levels of government to the regional and local levels of power, was invaluable. This book prepared the basis for understanding the transition to British rule. There was also a set of material on environmental history and the history of control of rivers, particularly the inspiring works by D'Souza (2007, 2009) on the Mahanadi river, Hill (1997) on the Kosi in eastern India, Klingensmith (2007), and Mishra's grounded narratives of embankment construction on the Kosi (see Mishra 1997, 1999, 2003). Recently emerging work on riverbank erosion in the Ganges—particularly in northern parts of lower Bengal around the Farakka barrage in Malda and Murshidabad—was useful in placing the proportion of internal displacement by riverbank erosion in West Bengal. One estimate is that about six hundred thousand people have been displaced by riverbank erosion in the Malda and Murshidabad districts of the state (Das 2005). Kalyan Rudra (1996, 2004) has consistently written about the uprooting of lives by riverbank erosion caused by the construction of the Farakka barrage on the Ganges. Another geographer and a South Asian expert, Graham Chapman, has also written about the disastrous flood of 2000 and how it was linked with the river control measures and riverbank erosion (Chapman and Rudra 2007). Bandyopadhyay et al. (2009) have focused on the vulnerability of human lives to riverbank erosion in this part of West Bengal. Also useful were a number of doctoral theses on fluvial dynamics that have been carried out in the region.

Related closely to the history of river control is the story of how the Damodar chars came to be settled. This process began in the late nineteenth century when groups of Muslim fishermen migrated from Bihar to these riverine locations. Bihari Muslims were initially employed as village watchmen and gatekeepers by the Burdwan rajas and were allotted land in the chars by way of payment. Besides fishing they reared cattle. Yet, unused to farming, they did not try to cultivate the chars, which at that time were mostly covered by bush, plum trees, and tall *bena* grass. Small amounts of *mesta* (a variety of jute), maize, and pulses were grown as crops. The population remained sparse, and floods were a regular visitor during the monsoons. After the Partition, Hindu communities began trickling into this part of India from East Pakistan in search of livelihood and secure social environments. Some charlands, designated as *khas* lands[22] without land records, titles, or owners, were seen by the government as suitable for resettling the refugees in camps in West Bengal. Some of the refugees were allotted *patta*[23] in existing chars; the shifting river courses have since made considerable stretches of charlands revert into the river channel, whereas some new lands have emerged from the riverbed. Moreover, considerable stretches of the river channel have been converted into seasonal croplands by the char dwellers. Settlement on the charlands gained pace after the Bangladesh Liberation Movement in 1971, leading to a significant increase in the flow of migrants into southern West Bengal across the Bangladesh border, migrants who still have to receive citizenship papers.

A source of critical literature was the writings on transnational migration within South Asia.[24] The Partition—the breakup of British-ruled South Asia in 1947 into different countries—is probably the most important landmark in the transborder movement of people in the Indian subcontinent. In the eastern end, the Partition forced millions of people to move across the new border between the newly created states of East Pakistan and India. For understanding the lives of those who came to build a livelihood on these chars, the literature on the Partition proved invaluable. This is a growing field, but again, the field itself is characterized by a number of (sub)partitions (as noted by Rahman and van Schendel 2003)—not only of rival nationalisms and differences in stories of human experiences, but also of disciplinary divides and divisions within the academic communities. Willem van Schendel's (2002) "Stateless in South Asia" has been an influential reading, where he shows that the very idea of an uninterrupted, homogeneous, contiguous, and bounded homeland is a fiction in South Asia. The unadministered "enclaves"—portions of one state that are completely surrounded by the territory of another state—compose a "landlocked archipelago" strewn along the India-Bangladesh border.[25] The territorial discontinuity in these islands of unequal sizes represents a violence of the Partition that has remained unparalleled in the history of South Asia. People living here, van Schendel has shown, develop fluid identities, practice new cultures, and juggle a combination of group identities. Books and papers on the refugees from Bangladesh tend to focus on metropolitan Calcutta and on the refugee camps, concerning themselves with the relationship between refugees and the state, both in terms of state policies toward the newcomers and in terms of the effects that refugees have on politics in Calcutta and the rest of West Bengal (Basu Ray Chaudhury 2000; Dasgupta 2001; Kudaisya 1998; Mallick 1999). A second strand in these writings brings out the voices and identities of a particular group of refugees in West Bengal, the Bengali *bhadralok* (the genteel, educated upper class), with their often traumatic and nostalgic memories of a lost homeland in East Bengal (Banerjee et al. 2005; T. Bose 2000; Chakraborty et al. 1997; B. Ghosh 1998). A third strand in this literature that was helpful to us privileges the voices of women as refugees inhabiting the borderlands of uncertain and ill-defined political terrains and territories (Bagchi and Dasgupta 2003; Banerjee and Basu Ray Chaudhury 2011). Against this backdrop of a refined and grounded understanding of place and displacement, this book tries to explore the livelihoods of people who neither benefited from rehabilitation programs nor were able to fully merge with the mainstream life.

Accessing the Chars

As trained geographers, we firmly believe in the value of fieldwork in research. We bear in mind Friedrich Ratzel's (1882) intuitive comment: "I travelled, I sketched, I described. Thus, I was led to the description of nature." Blok and Jensen, in elaborating Bruno Latour's environmental agenda, echo a similar sentiment: "[A]bove all, Latour outlines an empirical program for alternative explorations in a hybrid world of constant dynamism and change" (2011: viii). As a result, this book is based on a combination of field-based research methods. First of all, it moves along the geographical scale; in the Bengal delta, as a region cutting across the political border, it focuses on the lower Damodar valley and puts under the microscope twelve chars located on the riverbed in a small stretch of about forty-eight kilometers of the Damodar river along the border of the Bankura and Burdwan districts of West Bengal state in India (figure 1.1).[26] These chars lie in a small part of the lower part of the river valley in West Bengal. Figure 1.2 places the study area in local and regional locational perspectives. Roughly, these chars present a range of conditions that occur in different physical locations. Some of them are attached to the northern riverbank and are locally known as *mana* (for example, Kasba Mana, Bhasapur Mana), whereas others are islands locally known as *char mana* (for example, Majher

Char Mana, Kalimohanpur Char Mana). Figure 1.3 offers a cartographical view of the location of one such char, Majher Mana, which can only be accessed by crossing a stretch of water. Char Gaitanpur, on the other hand, is an attached char located near a large urban center, Burdwan. The surveyed chars were selected purely as a matter of convenience with attention to logistics such as ease of access. Even those chars that are located relatively close to the embankment require a fair amount of walking on the sand and crossing of water channels.

Our awareness of chars and the lives of char communities dates back to the respective doctoral research of Kuntala Lahiri-Dutt (1985) and of Gopa Samanta (2002), both focusing on rural transformation and urbanization processes in this prosperous part of Bengal. Yet, at that time, chars appeared only marginally in our vision. The study of the environments, the people, and their livelihoods in the small part of the lower Damodar valley in West Bengal that this book presents is based on our joint research done since 2001. We surveyed the chars in several phases between June 2002 and November 2007, and in a final phase during 2009 and 2010. After consolidating our familiarity with the char dwellers during the initial stage, we embarked on a household census with the assistance of a group of local students. This survey was carried out with a structured questionnaire on all the 1,312 households living in the twelve chars in the period from 2007 to 2009. The table in the appendix presents some of these results, mostly close-ended questions. To understand the livelihoods of char dwellers, their pathways of migration, the occupancy of land, the strategies to cope with poverty, and households' everyday occupations, qualitative methods were required. In four arbitrarily selected chars—Gaitanpur, Majher Mana, Bhasapur, and Kasba—extended interviews were used to record individuals' histories, subjective experiences of migration and homemaking, and perceptions of insecurity and vulnerability. In addition, interviews were held with around 80 women and 150 men from different age groups and economic classes living on the nine more accessible chars. We deployed qualitative techniques such as interviews, discussions, and participant observation (used by Limb and Dwyer 2001) to understand the perceptions of the char dwellers. A number of geographers have successfully used such methods recently, particularly those who study livelihoods, gender, and migration. One of the most inspiring works is by Gibson-Graham (2006), who believes that qualitative research that engages with research participants is able to best explore and reconstruct the personal worlds through

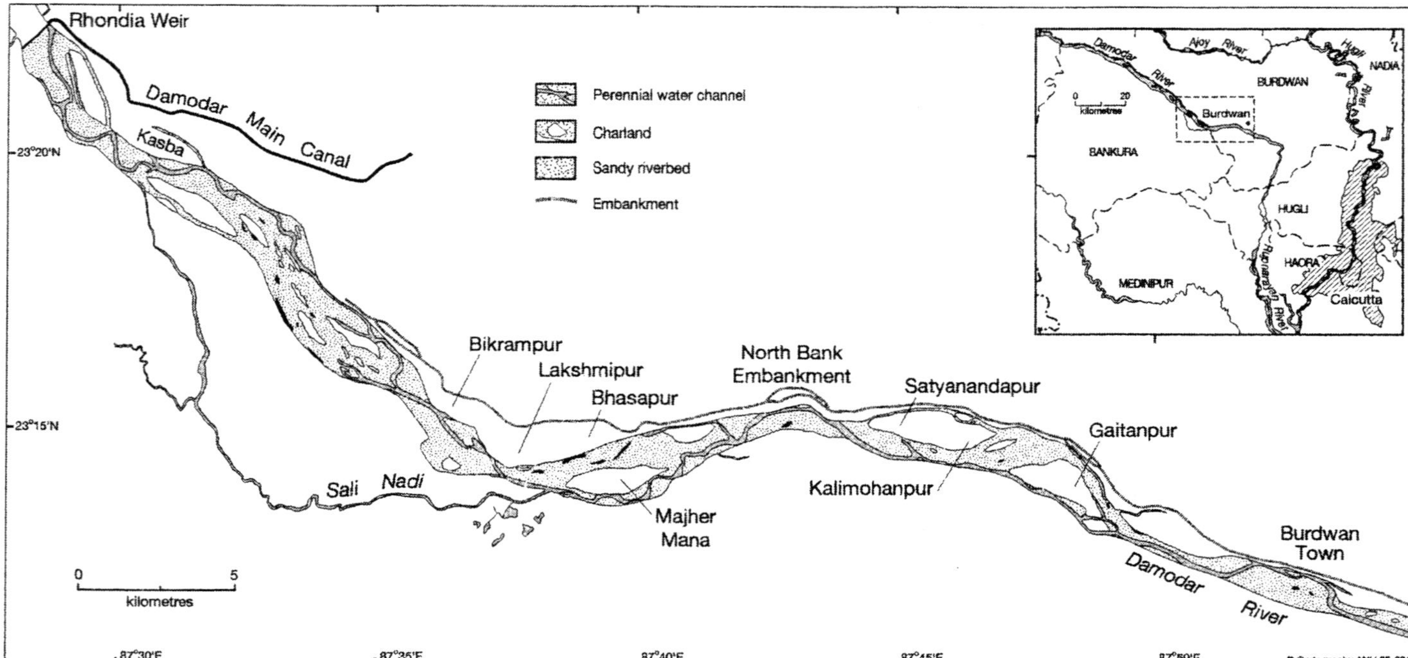

1.1 The General Area of Chars

Source: Compiled by the Australian National University (ANU) Cartography Unit from topographical sheets published by the Survey of India, Government of India.

Note: Not all chars that were studied can be seen in the map. Even within one char, there may be different parts that are named differently. For example, Simisimi and Namosonda are names of "areas" within Char Bhasapur.

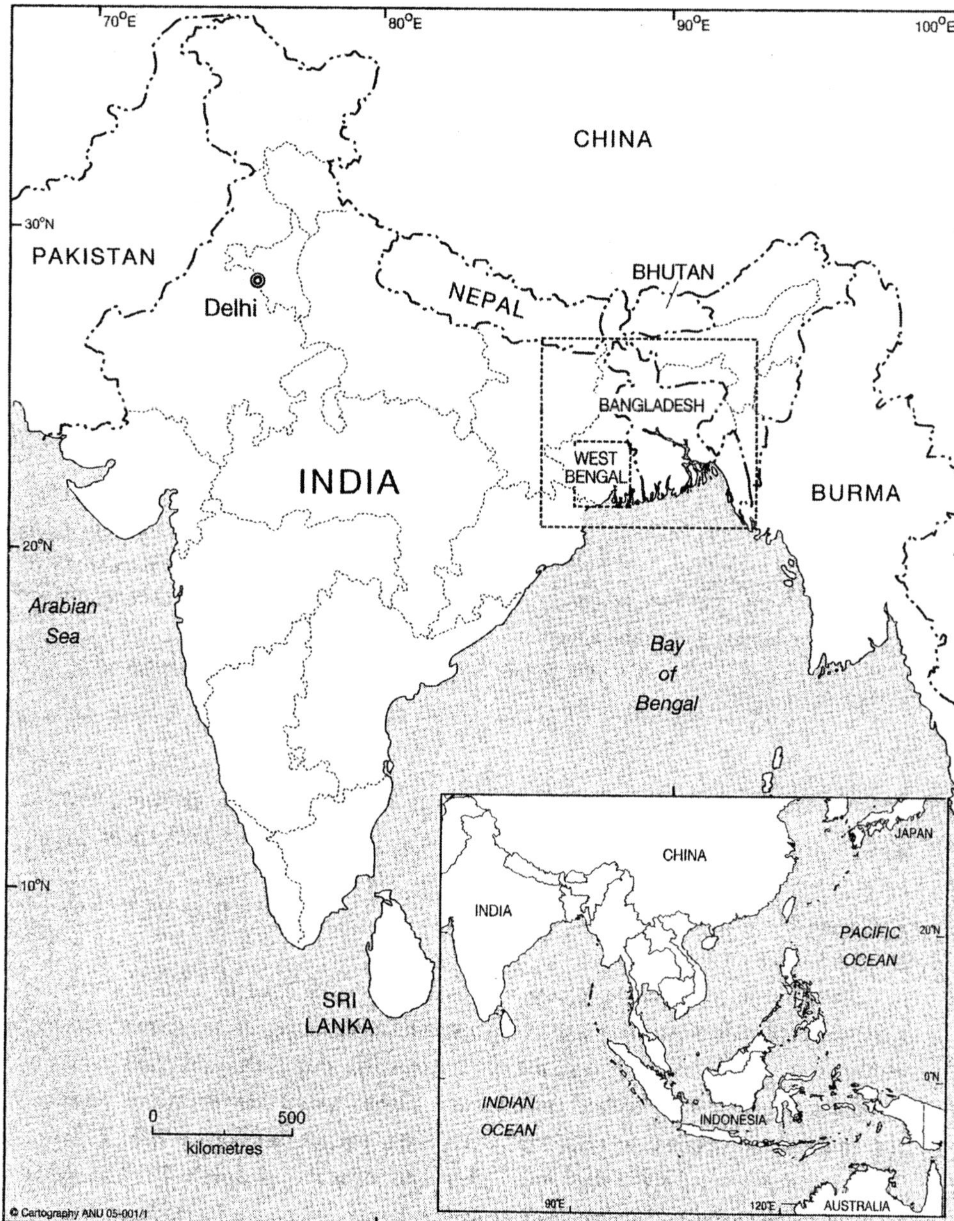

1.2 A Location Map

Source: Compiled from published sources by the ANU Cartography Unit.

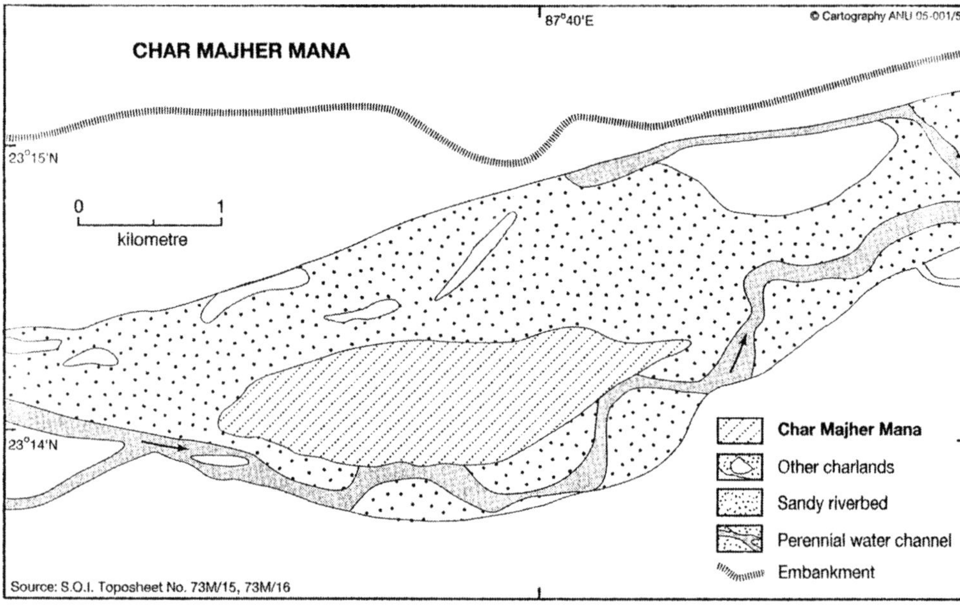

1.3 Majher Mana, a "Middle Char"
Source: Compiled by the ANU Cartography Unit from topographical sheets published by the Survey of India.

the interaction of cultural, economic, and social processes, through the individual experiences along with the social processes and structures of lives. Following Gibson-Graham's style of community engagement, we, particularly in the latter phases of the study, became involved with char people's lives.

As outsiders, securing access to the homes and lives of choruas was neither straightforward nor easy. During the first year or so, we spent a day almost every week casually walking along the different paths and tracks and speaking to anybody who had time for us. These casual conversations built the familiarity needed to allow us entry into their community life. This "acquaintance-building" also enabled us to observe people's livelihood characteristics in detail, which later came in handy when we formulated the survey questionnaire for the census. This phase was followed by more frequent visits establishing personal contacts with individual women and men. During this "friendship-building" phase, we explored more closely the life experiences of the individuals. One should not forget that these respondents were "self-selected"; strong relationships of trust could be built only with those who wanted to reciprocate, and no strict statistical sampling method could be followed. This ensured that the study involved only those who wished to participate. Although there was no conscious effort to conduct "scientific sampling," the resultant interviews may be described as a "sample" of lives of char men and women who were interested in the research and willingly participated in it. In this way, it was possible to obtain the richest data possible because of their interest in the research. Even in the interviews, personal conversations, and group discussions, we had to be opportunistic, engaging with whoever had time at a given moment. For this reason, we tried out different visiting hours, using extended hours on vacation days. Some individuals opted out of the research project in the initial stages once they understood our objectives. With regard to naming respondents, since names and surnames in India can be indicative of one's ethnic and caste location, we adopted a strategy in which the names are all real, but do not correspond to the actual name of any individual lest she or he be identified. Bihari names were used only for Biharis and similarly for Bangladeshis. Even then, the participants' names have been used with their full consent. The names of those mentioned in the early history of settlement on chars are real.

Small group discussions, widely used as a qualitative field method in social research, were also used once we gained enough trust from the communities. As is well known, these groups comprise numbers of people not exceeding six or seven at one time. During the research, these group discussions were organized quite informally: We would often sit on someone's open veranda adjacent to the main road and talk. Slowly, passersby with whom we were familiar would gather around. Once six or seven people had gathered, we would broach the issues we wished to explore that day. Those who were willing to or interested in speaking/discussing would stay back; sometimes they would even call others to join in if they knew of their interests or thought that the conversation would be useful for us. In this way, we carried out around ten or eleven group discussions on different chars. In groups that had more men, the discussions generally addressed questions concerning different aspects of migration, histories of occupancy, land rights, the vulnerability of the chars, and perceptions of security and livelihoods. On the other hand, in groups with more women, the discussions veered toward the gendered aspects of migration as well as vulnerability and daily livelihoods. To study women-headed households, broadly ethnographic qualitative methods were employed. In addition to spending time with each of these women, each woman was interviewed extensively. Most of these conversations could not be recorded, but nearly half of the women in women-headed households participated in the group discussions. Toward the last stages of our research, we invited local artists and photographers to express themselves and their views of life and environments on the chars. In the final stage, we were able to speak to the participants about keeping financial diaries and opening up about money management at home. There has not yet been a clear-cut disengagement process; although our visits are rarer now, we continue to remain in touch with those who contact us on their own.

Structure of the Book

The book is divided into eight chapters. We undertook field-based study in the general area, the lower part of the valley of the Damodar river, and chapter 2 outlines how and why tropical rivers such as the Damodar are different from the rivers about whose fluvial dynamics we were forced to learn. This chapter also discusses the previous char studies and other materials that were relevant for the research, and illustrates how the view of chars as hybrid environments is different from them. The discussion places the later, historical and empirical parts of this study in context and shows the geomorphological and ecological perspectives on char formation. The extensive material on Bangladeshi chars is presented briefly to bring to the fore the distinctiveness of the Damodar chars. Chapter 3 outlines the colonial and postcolonial history to delineate the factors of char formation and to substantiate the claim that chars are as much products of human intervention as they are of the ecology of Bengal. In particular, colonial interventions in governing land and water resources are analyzed to argue that the Permanent Settlement of 1793 led to the privileging of land in a riverine community, necessitating a series of legal interventions such as the BADA to make sense of the maze created by crisscrossing river channels that throw up river islands at nature's whim. This privileging of land as a superior physical element, as a more valuable "resource," created a legacy that continued well after India's independence. Rivers came to be associated with destruction and damage of valuable land, which needed protection from the violence of the rivers. How postcolonial river control measures have followed the ideological basis on which such interventions began, the social construction of the river as representing violent nature that is in need of human control, is also shown in this chapter. A brief description of the Damodar river is followed by a discussion of the colonial separation of land and waters as well as the river control measures that have given rise to the chars.

Chapter 4 analyzes the interactions between chars and "mainland" areas—areas that lie across the embankments within which the chars have formed. This region, seen by those living on chars as "inside communities," has in the recent past experienced rapid agrarian change and rural transition. The chapter begins with a brief history of the agrarian transition of the region, and the roots of its rural prosperity are then explored. Just as the chars are not "no-man's-lands," nor do they exist in isolation; they are in a constant interaction with the mainland. Chapter 5 outlines the migration history of the chars and shows that people arrived on chars from different areas at different times. Two main communities made their homes on the studied chars. Different communities, Biharis and Bangladeshi Hindus, arrived on the chars for different reasons, and their different ways of adjustment are shown. This discussion brings out the differences in cultural adjustment to a changing char environment by the two main char communities. This chapter thus presents culture as the key in influencing postmigration adjustment to the hybrid environment of chars. Chapter 6 explores the mental maps of char dwellers and shows the coping and adjustment strategies that they adopt to live in an environment of vulnerability and isolation. It makes an attempt to show that people live in a risky and uncertain environment not just because they have incomplete knowledge or because their rationality is bounded by compelling factors. They take a calculated risk, opting for a chance like that in a lottery or a gamble, a risk that is informed by the intimate knowledge developed over many years of living in a fluid and dynamic environment. This environment is seen from outside as vulnerable and risky, but for those whose lives are defined by water, the environment offers refuge and opportunities.

Chapter 7 lays out in great detail the livelihoods of char dwellers. It shows that not only have they honed a fine appreciation of the nature of the river in order to use every bit of opportunity available to them and create a hybrid livelihood, but they have also developed a "sense of community" that allows people to help each other in the struggle for survival. It also focuses on women and their experiences of migration, their roles in securing livelihoods, and their perceptions of chars as "home," and shows the vulnerability of women-headed households in securing a livelihood. Poor people have, by definition, only tiny amounts of cash and have to be deft in managing these small amounts to make ends meet. The last section of this chapter shows how the poor live on a diverse mix of minimal resources; to understand this complexity, we worked with families to see the income and expenditure flows in great detail. In this chapter, we look into the households and show how individual families manage their incomes and how people mobilize resources on an informal basis. The concluding chapter summarizes the work and indicates possible and future directions of research.

CHAPTER 2

Char Jage

A Char Rises

She [the Earth] will sink into the midst of the water.—VEDA SAMHITA, QUOTED IN GHOSAL (1930: 5)

As the rivers descend from the mountains and make their way to the seas, they bring down sediments off the mountains, eroded over long periods of time, that ultimately arrive at the mouths of the rivers. But before being dumped into the sea, much of this sandy, silty material is stored temporarily along the way. The river stores the material in its own "banks": floodplains and channels (see Morisawa 1985: 116). This is how chars are born:[1] they originate as part of a river's natural processes and are an integral part of the ecologies of almost all floodplains. To make it clear that chars are essentially the products of fluvial geomorphological processes, this chapter outlines the ecological processes of char formation with details of the Damodar chars.

From a geomorphological point of view, chars can be described as "sandbars," or river islands. Some bars may be "attached"[2] to the banks of rivers, extending as pieces of land from the edges into the beds. When they form on a riverbed, the river's channel is divided, forming a braided channel. Rivers store their sediments on floodplains and in their channels for a number of reasons. The dumping of sediments can occur because of the weight of the sediment load itself, when the load becomes excessive for the river to carry it along. Sand also gets deposited owing to a sudden loss of velocity of the river as it descends onto the flat lands from the hilly terrain. Such a decrease in the pace of the river currents further reduces its efficiency in carrying the sediments. Geomorphologists agree that "divergent flow," or the splitting of the channel into a number of branches, or "intricate braiding," is an integral part of the flows in large rivers.[3] Morisawa (1985: 118), an outstanding fluvial geomorphologist, also thinks that floodplains are "essentially ephemeral" because they are continuously constructed and destroyed by the river's own actions. The deposits of vertical and lateral accretions are reworked as the rivers scour the channel or surrounding plains or migrate laterally. To understand the floodplains of tropical rivers this point is the key. Chorley et al. (1984) have attributed various names to such river islands: bars and river islands. The presence of channel banks, in their view, gives rise to these bars that are essentially a class of large-scale bed form, or "macroform" (Jackson 1975). In this schema of scale-based categorization, the dimensions of the bars are controlled by flow, width, and depth as alluvial channel patterns evolve from straight, erodible channels to complex and braided channels.

Standard and established geomorphological texts view the alluvial channel as a neat category separate from land, as a geometrical unit; for example, Bridge sees a fluvial channel as having "a finite width and depth, a permeable boundary composed of erodible sediments and a free water surface" (2003: 141). As chars appear within a river's channels, these pieces of land seem to pose a problem to geomorphology: Are they to be considered as part of fluvial dynamics or are they to be considered as units of land? In other words, conventional geomorphologists' questions that are asked as starting points for their research assume an absolute physical world that can be exactly measured. The very existence of river islands and their nomadic nature are posed in terms of what natural things should be in the ideal physical world. In the case of chars, they would then ask questions such as: Are braided channels a "normal" and natural occurrence? If the answer is yes, at what *stage* of a river's evolution does braiding occur? If chars were to be studied by asking such questions, one would end up developing a mechanistic view of chars, a view that is explicit in the most widely known geomorphic perspective that Bridge gives of midchannel bars: "If deposition is less rapid and/or more continuous, sheets of sediments are formed rather than discrete bars. The resulting accumulations of sediment in mid-channel, or forming the convex banks on the inside of river bends, are referred to as braid bars and point bars, respectively. Braid bars and point bars can be thought of as compound bars inasmuch as they are normally composed of parts of multiple bars" (2003: 145). In his subsequent analysis of the complex history of erosional and depositional modification of bars, the "stage dependence" of channel pattern appears to be the most crucial factor. One of the early geographical works by Brice (1964) differentiates between midchannel bars and river islands based on the criterion of height, that is, whether or not they rise over water continually. In his plan of classification, midchannel bars are unvegetated and submerged at a bankfull stage (when the entire river channel is filled with water from one bank to the other), whereas river islands are vegetated and rise above the surface of the water; but whether or not a bar becomes an island remained unclear for Bridge. Consequently, Bridge comments that "such a distinction between bars and islands artificially separates depositional forms that may have a common geometry and genesis" (2003: 149). Brice has also attempted to classify midchannel bars as "transient" and "stabilized" on the basis of their permanence, but since such descriptions clash with geomorphological terms, terms such as "unstable" and "stable" were used to imply the degree of erosion and deposition within the channel and, hence, channel migration. Bridge comments that "terms such as transient, unstable, and stable should be replaced with quantitative measures of the lifespans and rates of creation, migration, and destruction of bars and channels" (2003: 149).

Different Rivers

Conventional geomorphological wisdom received a challenge when Asian river experts pointed out that tropical rivers and tropical hydrogeomorphological processes are different from temperate rivers and their hydrology. Of these Asian river experts, Avijit Gupta is the most notable. Modestly, Gupta writes: "In tropical geomorphology we are constantly surprised by new discoveries" (2011: 3). And indeed, "we have a limited understanding of the geomorphic processes, landforms and sediments in the tropics" because the early geomorphology books were written largely by experts who came from temperate countries and saw in the tropical world what they set out to see in the first place.[4] Standard textbooks on geomorphology were largely targeted at students in temperate countries of Europe and North America, and pupils studying in tropical countries rarely received the opportunity to explore the examples that were located closer to home. Although discussing a climatic region in essence, Gupta warns against seeing the tropics as homogeneous and points to the "considerable climatic variations [that] exist across the tropical zone" (2011: 3–4), the roles played by tropical oceans in shaping the climate, and the assemblage of active tectonic belts, ancient cratons, alluvial valleys, and subsiding deltas that physically make the tropics. He says: "The early tropical geomorphologists did not always recognise such wide-ranging geologic variations, putting too much emphasis on the hot and humid climate as the prime controlling factor. . . . The tropics used to be perceived as a set of climo-morphogenetic landforms, where physical features are primarily controlled by the ambient climate" (2011: 4). As a result of such preconceived bias, the landscape characteristics were generally explained by assuming that they evolved in a hot and humid location over a very long period of time.

Tropical rivers bring down enormous quantities of sediments along with their waters; writing about the Amazon, Meade says: "Massive amounts of sediment brought down from the mountains become the substrates over which and through which the flowing waters, with their accompanying load of even more sediment, must make their ways" (2007: 46). There are other differences; for example, the meaning of *flowing at a bankfull condition* is not similar for tropical and temperate rivers. Tropical rivers may have a channel within a channel, the smaller one fitted to the wet season flow and the bigger one fitted to larger floods. They may also alternate between dry beds and huge flows, depending on the season. Writing about large tropical rivers, Potter (1978) observes that they carry enormous amounts of discharge, are long, have large drainage basins, and commonly transport a large volume of sediments. Moreover, some of these carry enormous amounts of silt in their waters, particularly those rivers that drain out the monsoonal rainfall hitting the Himalayan slopes. Gupta's early work (1994) shows that the large seasonal rivers of India carry not only enormous amounts of water but also sediments,[5] giving rise to unintended consequences when they are impounded. Some of these sediments create chars or river islands that become an integral part of the river and land processes. Gupta (2007) also notes that many of the world's largest rivers either originate or flow in tropical regions. Arriving in tropical India, the British administrators did notice the difference between temperate and tropical rivers. Sir William Wilson Hunter realized that rivers had built up and destroyed civilizations in India long before their arrival. Hunter observed that "[m]any decayed or ruined cities attest to the alterations in riverbeds within historic times" (1882: 30) and thought that the history of India is linked to the changing courses of its rivers.[6] Obviously, such shifting of courses occurred because of the need to seek a new path when the older channel became clogged by the sediment load brought down by the river itself.

Coming back to the various roles played by rivers as geomorphological agents, one clearly sees that the rivers not only sculpt the earth's surface, but also act as the main conduits in transferring the sediments from the continents to the world's ocean basins. Tandon and Sinha (2007) consider the rivers key to this enormous "system" of sediment transfer. The sediments, as they are carried by rivers, give rise to a wide variety of "bedforms"; these can be beds, ripples, and dunes among the smaller-scale forms, and bars and bar-complexes among the larger-scale forms. Best et al. (2003), who have studied the Brahmaputra-Jamuna river system extensively, consider larger-scale forms as part of other sandy braided river systems as well and offer a detailed classification of floodplain sedimentation and an analysis of the morphogenic processes. In a later study, Best et al. show how the dynamic processes operating within the floodplains continuously erase and rebuild the floodplain, and how thick sand and clay deposits smooth out the initial topography; they opine that "the older parts of the floodplain . . . become more complex in topography" (2007: 414).

For rivers located in monsoonal tropical areas, the most characteristic feature is the seasonality and ferocity of flow. Those who are not familiar with the rivers in the Gangetic plains may have difficulty in even comprehending this essential difference. A river that has been lying nearly dry for a number of months may magically come to life suddenly with the onset of the monsoons and at any time during the wet season may spill over its banks. Toward the end of the rainy season, when the channel is full, it may cause widespread floods in the surrounding plains. This seasonality of flow in the tropical rivers of the Gangetic plains has great implications for chars and their inhabitants. It also means that while accretion gives rise to chars, they are also constantly eroded by the rivers that eat up their banks and shift their courses frequently. These large tropical rivers are most significant to the contemporary understanding of human-nature interactions in the past, and nourish human communities today; not only did they support great ancient civilizations, they also support biotic systems and are under threat from natural and human-induced changes, including the effects of climate change.

The Bengal Delta

Geographers and geologists have argued over the exact boundaries of the Bengal delta. Oldham (1870: 47–51) defined the delta narrowly by including the entire area lying between the Hooghly on the west and

Meghna on the east including the Sundarbans proper. Other experts such as C. S. Fox (1930) believed that the delta begins slightly below Rajmahal, situated much to the north, whereas Panandikar (1926) included only a few districts of (current) Bangladesh as composing the Bengal delta. K. G. Bagchi uses a broad outline: "The region between the Ganges and the Brahmaputra and that between the Brahmaputra and the Meghna . . . [has] no doubt been built up by the materials brought down by the rivers" (1944: 8–19).

The geomorphic unit of the Bengal delta is part of the geologic unit, the Bengal basin. The Bengal basin is described by geologists as "a large subsurface sedimentary province filled up by sediments of pre-trappean and post-trappean age"[7] (Dasgupta 2010: 198). Tectonically, the Bengal basin is a bowl-like composite formation created by the fracturing and fragmentation of the Gondwanaland. Recent geological studies believe that the Bengal basin was probably formed due to the stretch and sag of the Indo-Antarctican part of the Eastern Gondwanaland (Das Gupta 1997; Das Gupta and Mukherjee 2006). The Indian plate is thought by geologists to have collided with the Burmese plate about thirty-four million years ago (at the end of the Eocene) and to have begun to subduct below the latter. This gave rise in the Pliocene to a newly formed Bengal basin with an embayed coastline, and with the Indian craton on its western side and the Assam-Arakan folded mountain belt on its eastern side. By this time in geological history, the Ganga-Brahmaputra river system had come into existence and started to deposit the rivers' detritus into this newly formed basin. Since the Pliocene times, the sea has retreated and the delta has prograded farther southward. Most of the sediments are contributed by three major river systems, the Ganga, the Brahmaputra, and the Meghna, whose combined flow reaches the Bay of Bengal through the huge Meghna estuary. The subaerial part of the delta covers nearly 138,000 square kilometers and a very large subaqueous part lies beyond. Even at its northern parts, the surface is only about ten to fifteen meters above the sea level; but closer to the sea, the height is much lower. The more active parts of the delta have moved eastward, leaving the river systems in the general West Bengal part to decay. Two theories compete with each other to explain the eastward shift: The geological one points out the gradual rise of the northwestern part of Bengal and the subsidence of the Bengal basin together with a tilting of the crust (Burrard 1933), and the hydro-geomorphological explanation shows the different hydrological regimes of the Brahmaputra and the Ganga, creating a natural vent for the latter to the southeast (Franklin 1861). The lower part is also subject to tidal flows 4.5 to 6 meters high. Geomorphologists Morgan and McIntire (1959), Umitsu (1993), Michels et al. (1998), Goodbred (2003), Goodbred and Kuehl (2000), and Singh (2007) have studied the Bengal delta in detail.

Throughout the lower parts of the Ganga-Brahmaputra-Meghna basin, all chars are surrounded by water during the monsoon months. Chars are exposed to, and repeatedly affected by, floods and shifting of river channels. Near their mouths, many rivers do not follow the same course for more than a couple of decades and areas that are continually subject to waterlogging turn into a maze of moribund channels crisscrossing each other as the delta-building moves on. During heavy monsoons, continuous rainfall may even completely inundate the low-lying chars. In many seasonal rivers with braided channels, some island chars may comprise land that even in the dry season can only be accessed by crossing a river channel. Some chars can be much more than just a midchannel island that periodically emerges from the riverbed. Some of them turn into permanent or semipermanent islands located well inside the two banks of the river, but they almost always rise above the high water mark. The pattern of physical development of chars and the human use of their land and other resources differ from country to country, from one river system to another, and even within the different reaches of the same river. Majuli, the largest char in the world, which was formed by the great river Brahmaputra in Assam in northeast India,[8] has existed for at least two-and-a-half centuries. The Majuli island spreads over an area of 875 square kilometers and is about 85 meters above the sea level. It is formed in a stretch of the Brahmaputra where a large number of tributaries form their small, tributary-mouth fans on the north and south banks. Due to its stability, Majuli is a valid administrative unit, a *mohkuma* (subdivision), of the Jorhat district of Assam. Unlike Majuli, most newly formed chars are naturally transitory and fragile; their shapes change frequently and their edges may start eroding any time due to the river current; a whole char may even disappear overnight. Bank erosion is as much part of char dynamics as accretion; even Majuli suffers from a high rate of bank erosion.[9] Old charlands, inhabited for decades by hundreds of men, women, and children with their houses, livestock, and croplands, may be lost in a matter of days due to a sudden whim of the river. Yet some chars may house permanent human settlements, depending upon the silt and soil properties and the strength of river currents.

Chars in Bangladesh

The formation and people's use of chars are more intensively studied and their existence is somewhat better recognized in the part of Bengal delta that now is Bangladesh. Brammer's exhaustive work (1990, 2004) on Bangladesh and his work in designing the heavily contested Flood Action Plans contain some analysis of the Brahmaputra-Jamuna charlands. Rafiqul Hasan Mantu's and Abdul Baqee's detailed research work, both published in 1998, draws attention to these no-man's-lands. For example, in 1979, on Char Kashim of Chandpur in Bangladesh, about three hundred families who had been leasing the land on an annual basis from the government were attacked by people wearing police uniforms. Those who resisted were rounded up and abducted. Powerful local leaders also hired *lathiyal*s (literally, stick-wielders, but the term stands for local army or force). To explain these conflicts, Baqee, however, falls into the trap of a Homer-Dixonian thesis (of many people scrambling to access limited resources). To gain their rightful share of land in the newly emerged chars, poor peasants had to get accustomed to a violent way of life that involved the use of force, dispossession, murder, rape, and crop robbery (1998: 63). According to him, the covert understanding between local *matbar*s (leaders) and corrupt state officials at the local level and faulty land surveying that is ill at ease with the changing nature of chars give rise to the violent and complicated disputes that often end in bloodshed. Talking about the ineptness of charland laws, Baqee comments that "the laws are deceptively simple on paper but are very complicated in the implementation" (1998: 65). The five factors that he identified for why the charland laws are unable to ensure security for char dwellers in Bangladesh are relevant for this study as well. They include the opaque legalistic language used by land documents, the large variety of papers required to prove ownership (and the difficulty in obtaining them), the requirement of continued *khajna* (rent) payments for a lost land, access to land document officials, and the difficulties of establishing rights over resurfacing chars. A deadly combination of these factors means that those who lose their lands due to erosion fail to get them back even if they resurface or when another char rises nearby. A char takes three to four years to surface above the high water mark, and political machinations during that time ensure that such lands are already shown in official documents as sold and allotted. If this leads to bloody feuds during the harvesting seasons when many claimants assemble to resist, some settlement officials might even back one or two claims in an effort to bring peace. Not only in Bangladesh but also throughout the Gangetic plains, physical "possession" of the land is critical for establishing ownership or at least user rights; the principle is stated in a popular Bangla proverb, *Dakhal jar, jami tar* (Land belongs to the one who possesses it). One may somehow manage to produce some legal papers, but if the local matbar has designs on the land, the farmer can do nothing to establish and prove his rights or ownership of it.

Baqee focused on the processes of occupancy on chars that involve force and feud, as well as dislocation and resettlement, rather than livelihoods. However, since the publication of Baqee's work, the chars of Bangladesh have been drawn into the center of resource management and environmental policy debates and discussions around flood mitigation and human vulnerabilities caused by riverbank erosion. Chowdhury (2001) considered the greater awareness in Bangladesh of chars as populated places understandable because of the importance of the riparian areas to the country's life and economy. The Environment and GIS Support Project for Water Sector Planning (EGIS) study, conducted in 2000, considered chars to be a "by-product" of the fluvial dynamics—in particular, the sediment load, discharge, and morphological behavior—of the rivers of Bangladesh. Consequently, the project concluded that the erosion-accretion processes are associated with increase/decrease in char areas.[10] The study showed that chars covered over seventeen hundred square kilometers of the country (EGIS 2000: 5). This study updated an earlier and more extensive one by the Irrigation Support Project for Asia and the Near East (ISPAN) conducted in 1993. The ISPAN study was primarily concerned with riverine chars and looked into both the island chars and attached chars. It also investigated—besides the physical and demographic features—the social and economic dynamics of life in the chars. It noted that over 90 percent of the chars that are not eroded in the first four years of their emergence are used for either cultivation or settlement by the end of those four years. After about seven or eight years, both settlement and agricultural practices are supported by these chars. Cropping intensity in relatively lower reaches where land is more fertile can be high, although the chars can be less productive than other lands due to the sandy nature of the soils. Besides cropping, chars have large areas of grasslands, which support grazing and provide material for thatching. Many chars are mined for sand as building material. These studies were prepared for the Flood Plan Coordination Organisation, undertaken as part of the Bangladesh Flood

Action Plan on riverine lands of major rivers of the country, and used as a field inventory of resources through Rapid Rural Appraisals as well as formal interviews and the analysis of satellite images. Apparently, during the 1980s and the early 1990s, char areas increased in all rivers in Bangladesh, except in the upper Meghna region. An excellent summary of both the EGIS and ISPAN studies has been published by Sarker et al. (2003) which details the environmental dynamics of chars and presents them as one of the most vulnerable locations for human habitation (EGIS 2000).[11] The unstable environments of virgin charlands also give rise to subcultures that are distinctively different from the cultures of the mainland (Zaman 1989: 197). Baqee thinks that this cultural distinction of the chars makes them the "land of Allah *jaane*" (literally, "God only knows," an epitome of deterministic fatalism). Such nomenclature can be easily attributed to the risks and hazards of living on charlands. Baqee describes the chars of Bangladesh as being inhabited by "some of the most desperate people in the country." These people are locally known as "char dwellers" or *chouras*, as they are called in West Bengal,[12] a population that is as fleeting as the land they inhabit. The unstable nature of chars in Bengal makes them a no-man's-land, which in turn makes them immensely suitable for transitory settlers. In West Bengal, as shown in chapter 5, chars are used by the poorest and the most "wretched of the earth," such as homeless Bihari or Bangladeshi Hindu migrants entering without official documents.

Instead of focusing directly on chars, Elahi et al.'s (1991) and Abrar and Azad's (2003) studies focus on the other side of the coin—the fluvial dynamics of erosion and coping strategies of people with displacement. The latter gives an interesting threefold typology of bank erosion—*chapa bhanga, bhanga*, and *hanria bhanga*. "Chapa bhanga" literally means "the breaking of the bank in *chaps* [chunky portions]" and occurs during the rainy season when the rivers overflow in swift currents. The size of the chunks breaking away from the bank varies from the size of a golf ball to two meters in width, and the common perception is that chapa bhanga gives adequate time to the char communities to relocate and save their harvests and other belongings. "Bhanga," or "the breaking of the soil," can wipe out large pieces of land—from one or two acres—in a matter of minutes. The breakage is often preceded by a sound that can be heard from a distance and the formation of large rings of circular water currents called *ghurnis* that loosen the soil along the bank walls and make them slide immediately. "Hanria bhanga" means "the breaking away of the soil as if it is a clean sweep down to the bottom of a *hanri* [a round cooking pot]." In hanria bhanga, the strong, speedy, and sharp undercurrent of the river cuts through the soft, sandy layer and reaches two to three kilometers inland from the bank. At one stage in a riverbank experiencing hanria bhanga, a big mass of land can hang above without any support and may suddenly come down without any warning. People have little chance to survive or to save their belongings in hanria bhanga. Besides these three main types of bank erosion, people identify many other types with local names. For example, *chechra bhanga* occurs mainly in newly emerged chars and when the floodwaters recede. In these chars, the soil is usually sandy and the vegetation is sparse, allowing the receding floodwaters to wash away large amounts of loose sand. *Bhurbhuri bhanga* means the string of bubbles rising to the water surface from where the sand has been washed away; *nishi bhanga* is when the erosion occurs at night; and *probol bhanga* is when the bank erosion has devastating effects (Abrar and Azad 2003: 17–18). The range of terms manifests the range of close human experiences and understanding of rivers' behaviors.[13]

These studies contributed to the Flood Action Plan of the country, but more importantly, they were followed up with developmental interventions by the Bangladesh Country Programme of the Department for International Development (DFID) of the United Kingdom. The "chars livelihoods program" is a large-scale, multisector project that supports the "extreme poor households" who live in the remote northwest riverine chars region.[14] The earliest of such developmental intervention on chars can be traced back to the Land Reclamation Project that was initiated in the late 1970s with the assistance of the Netherlands government (Zaman 1989: 197). The Project ran in the Noakhali district of Bangladesh and primarily aimed at the construction of diked or poldered land by encircling the chars with embankments. It also intended to distribute khas lands[15] as per the government rules to ensure the ownership of the landless, which was followed by programs for rural development. The DFID started its five-year Char Development and Settlement Project (CDSP) by utilizing some of the experiences and lessons from this earlier project in 1994. It covered three large chars of the district (Char Majid, Char Bhatirtek, and Char Baggardona-2) and continued the work in the second phase from 1999 to 2005. The main difference between phase 1 and phase 2 of CDSP is that in the second phase, some chars were left unpoldered. The third phase of the project is currently under way, and altogether over one hundred thousand hectares of land have been brought under the project in its three phases. The fundamental principle of CDSP is to distribute the khas lands among the landless families of the chars, after building engineering works to protect the lands from flooding. The interventions under the CDSP project have been popular because they have been able to provide a sympathetic form of governance of chars to ensure that the poor receive landownership to assure them the opportunities for livelihoods. It has been claimed that the salinity of the soils has decreased, cropping intensity has increased, and protection from floods has helped the cultivation of minor crops and vegetables around the household lands and increased income opportunities from fishing.

Rural development and livelihood interventions on chars of Bangladesh have given rise to a "resource versus hazard" debate. Some experts note that while the rural development projects often create new opportunities for the establishment of settlements and the pursuit of livelihood activities, they also create a false sense of security and, thus, further expose char dwellers to the extreme vulnerabilities of bank erosion and flooding. The char dwellers, who once were mentally prepared to cope with floods, now expect to be protected from floods, which is almost an impossible task in a flood-prone country such as Bangladesh. Bank erosion has undoubtedly been proven to be the most important area of vulnerability for rural inhabitants all over Bangladesh. The unstable nature of the land that led to a determination combined with despondency that Baqee has described as an "unusual risk-adopting desperation" (1998: 1) is now changing. Consequently, the choura mindset that contributes to the formation of a "char subculture" has also been changing. Still, the presence of the state is minimal on chars. Although the CDSP worked with some government departments such as the local government and engineering department, agricultural extension, and public health, the role of the state in ensuring public welfare has been negligible. This leads to a sense of lack of fulfillment and heightens the sense of insecurity among the chouras in spite of the active presence of nongovernmental organizations (NGOs) in the chars pursuing human rights.

The Damodar: An Unusual River

The Damodar flows through the states of Jharkhand and West Bengal, across the area that is now the coal and steel belt of eastern India, before reaching the eastern part of Burdwan[16] district where the chars are located. The basin of the river—nearly 25,000 square kilometers of it—is marked by morphological differences. For the first one-third stretch of its 540-kilometer length, the river flows through the undulating hilly tracts of the Chota Nagpur Plateau and collects the monsoon runoff from a wide area. The lower two-thirds of the river descends onto a plain where, as described by Professor S. P. Chatterjee, it branches into "a mosaic of marshes, tortuous channels and closed interfluves" (1967: 3). An "elbow bend" below the town of Burdwan gives a clue to its geological history: Formerly, the river joined the Hooghly at Naya Sarai, some 50 kilometers north of Kolkata where the old mouth is still marked by Kansona Khal; in the eighteenth century, the Damodar spilled southward toward the Rupnarayan river, and finally, in the great flood of 1770, which almost destroyed Burdwan, the river abandoned its old channel and turned south to its present outfall. At the very end of its course, the permanent levees bordering the right bank of the Bhagirathi-Hooghly and the belt of marshes along the western edge of the levees prevent its joining the Hooghly, the main distributary of the Ganges on the Indian side. Eventually, the river meets the Hooghly near Falta point in Howrah district. The changing courses and the many distributaries of the Damodar have created an inland delta (Bagchi 1944) with Burdwan town at its apex.

In the environmental history of South Asia, the Damodar has been a source and site of contestations, claims, and counterclaims between the lowland-caste Hindu peasants and the upland tribal communities. Disputes begin with its name, which the Sanskritized cultures[17] claim is derived from *dam-udar* (the river with a fiery belly, indicating the existence of coal in its valley); but for the Santhals, indigenous communities who live in its upper basin, the root words imply sacredness, *dah* and *modar* or *Damuda* (sacred waters). In Bengali-Hindu texts, the Damodar stands out as a figure in stark contrast to the sacredness of the Ganges; the medieval Chandimangal Kabya refers to the river as Lord Krishna, a lover and also an angry young man (Maity 1989). Between the indigenous treatment of the river as sacred and the Bengali Hindu view of it as embodying nature's masculinity, a wide range of folk worldviews express the close links of local communities with the Damodar.[18] The upper and lower reaches of the river have contrasting ecological characteristics. The upper valley has a rugged relief with high slopes covered with forests and scrub jungles, and terraced, cultivated fields. The lower valley, on the other hand, is nearly flat, even bowl-like, building an inland delta with its numerous anastomosing distributaries and riverine chars. Kirk's (1950) early geographical account of the Damodar, the "valles optima," describes unstable river courses, water-sorted deposits through which they flow, and old river courses locally known as *bhils*, which are shallow, fresh-water lakes that are choked with aquatic plants or by pieces of detached ancient levees. Due to its hydrology, seasonal floods were an integral part of the Damodar's flow regime. W. W. Hunter's *A Statistical Account of Bengal* (1876) gives a vivid description of the floods of the Damodar, portraying how rainwater rushed off the hills through innumerable channels into the riverbed with such great force and suddenness that the water rose to form a wave sometimes rising up to 1.5 meters in height, leading to flash floods that were locally known as *harka ban*.[19] Further downstream, bigger floods washed away weeds and water hyacinths, cleaned up the drainage congestion in the lower channels, and helped maintain the Calcutta Port. Passing through Burdwan district in 1815, Hamilton wrote about the lower Damodar tract: "In productive agricultural value in proportion to its size, in the whole of Hindustan, Burdwan claims first rank" (quoted in Willcocks 1930: 20). The unusual concentration of agrarian population and settlements, the land and the water being the two primary resources for farmers, attests to the rural prosperity and the unusual concentration of small farmers and settlements that these floods led to in this particular deltaic stretch (Mukherjee 1938).

The geographical uniqueness of the Damodar basin has led to a great interest in the river, and there is a significant amount of literature on the hydro-geomorphological characteristics of the river. Beginning as Deonad, from the coalesced seasonal streams springing from the Khamarpat and Bijrangha hills, the river carries a large sediment load of 41×10^5 cubic meters every year. The upper two-thirds of the basin is in the Chota Nagpur Plateau of Jharkhand (formerly the southern part of the state of Bihar), and the lower one-third is in the *radh* (western bank of the Hooghly) plains of West Bengal (Bagchi 1944). The upper and lower reaches of the Damodar—with a transitional part in the middle—have contrasting ecological characteristics. Bagchi (1977) points out that the course of the Damodar is parallel, but in the direction opposite to that of the rainstorms, the average track is toward north and northwest. The monsoon rains in the hills of the upper catchment area occur subsequent to those in the plains, but descend quickly from the uplands carrying huge amounts of silt onto the flat land. The silty waters reach the lowland only to find the lower reaches of the rivers already inflated. Saha explains the floods as caused by "the simultaneous rise of two rivers which flow into each other" (1938: 55–56). The extremely low gradient of the river in this part of the basin also means that its waters can only drain slowly. Above all, the Hooghly being a tidal river with a high tidal fluctuation, it allows only the intermittent release of water into the Bay of Bengal each day.

Damodar Chars

The Damodar has been one of the more important rivers of Bengal for many reasons, not least for its hydrology and the density of populations, but also for its role in causing massive floods and drainage congestion, as well as for bringing prosperity to those living in its valley. The river has acted as a great "environmental laboratory" for the state, which has tried to protect the riverine communities by controlling the river. The Damodar is notorious for frequently changing its course, and though they are now almost obliterated by advancing farming lands, human settlements, and associated infrastructure, some of its paleo-channels may still be detected from remotely sensed images. Rural communities, frightened of its legendary floods, call the Damodar "the sorrow of Bengal." The fierce floods of the Damodar invoked early river-control measures such as low embankments along the riverbanks, which initiated a more rapid rate of char formation than before. It was the devastating flood at the height of the Second World War that disconnected Calcutta, the headquarters of the eastern command, for over a week, triggering a "Flood Enquiry Commission." The Commission recommended full river control, leading to the formation of the DVC in 1948 to administer multipurpose development in the basin through a series of dams, barrages, and canal network. The DVC—as will be shown in the next chapter—has been only partly successful in reducing the frequency and intensity of floods and in providing irrigation water to agricultural fields of the lower Damodar valley. In spite of the DVC dams, there were disastrous floods in 1978 and 1998, both of which inundated the chars and changed their morphology. The DVC has wrought remarkable changes in the river ecology and the physical environment in the lower reaches of the valley. The clearing of extensive natural forests in the upper catchments for the construction of reservoirs has led to high siltation rates in the reservoirs (Saha 2008). The unpredictability of floods also has caused unpredictable erosion of the chars, making their boundaries even more uncertain (figure 2.1). For example, the outlines of Char Gaitanpur have changed significantly in recent history (figure 2.2).

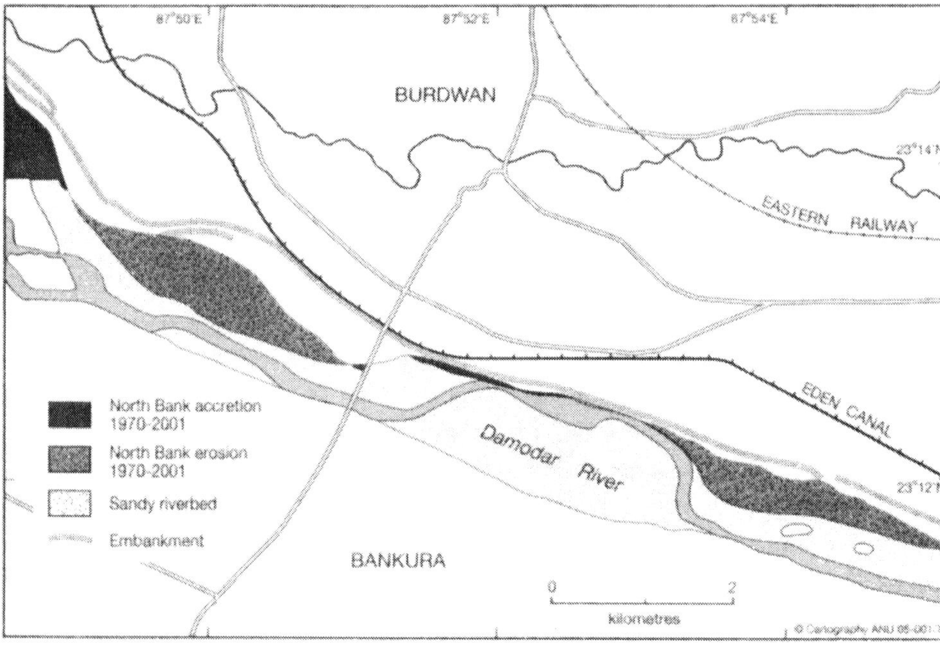

2.1 Shifting of Chars by Bank Erosion
Source: Compiled by the ANU Cartography Unit from topographical sheets published by the Survey of India; data from field surveys and remote sensing data.

Bhattacharyya (1998) shows that the dams on the river have reduced downstream water flows and altered the river regime enough to give rise to chars. According to her, river control was primarily responsible for the formation of chars in the lower reaches of the Damodar. She expands on how the sluices enhanced the formation of innumerable chars on the riverbed by releasing coarser and heavier sand through the lower parts of the gates. This is a purely anthropogenic explanation. We believe that char formation is more than just human intervention: Chars are an integral part of the geomorphology of the Bengal delta and we argue that the relationship implied between "river regulation" by the DVC dams and char formation is not entirely straightforward. If interventions are at all to be blamed, char formation in the Damodar needs to be placed in the background of early interventions—such as the construction of high embankments—in the river regime. This book shows that the meanings of land and river, to those who live on or near them and those who govern them, have been

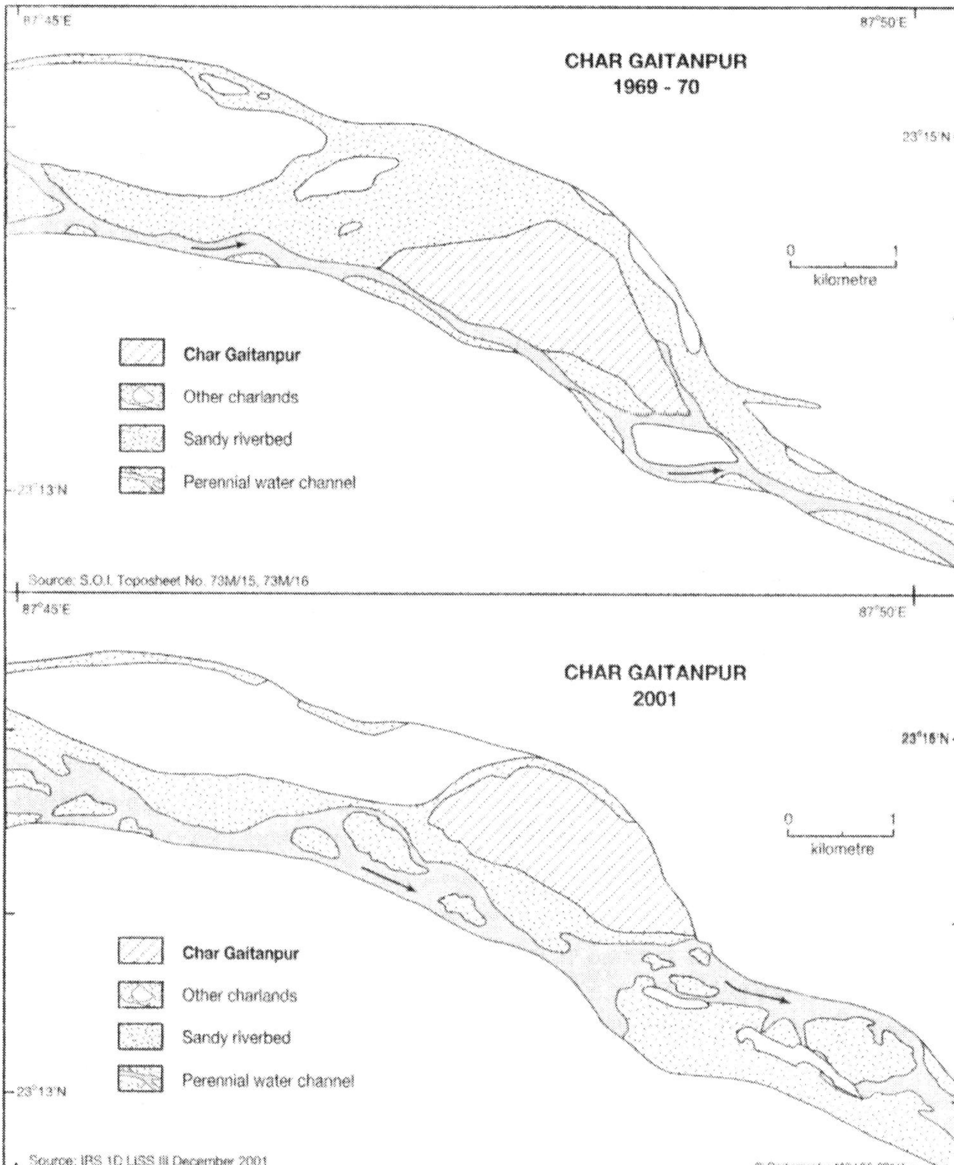

2.2 Shifting of Chars: The Example of Gaitanpur

Source: Compiled by the ANU Cartography Unit from topographical sheets published by the Survey of India; data from field surveys and remote sensing data.

historically responsible for the treatment the chars have received. These meanings have evolved over a complex process of precolonial, colonial, and postcolonial social, legal, and political processes from which neither the land nor the rivers of Bengal have remained isolated. What could be ascertained from interviews and anecdotal evidence are the connections between the decreasing frequency and changing nature of the floods, the construction of dams and barrages on the river, and the growing number of human settlements on the chars, described by Bhattacharyya (1998) as the "colonisation of the sandbars" in the lower Damodar valley.

Located on the western, moribund part of the Bengal delta, the bagri area on the western bank of the Bhagirathi-Hooghly branch of the Ganges has been traditionally known for rural prosperity. Part of this prosperity came from trade between the lower parts of the delta in the east and the forest-covered undulating tracts of the Chota Nagpur Plateau in the west. The trade was, until the early nineteenth century, largely river-borne, and the Damodar was known to have carried large vessels until the mid-nineteenth century. The rapid development of the jute mills in the Hooghly industrial belt and the growth of metropolitan Calcutta facilitated the establishment of the railways early in 1857 in the area. While the railways eased the transport of coal and other resources to Calcutta and stimulated the growth of the Raniganj-Jharia colliery belt, the introduction of this new mode of transport mostly erased a set of older settlements along the Damodar and the Bhagirathi-Hooghly in eastern Burdwan. Some of these settlements also had traditional industries—such as the cutlery industry of Kanchannagar on the outskirts of Burdwan—that died as they were cut off from what became the main transportation route (Lahiri-Dutt 1994). At the same time, early interventions—mainly in the physical form of embankments—into the deltaic river system began to create chars and cause drainage congestion near the mouth of the Damodar. The floodwaters of the river provided the foundation of agricultural prosperity based on the system of "overflow irrigation." Speaking to a gathering at the University of Calcutta in 1930, Sir William Willcocks expressed his belief that such irrigation could be reintroduced in the Ganges and Damodar deltas to bring in again the health and wealth which the western part of Bengal once enjoyed: "Let a return be made to the ancient irrigation of Bengal, and the country will be touched as with a magician's wand, and your ancient prosperity will be at your very doors. This will be so because the ancient irrigation was *flood* irrigation and not perennial irrigation" (1930: 128). The impending departure of the British and the Second World War prevented the restoration of the ancient irrigation system as per Willcocks's suggestion, and as will be shown in chapter 3, the Indian nationalists decided to "harness" and "train" the Damodar river through large dams and canals. The canals were also followed by the seed-fertilizer-water technology package that led to intensive rice farming and a consequent increase in rural prosperity. Parts of eastern Burdwan produce as many as three crops a year, and two rice crops are also commonplace. Generally, it is an area with relatively high agricultural prosperity, strong rural-to-urban links, and high levels of urbanization along the eastern end (Samanta 2002). The implication of the high visibility of this prosperity for the shifting charlands and their communities is that they have tended to remain largely unseen to the mainstream "mainland"[20] economy and society. Charlands were at the center of only small skirmishes in the 1950s and the 1960s, and these too have long since ceased. More subtle forms of power play are at work in rural West Bengal, particularly in this district, in the rural parts of which the Communist Party, ruling since 1977, has established a relatively stronger grip than in neighboring areas. The emergent rural prosperity not only attracts temporary and seasonal migrants from other, poorer districts of the state, but its complex power politics have also encouraged a number of scholarly studies (for a better understanding of the regional economy, see, for example, Bandyopadhyay 1995; Bhaumik 1993; Chandrasekhar 1993; Ruud 1994; Sanyal et al. 1998).

Char formation, therefore, is much more than just a purely natural process. The legal recognition of chars depends upon institutional arrangements such as land records for revenue administration. Most of the institutional arrangements established by the colonial government carried over by the postindependence state—even in the lower deltaic plains of Bengal—are aimed at stable lands and settled land-based populations. Thus, chars are also *produced* by official government documents and directives. For the colonial revenue administration, the erratic nature of such lands posed great difficulty. For example, in the diara lands of the Kosi, the need for political control necessitated ecological control of processes that were little understood by the rulers. Hill (1997), environmental historian of the Gangetic plains, has described in detail how the floodplains were treated by the British as a "great environmental laboratory." Further down the Ganges, in Bengal, the Permanent Settlement[21] was introduced in 1793 to inject a stable revenue system, but completely overlooked the ecological fact of the charlands and diara lands and the capriciousness of the river systems in Bengal. Hill observes that "[o]ne of the early and continuing problems with diara revenue collection [in Kosi river plains] was the fact that no land survey had accompanied the Permanent Settlement" (1997: 34). Consequently, the zamindars used different tactics to receive "illegal payments" from diara lands: Often they would delay issuing new leases on the pretext that they did not know the amount of cultivable land, or plead for the abatement of diara revenue. When rent abatements were disallowed and exactions on the peasantry failed, they tried to have their diara declared as wasteland, which was revenue-free. In fact, the best indigo lands were those that were subject to inundation during the rainy season and that remained submerged for two to three months. The cultivation of indigo was mostly confined to the low-lying charlands that, Iqbal (2010: 75) observes, the planters were always looking for. On some chars, indigo and rice even rivaled each other. Hill observes that the district officers were unable to distinguish between land that was merely lying fallow and land that simply had no productive potential. By the time of the survey conducted by Francis Buchanan in 1809–1810, more than 35 percent of Purnia district alone was considered wasteland.[22] Trained to treat only permanent lands as "land," the government officials who think of "systematic" surveys to register and control land have felt baffled about the chars even today. In Bengal, a char can only be accepted legally as "land" if it continues to exist for over twenty years. Some chars might stabilize enough and support enough people to gain legal recognition as land, but most of them do not quite fit the conventional description of "land" and hardly support any significant infrastructure such as roads and markets or water supply and sanitation facilities. Poor service provision also results from constrained access.

So far, we have presented the ecological factors of char formation in lower Bengal. In the following chapters, we show how char formation is also connected to river-control measures such as embankment construction along the rivers' banks and dams across the rivers' courses. The roles played by the colonial (and postcolonial) land tenure system in the formation of chars are also discussed in detail.

CHAPTER 3

Controlling the River to Free Up Land

For the first time in the history of the nation, the resources of a river were not only to be "envisioned in their entirety"; they were to be developed in that unity with which nature herself regards her resources—the waters, the land, and the forests together, a "seamless web."—DAVID LOWENTHAL (1967)

In the epigraph, David Lowenthal is speaking of the Tennessee Valley Authority (TVA), an American river-control project that became the model for controlling the Damodar. But a similar utilitarian and functional view of rivers and land, seen as "resources" waiting to be "developed," also prevailed in Bengal. The worldview arrived in Bengal with European colonizers attempting to tame the lands and waters to raise revenues. This worldview is also intricately connected to, and responsible for, the formation of chars. In the previous chapter, we explained chars as parts of the natural ecology of floodplains; in this chapter, we show that river-control measures lead to and exacerbate the formation of such lands. The river may be old; the ideas of control that encouraged the growth of the chars have a more recent antecedent. The Damodar river basin has a unique configuration—a broad upstream area of hilly catchment and a constricted funnel-shaped and completely flat downstream area—and the river has a monsoon hydrology. From the jungles in the upper parts of its catchment to the waterlogged plains in its lowest reaches, the river crosses a range of geomorphological conditions. The characteristics of its basin and its specific hydrology—monsoon rains passing the river course in parallel—is such that chars can rise naturally. The formation of chars, however, has been greatly enhanced by human interventions modifying the river's flow. The alterations have occurred during the last two centuries or thereabouts through a series of human interventions, both small and large and both physical and legal. For the Damodar, the strategic location of the river, the density of population in its lower valley, the rural prosperity, and the urban-industrial belt that has grown along its eastern end all encouraged the modification of the river system. Successive governments have made attempts over the years to exercise control over the monsoonal rush of waters in the river and to contain this flow within its banks. Above all, the privatization of property through the Permanent Settlement put far greater value on lands in the context of riverine Bengal, and created the ideological context in which the infrastructure of control could be justified. All these factors have had far-reaching impacts on the river and its chars. This chapter analyzes and outlines the history of these land- and water-control measures to show their relationship with char formation. In particular, it shows how the processes of transformation of the ecology of the Bengal delta, initiated by the colonialists, have been continued during the postcolonial times.

Much of this transformation involved not only physical constructions on the river to control and manage its flows, but also the separation of land from the rivers that gave rise to it. Modern European environmental and agrarian imagination needed to split soils and fluids into discrete domains (Cosgrove and Petts 1990). This exorcism of water from land, D'Souza (2009: 3) believes, was to turn it into useful property that could then be elaborated into socioeconomic-legal objects owned by individuals. This view of land was rooted in Adam Smith's view of what an economy should be like, and on conceptions of the environment based upon rural England; this is the reason why, Neale observed: "When the British came to India it never occurred to them that cultivated land could belong to no one, or, if one prefers, to a large number of people, each owning [it] in a different way" (1962: 51). If the state is the ultimate and absolute owner of the land, then the East India Company as the successor to the Mughal Empire had already become the natural owner of what was considered as "our estate," the land, and it appeared that there was no other way to make it productive but to put it under the plow (Guha 1963: 18). Neale (1962: 53) suggests that the revenue from the land on which the state asserted full ownership built the economic foundations of the British Empire; if, to the Indians, a claim to the land was a means of consolidating political power, to the English such a claim had logical implications for the distribution of income. The arduous attempts made by colonial British powers at transforming once soluble and precarious waterscapes into firm and durable landscapes, drying them out to turn them into settled agricultural lands, effecting "separations between water and land," required above all the mental or ideological construction of a particular kind of river, flowing over a land that needs protection from the river. This subtle process was accomplished through a number of changes in the land tenure system and in the ways lands were recorded and valued by the state, and by creating a legal framework to rule over the land and waters of Bengal. Laws that defined lands and waters into rigid categories were created in order to have "some degree of security of tenure and permanency of possession" (Thackeray 1889: 19). As a consequence, by the early 1900s, the Damodar came to be known as the "sorrow of Bengal" because of its unpredictable, violent, and devastating floods and its shifting courses. But as Kirk notes, "overabundance of water at one time" (1950: 428) was always counterbalanced by a lack of fresh flushing water at another in this land of a dying delta. The shifting courses of the river were preceded by a reorientation of the Ganges in the sixteenth century, when it turned southeast to flow mainly through the Padma and channel more of its silt-laden waters through the eastern distributaries of the delta. As the river swept down from the jungle-covered hills onto the agricultural plains, it brought with it enormous quantities of silt and sand, which enhanced the fertility of the plains, but which could destroy the productive power of the land, choke the wells and ponds, and destroy the homesteads of the villagers.

Separation of land and waters completely rearranged Bengal's economy. It is not unknown that early Bengal was never really a land of farming; farming was, at best, a secondary occupation, as evidenced by historical accounts. For example, in his book *Three Deltas*, van Schendel (1991: 66) recounts the eighteenth-century traveler Orme's (1805) account of a highly sophisticated artisan economy that grew on water-based prosperity: "[I]n the province of Bengal, when at some distance from the high road or a principal tour, it is difficult to find a village in which every man, woman and child is not employed in making a piece of cloth." Rice was the mainstay crop and was irrigated too, although by natural means, by rain and flooding, and the countryside was dotted with local markets attesting to a highly commercialized economy. This water-based artisan economy, van Schendel contends, did not lead to widespread urbanization, but boasted of impressive industries which tended to be dispersed in the countryside, as in the case of the textile industry. Till the early colonial period, as Buchanan (1798: 7) indicates, many inhabitants of densely populated parts of Bengal treated agriculture as a subsidiary occupation: "[I]n this part of the country, there is hardly such a thing as a farmer."

As the river's floods caught the popular imagination as disastrous and in need of control, the chars and the communities they supported rarely appeared in the periphery of vision of the general public. While experts and rich farmers endeavored to contain the waters within the banks of the river, often failing in these attempts, a completely new, hybrid world was taking shape within the river itself, giving rise to new communities and livelihoods. To understand this world, one needs first to illuminate the histories of land and water management in this part of Bengal. But, first, a brief background of the river that is at the center of it all.

The Damodar: An Imagined River

River control in the Damodar was primarily aimed at protecting land-based settlements, villagers' lives, and their farms. Yet, it was not as straightforward as it seems. Before any control measure was devised, there was a need to partition nature (as represented by the river) and the humans, and posit them against each other. This required the production of a certain kind of knowledge about nature, a knowledge that could justify the intervention. As is known, all knowledge is socially constructed; and, in this case, the statist ideology and state institutions became the production mediators between humans and nature that filled the gap in resource management literature and gave rise to discourses that were embedded within the institutional configurations of power, knowledge, and accepted authority. The representation of the floods as an aberrant and uncivil behavior in need of control legitimizes state intervention to protect its citizens from the river. The "recorded" history of floods in the lower Damodar valley begins in 1730, when one finds that floods of different magnitudes were taking place every eight or ten years. These inundations were portrayed as "abnormal" behavior of the river, leading to their elaborate and scientific classification based on their discharge.[1] Such a representation was based upon ideas of nature that hinged upon the subordination and transformation of rivers, leading to social, political, and ecological dominations. South Asian environmental history is characterized by such reinterpretations that colonists and colonized minds produced; social historians have hence offered a number of explanations. The political scientists Agrawal and Sivaramakrishnan (2001) explain this phenomenon as the partitioning of the autonomous nature from the human agency, and show how this kind of representation can lend easily to statist modes of the governance of nature.

The Indian sociologist of science Ashis Nandy critiques the description of rivers as "wayward," and notes that such images have "not only persisted but powered many of the contemporary efforts to contain or tame rivers in that part of the world [in eastern India]" (2001: 711). Environmental historian Hill (1997) explains this as the treatment of riverine floodplains as a great "environmental laboratory" in which to test European ideologies on the purpose, use, and control of nature in all its manifestations. Writing from a Marxist perspective, D'Souza (2003, 2007) explains this need to dominate nature as the salient feature of colonial capitalism, and elaborates his point through historical studies of the Mahanadi river of eastern India, over which the Hirakud dam epitomized human control. The Damodar is another example of a similar experiment in river control and regulation. Words such as "river training," "river control," "taming," and "harnessing" added a scientific legitimacy to an imagined river (Lahiri-Dutt 2000). The presence of the newly independent state and nationalists gave this state project further legitimacy.

It is not folklore that before the interventions began on the Damodar, the village communities had developed—from years of coping with floods—various means of adjustment to the excesses of water. Even today, one might encounter houses in flood-prone areas that were built on raised plinths that withstood the onslaught of the worst flooding. Crops in the farms depended upon and actually thrived in floodwaters, growing taller as the floodwaters rose. In his seminal lectures, William Willcocks (1930: 9–12) describes this flood dependence as the "overflow irrigation" in which broad and shallow canals carried the fine clay and humus-rich crest waters of the floods into the fields, and frequent cuts on the banks of the canals—spill channels which were called *kanwa*s in Bhagalpur or *hana*s (in the lower parts of the valley)—inundated the fields to fertilize the soil, checked the spread of malaria, and helped turn rural Bengal into the productive land that it was. The indigenous crop varieties grew rapidly ahead of the floodwaters, and the cropping calendar too was often suited to phases of inundation (Brammer 1990; Hofer and Messerli 1997). Even standing water had its use: Jute crops were retted in the stagnating water of the swamplands (Chapman and Rudra 1995). An intricate network of ponds, aqueducts, and water tanks provided seasonal storage of water as well as drainage.

One might ask: Why did this system of overflow irrigation not survive in Bengal? Willcocks blames the governance chaos during the postbreakdown of the Mughal Empire. He considers that those who fought for and colonized Bengal for its riches did not look after the irrigation system: "[T]he Mahrattas and the Afghans had disorganised the ancient 'overflow irrigation' of Bengal" (1930: 20).[2] He quotes François Bernier (1891 [1815]), a French physician who visited Bengal between 1656 and 1668 and whose perceptive travel accounts are still a good source of information on Mughal Bengal: "[T]he knowledge I have acquired of Bengal in two visits inclines me to believe that it is richer than Egypt. . . . From Rajmahal to the sea is an endless number of canals, cut in bygone ages from the Ganges by immense labour, for navigation and irrigation" (1930: 18–19). By 1815, the zamindars and tenants of Bengal had neglected the maintenance of the canals to such an extent that they choked up with the silt and became unable to carry the rainy season flows. Willcocks notes: "As the uncleaned canals took less and less water, more water remained in the Damodar and it became a menace to the country. The Damodar banks now assumed a fresh importance" (1930: 21). This was probably the beginning of large-scale char formation in the river and the commencement of the formation of chars that stabilized over time rather than being flushed away during the monsoons.

Colonial Control of the River: Profiting from Land?

Although Willcocks was a great enthusiast for revitalizing the ancient overspill irrigation system with minimal interference into the river hydrology, a different kind of power politics had begun in 1760. The East India Company took the *dewani*[3] of Bengal, Bihar, and Orissa from the Mughal Emperor Shah Alam in 1765, and took over the role of direct management and control in 1772, that is, within this short period of twelve years, the East India Company became "the permanent rulers" of one of the richest tracts in the world (Pal 1929: 2). The problem that followed was one of knowledge: of land tenures and taxes of the country that they were now owners of, of surveying and assessing to ascertain the values of property, and of fixing the rent of estates. Describing the quandary, Baden-Powell, in his book that became a manual for land revenue officers, wrote: "The whole theory of the Indian Land Revenue was absolutely strange to the English authorities. They could not tell who owned the land and who did not, nor what category to place the different native officials they found in the districts" (1892: 393). They must have found the shifting rivers and dynamic lands messy, the Mughal system of property ownership complicated, and the ancient Hindu quite incomprehensible. The first priority in establishing an absolute and irrefutable authority on the land was to prove beyond doubt that the state owned all the land according to ancient Indian systems. Toward this, the Company even asked one Bengali Sanskrit scholar, Jagannath Tarkapanchanan, to write a "digest of Hindu laws" (Pal 1927: 18), but when he suggested that under the ancient laws and customs of India, property was vested in the peasants[4] and the landlords, who were not much more than revenue farmers, the Company officials were reluctant to accept the view.[5] A policy, based on the principle of property, was needed to establish that the government is justly the owner of the land, the "estate" that was Bengal; then what it took from the cultivator could be regarded as rent and it could be entitled to claim all the lands and waters of the estate and the products from them. Neale says of the Company officials that they "all shared the belief that a sound administration must have the security of landownership as its basis, and nothing but a Permanent Settlement could ensure this" (1962: 17). Consequent to the realization that it would be futile to look back in history for ancient traditions and that the Bengal society was to be fashioned after the image of England, the Company set off to create its own rules, primarily aimed at the creation of a profitable system of revenue collection from land, which they deemed as the key source of profit and power. Pal quotes Backerganj Final Report, paragraph 210, suggesting the sole objective [of the East India Company] was "to squeeze the sponge as thoroughly as possible" (1929: 3).

The philosophical basis of valorizing land lay in the contemporary British politics of confirmed physiocrats. The idea was that the key to public revenue lay in the concept of private property (Hill 2008: 222). Consequently, the Company officials envisaged Bengal to be an agrarian economy, an economy in which the rivers were only seen as instrumental because it was land that yielded revenue and, hence, riches. Obviously, whoever could own more land had more riches, and the less they had to pay to the Company as rent the better. The process began when in 1786, five years after his defeat at the battle of Yorktown, Lord Charles Cornwallis was appointed the second Governor-General of India.

As Cornwallis embarked on the task of a complete overhaul of the agrarian system, he kept in view the primary goal: to ensure that the East India Company had a constant, guaranteed annual revenue so that budgets, in terms of income and expenditure, could be figured on an annual basis without having to deal with any unexpected fluctuations in revenue. The first task toward this end was to rework the Mughal land revenue system and to change the agrarian hierarchy and to fashion a new Bengali society after the image of England (Guha 1963: 17). Stokes has argued that Cornwallis represented the general ideas of his country at that time and was not alone: "[T]he British mind found incomprehensible a society based on unwritten custom and on government by personal discretion" (1959: 82). The Bengal Permanent Settlement Act of 1793 incorporated this philosophy,[6] and the implications of it were breathtaking, according to Hill (2008: 223); with a stroke of the pen, the agrarian world was turned upside down. The law made the former revenue collectors, the zamindars, into British-style landlords, and the vast territories from which they collected revenue were now their private estates. Throughout the Bengal Presidency, settlement officers began to undertake surveys to figure out the quality of the lands and crops that were grown on them and settle the revenue owed to the Company by each estate. Once the settlement was agreed upon, it became fixed in perpetuity, never to be raised or lowered. Hill discusses how monumental the ramifications of this aspect (the "permanence") of the settlement were, how it completely stripped the peasants of their rights to occupancy, and how it was not until the passage of the Bengal Tenancy Act of 1885 that the cultivators gained some rights to the land they cultivated.[7]

At the time of the transfer, Burdwan Raj was fourth in a ranking made by the Calcutta periodical *Capital*, after Dwarbhanga, Cooch Behar, and Orissa Temple Endowments (Henningham 1990). Consequently, the rent for Burdwan was set at a considerably higher rate than that of any other zamindari jurisdictions of the *subah*, and consequently the first appointed English superintendents, Messrs. Johnstone, Hay, and Bolts, set out to acquire a closer knowledge of the resources and capacity of the lands placed under their charge. They began to identify and classify the lands as cultivated, uncultivated, alienated, and "most productive." This way, they allocated a large amount of land as *baze zameen*, or wasteland. The Company officials also leased the most profitable *pargana*s to themselves and often went to great lengths to acquire the rights to the most valuable lands. Based on their study of land revenue records, Chaudhuri et al. give a detailed account of the corruption over landownership by Company officials and comment that "these possessors are, undoubtedly, for the most part, the official land-owner himself clandestinely, his minions, and the *mutseddies* of the *Khalsa;* whose acquiescence to such collusive benefices, under the sanctified appellations of religious or charitable gifts at different times became necessary, as they were in their nature wholly fraudulent and sure to be resumed if made known to the Mussalman Government" (1994: 381). The Permanent Settlement of 1793 gave land away to zamindars in perpetuity to reduce the complexities of revenue collection and to prevent defaulters in the payments of rent since many landowners, including the Maharaja of Burdwan, were unable to pay the rent and were thus selling portions of their estates. For the Maharaja, the settlement was on the higher end and he often failed to pay up by the due date. Alarmed at the rate of dismemberment of his estate, the Maharaja decided to bind tenants to the same conditions to which he himself was bound by the colonial government, and one of his actions was to create *patni* tenures, or perpetual leases. Chaudhuri et al. interpret this new tenure system as "the hypothecation of the land as security for the punctual payment of the rent, and the liability of the tenure to summary sale in the event of default" (1994: 384–385). It also meant that the right to collect rent from the tenants (and the right to use noneconomic compulsions such as physical force to exact rent from the defaulters) devolved to the lower layers, and the upper-layer zamindars became more of a legal or juridical presence rather than a real social entity for the peasants. More than the subinfeudation on the land itself, this distancing of the state from the peasants had long-term implications for the power politics of Bengal. Quoting a Bengal Administration Report of Sir George Campbell (1921), Bhattacharyya points out that "all the under-tenures in Bengal have not, however, been created since the permanent settlement. . . . Dependent taluks,[8] ganties,[9] howalas[10] and similar fixed and transferable under-tenures existed before the settlement" (1985: 9–11). Another interpretation of the system introduced by the Permanent Settlement is that it aimed to give all underholders of land, down to the *ryots*, or the peasants, the same security of tenure as against the zamindars, which the zamindars had as against the government. Subject to the payment of the established revenue, the rights of all subholders were recognized and protected. It is probably this security that saw the patni system gradually extend, and by 1825 nearly the entire estate of the Maharaja was leased out in this manner. The *patnidars*, finding how much trouble this arrangement relieved them of, created *dar-patnis* (patnis of the second degree) upon the same terms and with the same rights over the land as they themselves had. The dar-patnis created *se-patnis* (patnis of the third degree). Neither did the zamindars of Bengal develop into capitalist farmers following the English model, nor did they shape themselves as French *fermiers*. Instead, the process of subinfeudation created a sprawling class of landed gentry who earned a living as revenue farmers.

What developed in Burdwan is of significance to understanding the agrarian transition of Bengal because while other zamindars also began to lease and sublease their lands, the Burdwan Raj initiated and almost perfected the structure, and the Burdwan Maharaja did so first, before other rajas could even understand the implications of the Settlement. In the model he created, the layers were not just a few (such as patnidar, dar-patnidar, and se-patnidar), but were well above twenty in some zamindari estates. Each link between these formations of revenue farmers resembled the others. Soon, the Burdwan model became so definitive that it was widely imitated by other zamindars. The East India Company, therefore, had to legalize, through Regulation VIII of 1819, the creation of such formations, thus giving a *de jure* recognition *post facto*. The Regulation, although innocuous and simple, was of great historical potency; it became the key that unlocked the door of social and economic changes of unparalleled magnitude. From a riverine community, Bengal moved on to become a land-based community. This had unforeseen impacts in shaping the meaning of place and environments in Bengal. Events progressed ahead of the lawmakers, who thus found no other option but to formalize them with legal sanctions. The legal basis of such infeudation was the concept of zamindari tenure or the nature of property rights that it connoted. One of the experts on colonial land regulations, C. D. Field (2010 [1883]: 509), following Harrington, enumerates the characteristics of the zamindari property as an absolute right of proprietorship in the soil, subject to the payment of a fixed amount of revenue to the government. Roy (2010) thinks that this absolute right allowed the colonial British to accumulate primary capital through land taxation, determine the agrarian relations as well as the relations between land and the waters, and alter the meanings that these elements of nature held to local residents. The innumerable undertenures that had developed in this new system indicate the growing importance of land in Bengal. Philips (1876: 29) notes that it was impossible to give an exhaustive account of them since "in many cases what is called a tenure has no distinctive feature; and the name it bears is given, not an account of any peculiarity in cultivate or the crop produced, or the mode in which rent is paid." There was *sali* land, which was wholly submerged during the rains; *suna* land, which was not so submerged; *nakdi* or *nekdi* land, for which rent was paid in cash at a certain rate for the *bigha*, *bhaoli* land, for which rent was paid in kind, the rent being a share of the produce; *bhiti* land, which was the raised site suitable for building homes; and *uthbandi* or *ootbundee* land, where the ryot paid for as much of his holding as he actually cultivated. These names were frequently met with as names of tenures.

A series of actions and measures followed the Permanent Settlement of land, the most significant being the initiation of surveys of rivers and lands. The East India Company assigned its surveyor and engineer, James Rennell, to conduct a survey of the river systems in Bengal and to prepare detailed maps of these rivers. From 1763 to 1773, Rennell compiled a set of maps of Bengal for the British Government, published in 1779 as the *Bengal Atlas*. This *Atlas* became the most authentic and legitimate source of information on the rivers of Bengal and was regarded as vitally important for commercial, military, and administrative purposes. Rennell's *Atlas* has come to be regarded as an information datum; a comparison of contemporary maps shows the changes in river courses since the Permanent Settlement. To survey and assess the land, the Board of Revenue was established after 1793 to monitor the zamindari systems. As the importance of land rose, the Board was deemed insufficient, eventually leading to the formation of the Directorate of Land Records almost a hundred years later in 1884 to promulgate the Bengal Tenancy Act in 1885. Under its command and supervision, this Directorate initiated the first major settlement operation for preparing the Cadastral Maps[11] as well as for recording rights under the provision of the Bengal Tenancy Act of 1885. It goes without saying that the state tended to side with the richer landlords during the cadastral survey, recording the new lands in their names. Large amounts of money changed hands; the frustration of the rural poor was reflected in the proverb *Deshe elo jarip, praja holo garib* (The villagers become poorer when the survey comes to the village). Not all of the poor villagers accepted the change quietly; McLane (1985: 26–27) has argued that due to changes in land revenue obligations, tenant-landlord relations, and the organization of policing and judicial systems, dacoity and banditry flourished in post–Permanent Settlement Bengal. The fact that the typical bandit gang was made up of lowland villagers who led "ordinary lives" as field laborers, cowherds, palanquin-bearers, village watchmen, or lathiyals (men employed to use *lathis*, or sticks, to collect their master's rents or to fight with neighbors for the possession of disputed land or crops) reflected the dissatisfaction with the substitution of discretionary and paternal authority at the village level with the state's impersonal governance. These people were not *janam chuars* (born robbers) and did not belong to what administrators came to call "criminal tribes and castes," but were most likely village poor "turning to gang robbery out of economic desperation" (1985: 32).

On the rivers, the net results of the heightened importance of land as against that of the river were that more embankments were constructed and the heights of the older ones raised. The meaning of the embankments also changed; as the river was unable to spill over its banks, the administration began to imagine that the embankments were meant solely for flood protection. Irrigation went on as local farmers as well as zamindars secretly cut breaches into the banks for irrigation.[12] Excessively high tax on the land resulted in the comparative neglect of the rivers and their banks. That the land tax was high was maintained even by Lord Cornwallis. In a letter dated March 6, 1793, to the Court of Directors, he said: "[I]t is the expectation of bringing them [the extensive waste and jungle lands, and the chars] into cultivation and reaping the profits of them that has induced many [of the zamindars]. . . . It was their additional resource alone which [could] place the landholders in a state of affluence and enable them to guard against inundation and draught."

Colebrook in 1806 wrote that dealing with the annual inundation that lower Bengal experienced required "patient industry" and the labor of the peasants and the landowning classes. The banks and dikes also required an enormous amount of capital for their building and maintenance. Until the Permanent Settlement, the responsibility for this investment was vested in the state, which used its own revenue. Even prior to the Permanent Settlement, it was clear that many of these embankments needed regular repair. It is possible that the lack of direct benefits from them made the Burdwan rajas disinclined to maintain them. Now this was supposed to be done by the zamindars, who were already heavily in debt. Not only were the embankments neglected, the local ponds and tanks that absorbed some excess waters and provided drinking water to local communities also fell into disrepair. Besides, the zamindars devised various means to delay their annual installment payments, or *kists*; they also found that reclamation of new land from the riverbeds was the easiest way to enhance their economic solvency. These reclaimed or cleared lands from riverbeds (and elsewhere), considered as baze zameen, were tax-free lands, and even when the zamindars settled communities on these lands, the tax was payable only to the zamindars. Mitra's compilation of letters from the Governor-General in Council's office to the Collector of the district show that the question of maintaining the embankments was forced on the colonial government; there are repeated orders to the raja to undertake repairs of the old *bandhs*, or embankments, and grants of additional funds for the "repair of the embankments of the district under your charge" (1955: 67).[13] It appears from some of the letters that the maintenance of these bandhs had become a major cause of disagreement between the colonial state, local landlords, and peasants. Sometimes the devastating floods destroyed not only the peasants' farmland, but also the silk and indigo factories, underlining the need for proper maintenance of the banks. The overflow canals came to be known as "dead rivers," or *kana nadi*. Willcocks's observation is supported by historical records that show how the banks came to be known as "zamindari banks."

The decay of the overflow irrigation system was followed by increased shifting of the courses of the Damodar. Chatterjee observes that the consequences of these shifts have been "vital" as they have almost always been accompanied by "catastrophic breaches as a sequel to high spates" (1967: 2). As the river began to change its course more frequently, he notes, "the people of the region had to adapt themselves to the changes and began cultivating the *kana*s, blind or dead channels, when fields were devoured by newly formed spill channels" (1967: 2). The settlements that began with the blessing of the river now needed protection from the river, and people, he says, "often agitated for embankments along the main stream and those connected with it. Zamindars were ultimately prevailed upon and the Damodar was embanked" (1967: 3). The Land Revenue Records of 1851 note that "many voluminous reports on embankments" existed, often dating back to 1818, 1819, 1820, and 1824 to 1829. One of the conundrums of colonial British administrators of Bengal—from 1772 until around 1850—was how to track the origins of these bandhs. Generally, it was agreed that these had existed long before the colonial government acquired possession of the country and the officials lamented that there was no record whatever of the period when or with what design the first bandhs were constructed. At times their contradictory characters and different purposes of use baffled the administrators, who decided that "it seems obvious that they must have been erected in order to prevent the incursions of the sea, and the River into the cultivated lands" when the waters rose. A committee was set up in 1846 to examine the "Damoodah Bunds." From the "disjointed nature of Bunds," the committee considered that originally bandhs must have been constructed at different intervals of time and in detached pieces to protect the "country," and that "they must have originated from inundations and in the fears and whims of individuals," and that "no uniform system could have prevailed" (as noted by Capt. W. S. Sherwill [1858]). The committee also observed that the bandhs that had been raised since they had come under the control of the government appeared to have been constructed merely on the grounds of the popular belief of their necessity and usefulness in protecting the lands and the lines and property of the taluka lands from inundation, and for the improvement of agriculture (Land Revenue Records 1851: 27–28).

Some of the customs and systems of administering land, developed in ancient India, remained more or less unchanged even during the Mughal times. The rules of usage "not being generally known,"[14] and with the Permanent Settlement established, the British rulers began to contemplate the problematic issue of legalizing the fictional entities of chars and attempted to resolve the maze of problems of accretional lands and the erosion of existing lands by the rivers (see Ascoli's 1921 history of revenues of the Sundarbans). The law that was created for this purpose, the law that still rules the rights of ownership of chars, is the Bengal Alluvion and Diluvion Act of 1825. Being the first legislation on the chars, this Act probably gave rise to the popular folk term "*badajami*" for chars. The Act was meant to establish a set of rules to guide the courts to determine the claims to land "gained by alluvion," or accretion, and the resurfaced land previously lost by diluvion, or erosion. The preamble describes the administrative observation of the frequent changes that take place in the channels of the principal rivers of Bengal, and the shifting of the sands on the beds of rivers. The full text of this Act, available in Hunter's *Imperial Gazetteer of India*, states that "chars or small islands are often thrown up by alluvion in the midst of the stream or near one of the banks, and large portions of land are carried away by an encroachment of the river on one side, whilst accretions of land are at the same time, or in subsequent years, gained by dereliction of the water on the opposite side" (1887: 137).[15]

Two main categories of land are considered by the BADA: *in situ* and new accretions. The right to land that once existed but was diluviated, and subsequently resurfaced in the old site, is one thing, and determining claims on it may not be difficult. The BADA considers the rights to such lands to be incidental to one's title to a tangible property, derived from the principle of justice and equity. The right to property is not affected only because it has been submerged under water, and the owner is deemed to be in "constructive possession" of the land during the time of its submergence and can claim it back when it reappears out of water and can be identified as land. For this, the owner must continue to pay rent for the diluviated land.

The BADA ensures that when new land rises within a river, it should be considered as "an increment to the tenure of the person" to whose land it is contiguous, subject to the payments of revenues assessed by the state. Such a rule will not be applicable if a river suddenly changes its course and separates "a considerable piece of land from one estate, and join[s] it to another estate without destroying the identity, and preventing the recognition, of the land so removed" (Hunter 1887: 138). Newly rising chars in large navigable rivers are the property of the state, but if the channel between the island and the shore is fordable at any season of the year, it is considered an accession to the land tenure of the person who is "most contiguous to it." The BADA applied only to the large and navigable rivers. In "small and shallow" rivers, fishing rights were given out as *jalkar*, which gave the rights of the river to individuals.[16] Clearly, such an elaborate schema of landownership was required for revenue collection purposes introduced by the British.

Barkat (2004) thinks that the BADA was designed primarily to protect the interests of the original owners and saw chouras as infiltrators. One aspect of this was the complexities in defining and regulating the relationship between landlords and tenants. The Bengal Legislative Council Act III (popularly known as Bengal Tenancy Act, or BTA) of 1885 was enacted by the then Bengal government, which identifies khas (government-owned) water bodies (such as *haor*s [low-lying depressions between two or more rivers], *beel*s [lake-like depressions], *khal*s [drainage channels], and *baor*s [ox-bow lakes of former meandering bends of rivers]) as a subset of khas lands. Yet the key to establishing land rights in the court of law remained the payment of rent, even on diluviated land. An amendment of the BTA made in 1938 provided for automatic abatement of rent if the land was diluviated, but restitution of this right if it reformed within twenty years of diluvion. Successive laws attempted to clarify gaps and establish sovereign rights of the state over all land; for example, the East Bengal State Acquisition and Tenancy Act (EBSATA) of 1950 was enacted after the Partition during the Pakistani rule. It further changed the rent provisions to favor either the state or the bigger landlords against the poorer peasants. After the independence of Bangladesh, the Presidential Order No. 135, which aimed to rehabilitate the landless, was promulgated in 1972. This order clearly indicated that all newly emerged lands that were previously lost by erosion should be treated as khas land and restored to the government and not to the original owner. This order might have been meant to recover chars from the more powerful local elites in order to redistribute them among the landless farmers. It did not operate on the ground in that way, however, and failed to fulfill this promise. For this reason, an amendment of Act XV was made in 1994 for the abatement of rent of land lost by diluvion, and for the subsistence of the right to land that is reformed *in situ* within thirty years, subject to the ceiling of sixty bighas. For land that rises in a new location, the rights depend upon the ownership of the riverbed. As jalkar rights over smaller rivers have been withdrawn since 1956, the right of ownership of chars rising on them belongs to the state. The general rule of thumb at present is that chars formed slowly and imperceptibly in continuity of someone's land will be considered as an increment to the land of that person subject to the payment of rent for the increased land. When a char rises in the middle of a river and is separated from the banks by a channel, it becomes the property of the state. If the channel is not deep enough to be navigable and can be crossed on foot, however, the char will be considered as an increment to the land most contiguous to it.

As mentioned in the beginning of the book, there has been more thought about the chars in Bangladesh than in India. It might reflect an awareness of the use of force to gain and retain control over these newly rising lands. Initial possession of chars creates advantages on the ground as well as in the court of law. This was the reason for the enactment of the Bengal Alluvial Lands Act in 1920: to prevent disputes over the possession of such lands. This Act assumes the district collector or the local administrator to be well informed, and devolves the rights of decision-making on the ownership of such lands onto him. A number of calls have been made in Bangladesh for reform of these laws because of their complexities and ambiguities in contemporary management of the land. Again, it is their complexities, layered over the years, that prevent serious rethinking of their usefulness for the poor. In riverine Bangladesh, land continues to remain the principal source of livelihood and security, and its ownership attributes social status (Alim 2009). Yet those who live on the chars have no legal rights over or even access to khas water bodies and khas lands. Even the fishing communities' access to inland water sources is partly determined on the basis of jalkars, which too are usurped by the elites (Barkat 2004).

Changing ideas of and valuations of land and water have had far-reaching effects on the rural economy of lower Bengal. Bengal was never really a land of farming; farming was, at best, a secondary occupation. Van Schendel (1991) contends that the water-based artisan economy of Bengal might not have led to widespread urbanization, but boasted of impressive industries that tended to be dispersed in the countryside, as in the case of the textile industry. Slightly over a hundred years after the introduction of the Permanent Settlement Act and the BADA, Bengal turned into a land-based peasant milieu. Social relations changed in response since land and water are at the heart of many social norms, including gender relations, in farming communities. Interventions on land and water change production relations and exacerbate power inequalities within communities, which may be reflected in the spatial layout of rural settlements. Many villages that stood next to the river gradually moved away from the river in the last sixty to eighty years as dependence on its water and the use of the river as a means of transport lessened. One village, Natu-Haripur on the southern bank, has shifted at least three kilometers in the last forty years. Older houses located closer to the embankment became dilapidated and newer housing came up farther away from the river, where the source of water for farming is the ground surface. Often the full extent or the depth of the interdependence of the two is not quickly apparent to those without a historical knowledge of the area. Changes may also take many decades for the full consequences to be manifested. Changes in gender relations have also followed the changes in production relations (Lahiri-Dutt 2012); thus, the control measures have "engineered" not only a physical infrastructure, but also a masculine social order.[17]

Control Measures

The control measures for the Damodar are broadly of four categories: the pre-British *pulbandi* banks; the higher embankments (or dikes) that were built under the Burdwan maharajas; the sluices and the cross weir across the river; and the dams and barrages built by the DVC. Chronologically, the pulbandi banks were the first, but they were usually low-lying, not extensive, and poorly maintained, allowing spillovers or breaching into the fields. With time, the interventions tended to become stronger, more permanent, and taller. Such higher interventions, which are in the second category, were generally built during the post–Permanent Settlement period. As "containing" the river's waters—when in spate—within its banks became the core objective, bandhs, also known as dikes or levees, became crucial to the well-being of the populations. Early observers (such as Gastrell 1863 and Sherwill 1858) were of the opinion that embankments were built by local zamindars to protect their land and property, but according to Sengupta (1951: 33) they were meant to protect paddy, the main crop.

These embankments reflected local power politics as well as played a major role in enhancing the status of some areas by "protecting them" at the cost of the others. Public discussion intensified in 1851–1852 on removing the embankment on the right bank of the river, which reflects their complex roles (Inglis 1909). The left or north bank embankment—protecting the town of Burdwan and the major roads and the newly built railway line—was always stronger and better maintained than the one on the right. This is because the area beyond the right-hand embankment—the southern part of Burdwan and parts of Bankura districts or the trans-Damodar area—was primarily an agricultural land inhabited by poorer castes and, hence, was left to be inundated during the monsoon flushes. The right embankment also had a larger number of hanas to let out the waters on the southern paddy lands. On the north bank of the river was the prosperous country town of Burdwan, the headquarters of the district and eventually the seat of the rajas. The trans-Damodar area across the right bank of the river—the *nikashi*, or the drainage outlet area—suffered, in comparison to the north bank, from poor access and was more agricultural in nature. Such unequal treatment has been explained differently; according to Bhattacharyya (1998), the attention given to northern embankments was due to the repeated floods in 1840 caused by breaches on the left (north) bank that submerged the town of Burdwan. As apparent from the notes of Major Baker, the consulting engineer for railways to the Government of India, the attention could also have emerged from a growing concern over the possible threats of inundation of the railways (as mentioned by Inglis 2002: 360).

The embankments gradually turned the trans-Damodar area—Dakshin Damodar, as it is called locally—into a rural hinterland of the "protected" northern urbanized tract. The region turned into an unhealthy swampland ravaged by complicated problems, one of them being the notorious Burdwan fever (O'Malley and Chakravarti 1909). Rampant malaria, caused by congestion of drainage in the lower part of the valley, was a spin-off of the embankment construction.[18] The effects of these high embankments, in terms of char formation on the riverbed, began to be felt by the middle of the nineteenth century, and the Expert Committee on Embankments in its report of 1846 actually advised that the river should remain unconfined by such high bandhs. The report also noted the gradual shallowing of the riverbed that had helped to increase the magnitude of the floods in the lower reaches. After about eight years of debating, significant lengths of the right-bank embankment were removed and stretches of the left-bank embankment were further strengthened.[19] Banerji quotes S. C. Bose that the decision to abandon the right embankment to decrease pressure on the left was, from the outset, an "unbalanced remedy" since "this very extraordinary situation of an erratic river, debouching into a dead flat flood-plain after draining a badly eroded plateau, being embanked only on one side has prevailed for over a century. It has led to a one-sided building up of land and various other complicated problems" (1972: 34–35). The justification behind embankment construction lay in the efforts to protect the fields from erosion and floods. This ensured a regular revenue collection and was based on the notion that the dikes would help to increase the river's velocity and help wash off the sediment load, preventing it from spilling over onto the surrounding fields (Inglis 1909). In reality, the embankments helped to raise the riverbed and the chars on it, clogged up drainage, enhanced flood heights, and disjointed the distributaries and encouraged social, political, and economic disparities at the local level. In many parts of the river course, these embankments have created extremely complex networks of high walls, trapping some villages and communities inside them, and making them more vulnerable to breaches than ever. For some villages, they have increased vulnerability rather than reducing it. Dadpur village, located a few kilometers downstream from Burdwan, is walled in by a series of embankments that lie at a higher elevation than the village, and that have grown taller over the years (figure 3.1). The residents are worried that a major monsoon flow could potentially break the barrier and submerge the entire village.

As higher grounds in a low-lying and watery environment, the embankments have come to be seen as useful spaces by the villagers. Over the years, these have developed into significant features in the local landscape in the lower valley. They have also turned into usable spaces by the villagers. They provide local community spaces for keeping smaller domestic animals like goats and poultry and for drying the grain, as well as for playgrounds for little children and spaces for recreation for the elderly. The transport routes generally follow the embankments, and chars are generally accessed from these gravel roads. More crucially, because they are high, the embankments provide shelter during the monsoon inundations. The spilling-over of the right bank or outlet through hanas has decreased in recent years because

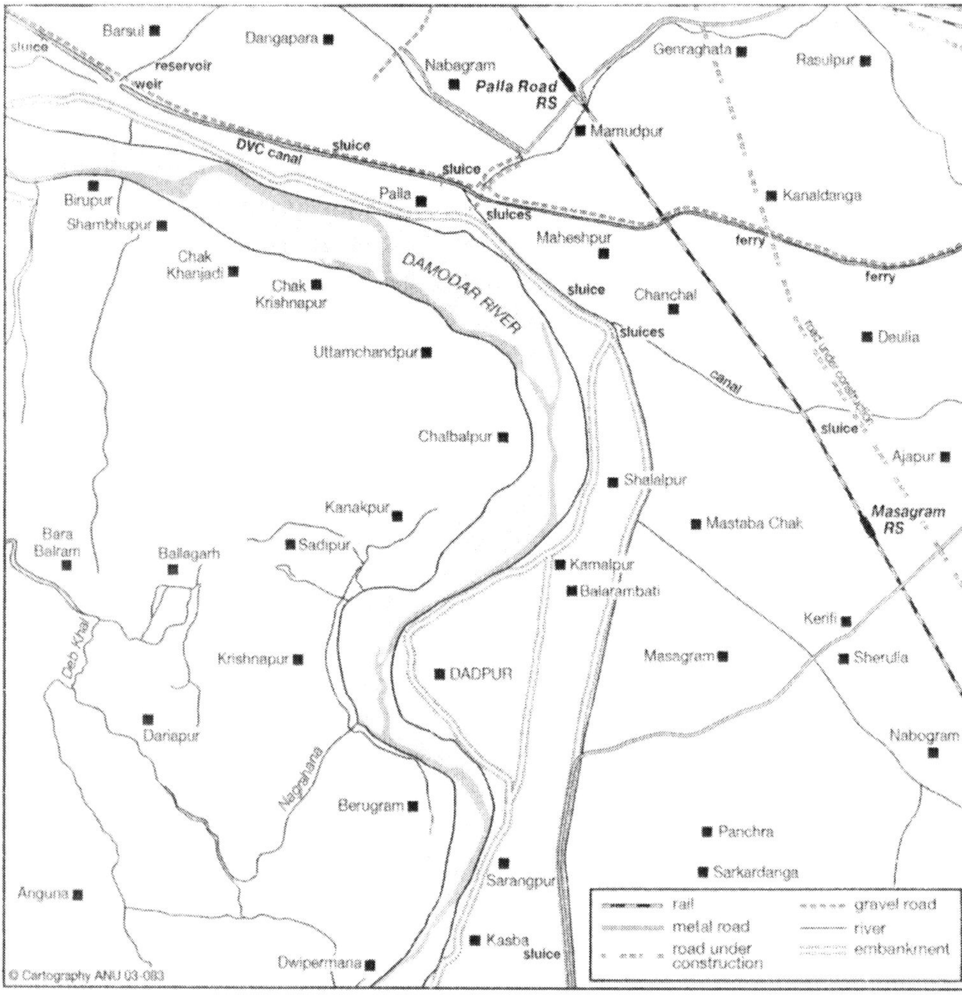

3.1 Dadpur Village Surrounded by Embankments
Source: Drawn by the ANU Cartographical Unit based on Survey of India topographical sheets.

of steady rises in the height of the embankment and the closing of many hanas.

Yet another set of interventions includes transverse structures of various widths and heights across the riverbed. Although they serve as control measures to direct water flow into canals, these measures had flood control as their core purpose. As per Inglis (1909), the origin of these schemes lay in efforts to control malaria fever (that was probably caused by waterlogging).[20] The Anderson Weir in Rhondia, over a kilometer long and around three feet above low water, was designed to help divert water from the main river to the channels of the Kana Nadi and the Kana Damodar to irrigate rice-growing areas. This was followed by the construction of Joojooty (or Jujuti) sluice in 1880 near Burdwan to obtain a better command over irrigation. The Eden Canal was built in 1881, mainly to reassign water from the Damodar to the decaying distributary system. As the bed of the river rose higher than the water level of the Hooghly due to siltation, a system of sluices was built on the left bank. Experts agree that the embankments "did more harm than good" (Banerji 1972: 36). The waterlogged area turned into a series of stagnant cesspools. S. C. Bose notes: "A large part of the district being very little above mean sea level is liable to be flooded every year by the principal rivers and their branches" (1948: 49–50). The embankments had the effect of gradually closing off the headwaters of some of the distributaries, turning them literally into kana nadis and enhancing the southward shift of the river course. Banerji (1972: 34) also observes that under the British government, a marked change was noticed by 1845, when no fewer than eighty-nine masonry sluices were constructed, replacing the cuts made by the peasants. Looking at these interventions, one can clearly note the ascent of technological means of control and the separation of the river from the land and land-based farming communities. Revenue collection from land and the sedentarization of farming and peasantization of communities in Bengal meant that wealth became associated with land, which increased in value and knowledge about which was enhanced. The heightened importance of land relegated the river further away from mainstream life, and gradually the rivers in riverine Bengal came to be seen as evil forces of nature. This was the local context in which the multipurpose project of the Damodar valley was proposed.

Large Dams under the Damodar Valley Corporation

In 1943, at the peak of the Second World War, when Calcutta was the head of the military operations in the eastern front, where the Indian National Army of Subhash Chandra Bose was advancing across the Burma border from Rangoon, the river breached its left bank levee a few kilometers downstream of Burdwan.[21] Not only did the ensuing flood devastate the fields, it cut off all communication and supplies to Calcutta. This prompted the establishment of the Damodar Flood Enquiry Committee to advise the colonial government on permanent measures to control floods caused by this river. The Committee was led by the Maharaja of Burdwan, whose seat of power, Burdwan town, was at stake. The Committee also had notable scientists, who, in 1944, arrived at the conclusion that the river needed control measures, and the Tennessee Valley Project was to be the model for the "multipurpose" use of the Damodar river. To replicate the Tennessee Valley Authority model fully in this part of the world, one of the engineers of TVA, W. L. Voorduin, was hired. Voorduin's plan was to build a series of seven dams, backed by large reservoirs, to stop and store the monsoon waters just before they reached the plains as they ran off the hills. The Damodar Valley Corporation (DVC) was set up by a special act in 1948, and construction of the dams at Tilaiya, Maithon, Panchet, and Konar with hydroelectric stations connected to each dam began in earnest. Given the rich reserves of coal in the upper valley of the Damodar, thermal power stations were also built. It was envisaged that the second phase would cover the construction of four more dams and hydroelectric stations; however, only the first phase was completed by this "dream-child of Nehru." As the number of dams was reduced, to have better control over the run-off, the Durgapur barrage was constructed in place of the weir suggested by Voorduin. The barrage, located close to the plain, was built to lead off two main sets of canals along the two banks of the Damodar to irrigate the rice-growing lands. The government of Bihar later constructed the fifth dam at Tenughat in place of the Aiyar, funding for which was given as a loan to the state, and which is not integrated into the DVC system. It supplies water mainly to the Bokaro Steel Plant and the thermal power station. About 93,000 people were removed from 27,500 hectares of land on which they had lived traditionally, and 45,000 houses owned by these families were submerged. At that time, the policy was to offer equivalent land for land, only if the displaced persons indicated their choices by a certain (and fixed) date. Not much is known about these recipients of land or even those who did not receive any land due to their lack of knowledge of government rules.

A number of publications including DVC's website[22] give a detailed outline of the project. As early as 1960, dams were proposed to be built in the upper catchment of the river, but were always thought to be economically unviable. The recommendations made in 1944 and the subsequent construction were possible because, although flood control was its main objective, the DVC Act of 1948 that brought the corporation into existence had a number of other purposes thrown into the project. The expansion of

Western enlightenment in colonial Bengal must have also been responsible for the philosophy behind this unquestioned acceptance of a positivist nature of scientific intellectualism (Forbes 1999 [1975]). It was therefore not surprising that the Western-educated middle class hailed the DVC as one of the "great engineering projects," and used superlatives such as "amazing," "a mighty experiment," and "a great adventure" to describe the project. The DVC was also seen as the dream child of Nehru, the first prime minister of the independent nation; Nehru's famous words describing large dams as the "temple of modern India" were supposed to have been spoken while inaugurating one of the four dams of the DVC project. Numerous research articles portrayed the DVC as a symbol of the new nation, which was keen to sacrifice in the interest of the "greater common good." As yet another body of literature has shown, the DVC neither has fulfilled its promise of flood control nor has committed itself to providing irrigation water to the farmers, particularly when they need it (see Lahiri-Dutt 2008 for more on this). Indeed, floods have decreased in frequency and intensity; they have also changed in nature. The residents of the lower parts of the valley point out that the floods, when they come, now last longer and are more destructive. The floods can cause more destruction because a false sense of security has now permeated through the residents of the valley (Lahiri-Dutt 2003). The post-DVC period has seen three major floods—in 1958, 1978, and 1998—raising concerns that perhaps the DVC was more of a calamity than a boon (Basu 1982), and generating a range of economic appraisals of the project (Ganguly 1982). The blame has been laid on the "uncontrolled" parts of the catchment below the dams that bring additional runoff into the lower system of the river. Aich (1998: 81) also held responsible "administrative bottlenecks"—particularly the inability of the DVC to acquire land—for leading to the failure in the provision of full flood control by the Maithon and Panchet dams, as their capacity was reduced to half of what was originally envisaged. Disputes between Bihar (now Jharkhand) and West Bengal on irrigation water allocation from the reservoirs have also caused some of these bottlenecks. In addition, the regulation manual, prepared long ago by the Central Water and Power Commission (GoI 1969) has been inadequate in dealing with occasional years of excessively heavy late monsoon rains.[23] Ganguly (1982) also accuses poor governance and internal corruption within the DVC for its lackluster performance.

Over the years, the DVC has metamorphosed into an authoritarian state instrument of centralized water control, but with only limited powers. As early as 1979, Chakraborty et al. (1997: 303) argued that the DVC project "has been far less than comprehensive" mainly because of the deficiencies in the DVC Act. It has suffered from the difficulties of resolving conflicts between its validated fields of activities, which demand an autonomy of decision-making that the two states of Bihar and West Bengal do not have. A similar view is expressed by Pathak (1981), who noted the dismal state of internal affairs—power squabbles, inefficiency, and failures of personnel management, to name a few. More importantly, he notes that with regard to the resettlement of dam-displaced persons, the DVC has suffered from the conflicting interests of the two states and notes that the "performance of the Corporation has never been reviewed during its lifetime and could not be given a good leadership from the third plan period" (1981: 634). The DVC has presented itself as an icon to the modernist urban elites, symbolically representing a centralized and systematic river control. This kind of control, however, is impossible to manage in deltaic Bengal, given its hydrology and its complexity of river-based irrigation history. Some experts still believe that if the DVC had been completed as per Voorduin's vision, the problems would not have occurred: "As the system was not built up to the design capacity, the capability of the system is restricted and supply of the desired output cannot be guaranteed at all times" (Banerjee 1991: 201). The rapid rates at which the reservoirs are filling up with silt indicate that this is probably far too optimistic a belief. A greater number of dams would likely have caused further impacts on downstream ecology and hydrology.

The formation and stabilization of chars on the riverbed have been one of the direct consequences of the controlled flow of the river. Downstream from the Durgapur barrage, where the river meets the Hooghly, vast quantities of sand deposited on the riverbed continue to raise the height of these river islands. The flow of the river is not enough to flush this sand away into the Hooghly and out to the Bay of Bengal during the monsoon floods. The amounts of sand brought in by the river have also increased, the reason being excessive soil erosion in the upper catchment area. Forests in the upper catchment were cleared to build the dams, and accelerated erosion in this part of the river basin has further increased the sediment load in the lower part of the channel. The high embankments have held the alluvium well inside the banks of the river, encouraging braiding of the channel and stabilization of the chars.

James Scott (1998: 263–64) has investigated such large engineering projects that represent modernity, and is of the view that such projects are based on certain simplified and formulaic assumptions. These assumptions are typical of high modernism, which puts faith in scientific and engineering expertise, imposed through the agency of state power. In exercising power, the original schemes are continually adjusted to cope with the contingent situation and the power of officials and state organs. Scott, of course, did not see the Damodar, but his text reads as though he were explaining the systemic failure of the DVC. The supremacy of positivist thinking among the Bengali educated elite (Forbes 1999 [1975]) must have contributed to the complete faith in the kind of river control that the DVC represented. The original proponents of the Damodar Valley Corporation in 1948 emphasized the wealth-creating potential of the scheme and the specificity of the river and the need to understand the specific geographical and historical context of the river. Nevertheless, over the years the river-control measures of the DVC became a "model" and any contextual specificity was lost in the explicit efforts to push through this agenda. As one of the pamphlets published by the DVC states: "Once a successful demonstration of comprehensive river harnessing has been provided in the Damodar Valley with its manifold benefits, it will be easier to undertake similar experiments in other river valleys of the country in the light of the experience gained here" (1948: 8). This reveals that a Western engineering concept was transplanted in its entirety into a very different context. The project was seen as an "experiment," and the context was probably seen as not much more than a mere laboratory. The local and regional setting was treated as one without a history and without politics, an empty environment that was devoid of a history and people. The chars and their peoples became collateral in this great experiment.

River Control and Chars

As shown earlier, the Damodar has been the subject of control in different ways at many stages in recent history. The physical environment of the Damodar delta has undergone considerable changes since early colonial times, as civil engineering techniques have replaced traditional irrigation. The first phase saw the construction of low bandhs, which were raised gradually and turned into full-scale embankments. Later, the Maharaja of Burdwan took over the construction and maintenance of embankments along the course of the river to contain its floods, and then in the early 1950s, the DVC constructed dams and brought its canals through the region. The

DVC dams were only partially successful in reducing the frequency of floods and providing irrigation water through canal networks to agricultural fields. These interventions brought several changes in the physical environment to the lower reaches of the valley. The clearing of extensive natural forests in the upper catchment areas for the construction of reservoirs resulted in increased siltation rates and in the formation of more permanent chars on the riverbed. While flooding in the lower reaches of Damodar's valley has been reduced, low-intensity floods have become longer in duration. Moreover, in the lower Damodar valley, floods now dump coarse sand and thus destroy the fertility of cultivated land (figure 3.2). A purely physical interpretation of char formation is offered in figure 3.3.

Since the behavior of the river has now become more unpredictable, chars face a more uncertain existence. The physical character of the Damodar chars, however, is somewhat different from the physical character of those located in the active delta areas of the Ganga-Padma and other rivers in deltaic Bengal. Being more permanent in nature, Damodar chars do not experience the regular and annual flooding that is characteristic of the active delta chars of Bangladesh. Floods, more devastating in nature and of longer duration can and do occur, such as those in 1978 and in 2000. As the nature of floods has changed in the lower Damodar valley, the ways in

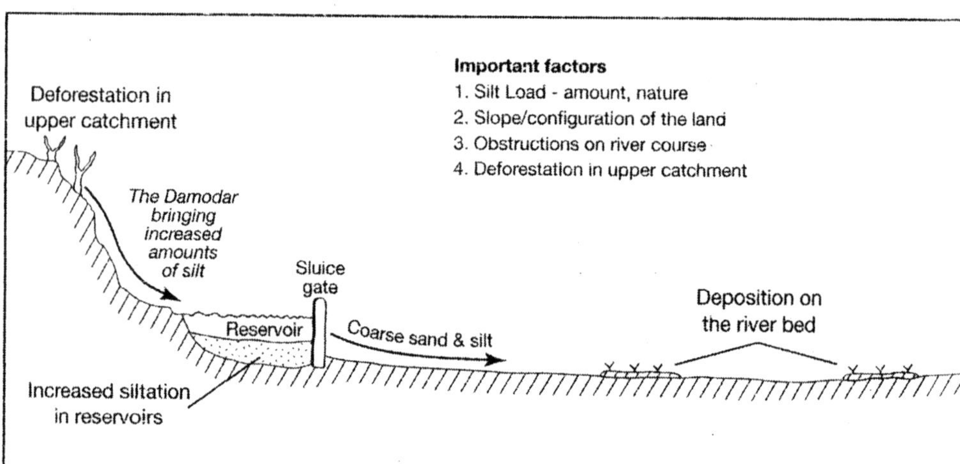

3.2 Human Intervention: Formation of Chars

Source: Schematic diagram drawn by the ANU Cartography Unit based on the interpretation of literature and data from field surveys.

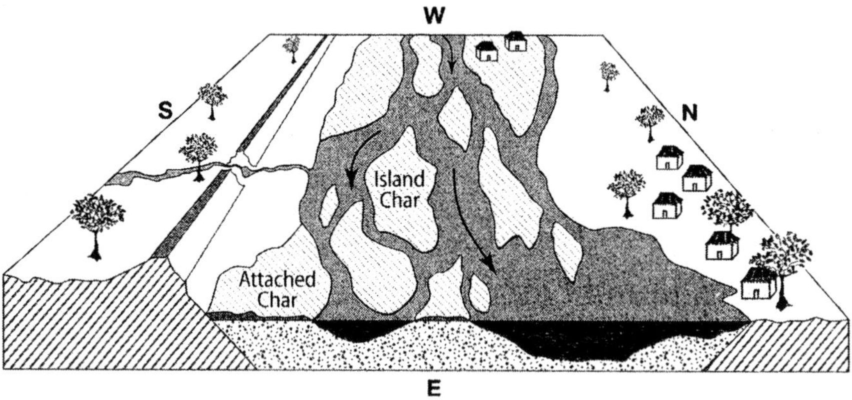

3.3 Physical Interpretation: Formation of Chars
Source: Schematic diagram drawn by the ANU Cartography Unit based on the interpretation of literature and data from field surveys.

which local people traditionally have dealt with them have also become ineffective or have had to be modified. In the following chapters, we will deal with the implications of these changes to the lives and livelihoods of people who arrived on the chars to settle down.

In this chapter, we have traveled through a very long period in history in an effort to explain how the hybrid environment of chars came into existence. Colonial land systems not only left their imprint on Bengali social and economic lives, but made far-reaching impacts on the ecology. The separation of land and water as two separate physical elements, the valuation of land for its revenue-yielding qualities, and the perception that rivers in Bengal were in need of control were colonial contributions. We have shown that, above all, by changing the way lands and waters were valued by those who lived in Bengal, these factors prepared not just the context but the intellectual atmosphere in which interventions in the river's system could be legitimized. Therefore, one might say that what happened during the colonial period was critical to understanding the production of an environmental discourse that was also part of the Bengali milieu. Environmental changes created and were created by a mindset that legitimated and encouraged rivers to be controlled in riverine Bengal, and in the midst of all the focus on the rivers and their floods, the chars turned invisible.

CHAPTER 4

Bhitar o Bahir Katha
Inside and Outside Stories of Chars and the Mainland

Ghareo nahe, pareo nahe je jan achhe majhkhane [One who is in the middle, neither at home, nor outside]—RABINDRANATH TAGORE, 1905

The inhabitants, villages, and livelihoods in the Damodar chars are marginal from, yet interact with, the people, settlements, and occupations in the lands that lie across the banks of the river. The land beyond is locally known as *danga jami*; it is higher and drier land that is almost always beyond the water—the land that most people recognize as *land proper*.[1] To char dwellers, the world lies within and ends inside the bandhs. It is not unsurprising, then, that char dwellers perceive the land that lies beyond the embankment as *bandher bhitarer jami* (land lying *inside* the embankments), that is, land bound by embankments. This reveals the attention and care that this land receives as against charlands. The implication of this nomenclature is that the mainland, or danga jami, is protected by embankments, and charbhumi is the land that lies outside them. To describe this world that is external to the charlands, we use the term "mainland." This is where villages and towns are located and where roads exist. This is the land that is officially recorded and mapped, accounted for, and governed. And this is the land for which government programs and schemes for rural development are implemented.

Located at the margins of the mainland, chars remain at the periphery of social, political, and economic processes, of which one major factor of change has been the government's effort for rural development through a number of projects and schemes pursued since the 1960s. In response to government investments, farming systems in mainland Burdwan have changed fundamentally. Without legal recognition, chars have remained at the margin of most of these changes, changes that have deeply altered the lives of village communities in danga lands. Although chars lie at the margin of the mainlands, substantial exchanges and interactions between them can be detected with a closer look. In spite of the embankments, which create a physical barrier that separates the islands from the lands beyond, it is not incorrect to say that chars coexist with danga jami.

In this chapter, we draw attention to the rural transition of the adjacent region within which chars are placed, and outline the interactions between the two. In particular, the so-called agricultural miracle of the region is looked at and the factors of change in mainland farming systems are discussed. The government-sponsored schemes and projects of rural development that were introduced in mainland villages neglected chars and char dwellers. Yet one cannot say that all these changes completely bypassed the chars, leaving its inhabitants isolated. We introduce the readers briefly to the agricultural economy of the mainland region across the riverbank in order to set the backdrop. This chapter also shows how people on chars interact with those on mainlands and illustrates the close connection between the two. Above all, the chapter temporarily refocuses attention away from the river to land-based changes that have taken place around the chars. Since we showed in the previous chapter how this part of Bengal turned into a land-based rural economy through river control, we illustrate here how postindependence rural developmental planning changed the nature of the coexistence of the land- and water-based worlds. The rural prosperity of the mainland led to its being known as the richest district of West Bengal, but chars became more marginalized as the lands beyond the riverbank became more prosperous.

The mainland areas in Burdwan district across the northern bank of Damodar are some of the most prosperous parts, arguably, in all of South Asia. Administratively, most of the south bank of the river belongs to the Bankura district of West Bengal. We showed earlier that for a variety of reasons the south bank has never attained a level of agricultural prosperity comparable to that of the north bank of the Damodar (see Samanta and Lahiri-Dutt 2003). Conventionally, as the drainage, or nikashi, area, the south bank would receive the excess floodwaters of the Damodar on a regular basis. Consequently, for the intensive rural development program in the 1960s, Burdwan district, lying on the north bank of the Damodar, was chosen. Although chars have largely remained outside the purview of rural development programs, the prosperity of agricultural Burdwan continues to attract migrants to the chars. Understanding this regional and local context of rural prosperity is necessary to appreciate char communities, their livelihoods, and their perceptions of vulnerability.

Burdwan: A "Gift of the Damodar"?

Burdwan's agriculture is particularly well endowed, and its prosperity dates back to historical times. Located on a rich alluvial plain, the region has always been agriculturally more prosperous than the rest of West Bengal, where the fertility of lands in the moribund delta was exhausted and malaria raged in waterlogged lowlands. Throughout the nineteenth century and early part of the twentieth, Burdwan's rice-farming economy remained better-off because of efficient drainage provided by the Damodar. Burdwan town, in fact, grew approximately at the apex of an inland delta created by the Damodar's numerous distributaries, of which the Banka, Khari, Behula, and Bhalluka were the major channels. These channels flushed out the excess monsoon waters into the Hooghly, which in turn drained out the sediments into the Bay of Bengal, keeping the local river-borne trade active throughout the year. They also provided water for irrigation and acted as sources of drinking water. Over time, the growing height of the embankments led to the deterioration of the drainage efficiency of these channels, which were eventually used as productive farming land by the growing agrarian population. Today, some of these channels can only be detected from secondary evidence such as paleo-sediments, or during the monsoons when the flow of the water seeks out natural wrinkles on the land. In the past, these channels, except for the bowl-like area around Samudragarh-Pandua, kept the area well drained.

Part of the rural prosperity in the region also came from village-based small crafts and industries such as the ironworks of Kanchannagar. The navigability of the Damodar allowed a thriving river-borne trade and encouraged the growth of secondary industries. Exchanges of goods and commodities between the higher lands of the Chota Nagpur Plateau fringe on the west and the eastern waterlogged lands were regularly carried out along the Damodar. In fact, it was not only the Damodar but the series of rivers flowing down from the west—such as the Ajoy—into the Bhagirathi-Hooghly that performed this role. Consequently, they gave rise to a number of settlements that acted as centers of trade along their courses. The district of Burdwan and the settlements located in the district were the richest. Traders came to Burdwan from all over the country, and it was one of these trading families that eventually assumed the title of the Maharaja of Burdwan. The biggest port on the Damodar was Satgaon (or Saptagram), located farther down the river from where these chars were studied. Looking at the history of Burdwan's rural economy, one is bound to feel that the Damodar was much more than just a channel for carrying waters and trade; in the past, it constituted the lifeblood of Burdwan.

Another reason for Burdwan's relative and continued rural prosperity could be the resilience of local communities, in particular the Ugrakhatriya (or Aguri). The exact origin of this community is mired in controversy,[2] but this landed caste has been well known for characteristics such as courage, physical strength, devotion, hospitality, and generosity. The community is often thought to be the warrior caste, or Khatriya (variously spelled as Kshatriya or Chhatriya), based in Bengal. R. C. Mazumdar's (2004: 417) understanding that "[t]he Ugras were to follow the vocations of Kshatriyas and practise military art" resonated in the *District Gazetteer:* "The Aguris are popularly believed to be the modern representatives of the Ugras or Ugrakshatriyas mentioned in Manu" (Paterson 1910: 45). Paterson thought that the Aguris were born from the "illicit" unions between the Khetris of the Burdwan Raj family and the Sadgops (also the original inhabitants of Burdwan, the cattle-herder castes settled on land), and formed a distinctive cultivating caste. Such is the peculiar concentration of these caste groups in rural Burdwan that a number of researchers have explored the local history of Burdwan, and, more recently, the consensus seems to describe the Aguri community as a Bengal version of the Kshatriya, who received in pre-Moghul times an *agrahar* (equivalent to a Moghul *jagir*), "an endowment of land or village by a Raja to a Brahmin or a Kashtriya for his meritorious actions" (Bandhu 2008: 31). Dutta agrees and describes them as forming the stratum of powerful peasants who were structurally situated between the zamindar and the direct peasants in the years before or the formative years of colonial rule: "They were an influential and powerful section in the rural society of the district . . . the zamindar dominated the scene, while the agricultural castes, the Sadgops and the Aguris, formed the economic backbone of the village" (2002: 25). The lending of cash and grain allowed them to exercise their domination over poorer peasants. Even to this day, the Aguris of Burdwan district compose a group of landed farmers with distinctive social characteristics. It is possible that Burdwan's rural economy survived the decay that took over other parts of rural Bengal due to the presence of the Aguri community in large numbers.

If Bengal as a whole was described as "the gift of the Ganges" (Mukherjee 1938), an area containing the highest congregations of settled rural populations in the world, who feed off the crops yielded by the fertile fluvial alluvium, then Burdwan's economy and social milieu can easily be described as an endowment of the Damodar. Among the districts of Bengal, particularly those located in Radh[3] Bengal, as long as the Damodar was still able to carry large vessels and barges,[4] Burdwan continued to play a pivotal role in the regional economy. Although the railways were constructed to carry coal from the Raniganj-Jharia fields to the industries located in Calcutta's backyard, much of the coal was still transported by the Damodar till the late 1800s and the early 1900s.

With the beginning of embankment construction, initiating the retaining of silt in the river channel itself, the role of the Damodar in the rural economy of Burdwan declined over time, and local prosperity began to wane in the late eighteenth century. The stagnant waters accumulated along the raised embankments bred mosquitoes: This was the period when malaria began to ravage the Bengal countryside. As some caste Hindu peasant communities dwindled due to malaria epidemics and rural depopulation, lower-caste Bauris and immigrant tribal labor took up agriculture on the fallow lands, which were gradually being covered by new jungle. Much later, after independence and particularly during the 1960s, a renewed rural prosperity began to characterize Burdwan. This prosperity was based mainly on surface canal water and later on groundwater-intensive irrigation (and other technological inputs). This, again, played a crucial role in drawing popular attention further away from the river.[5]

Although rural Burdwan has always been more prosperous than its neighboring areas, its mainland areas did not fully escape the overall decline in rural prosperity as the delta system clogged naturally. Bengal's river system experienced a "revolution" in the late 1700s, in response to which the region's economic history was "re-moulded" and "both geography and history" of Bengal were remade by introducing as many as six new rivers (Bandopadhyaya 2009: ii). Bandopadhyaya (2009: ii–iii) draws upon three major effects of these topographical changes: (a) the shifting of the most active parts of the delta to the east by the middle of the nineteenth century; (b) the choking-up of the moribund parts of the delta in central and western

Bengal where soil fertility began to decline; and (c) increased waterlogging due to construction of roads, railways, and embankments along the rivers. The annual floods that enriched the land with silt and kept down the mosquito populations were contained within the rivers' channels by the embankments.[6] The impacts varied across different parts of the delta, and Burdwan suffered the least because of the release of the waters in the trans-Damodar nikashi areas on the south bank of the river. Eastern Burdwan was also affected by depopulation caused by the outbreak of malaria and decline in the fertility of land, but its economy quickly bounced back to become a "small pocket of growth" in this overall bleak scenario.

The Region's Agrarian Changes

The contemporary configuration of the region's agricultural economy is a continuation of this past, but with major differences in irrigation, various government schemes for rural development, and land reforms. Being one of the selected Integrated Agricultural District Programme (IADP) districts in India, Burdwan received a significant portion of postindependence rural development programs. Besides government initiatives, intensification of cropping was enabled by the innumerable shallow and deep tube wells that dot the rural countryside today. The availability of irrigation water made possible the cultivation of *boro* rice, which is harvested primarily as a cash crop. Tube-well irrigation played a more significant role in Burdwan than in other districts as the system of the DVC largely failed to deliver water to the fields when it was needed. Basu and Mukherjee (1963: 2) note that the "direct primary benefit of the Damodar canals" was increased production of *aman* paddy, the major subsistence crop of the area, which led to increased income for the farmers. The agrarian prosperity of Burdwan became evident with the town's rapid expansion; the rural landscape of the town too changed by the late 1960s and the 1970s—the whirring of tube wells in rural areas that were green with crops during the winter months, husking, and rice mills spouting smoke into the unpolluted sky. Burdwan turned into one of the most prosperous districts not only in the state, but possibly in South Asia.

Politics was critical to the agrarian changes of Burdwan. The Left Front, led by the Communist Party, which came to power in 1977, took advantage of this technology-led rural prosperity to restructure rural society through Operation Barga,[7] which sought to redistribute land to sharecroppers. The post–land reforms rural growth in the 1980s was so spectacular that a number of international research projects were conducted in the mainland areas. One complex problem was determining whether the rural growth was spurred purely by technological advances or if institutional changes accompanied or preceded the growth. Bose (1999: 47–51) refers to Gazdar and Sengupta's (1999) view that explanations for such rapid agricultural growth need not be viewed within "institutional versus technological" or "state action versus private incentive" kind of dichotomies, and suggests that private investments and incentives have to be seen in the context of political empowerment and government intervention at the local level. In his work published in 1993, Harriss put forth the view that agrarian breakthroughs in the state of West Bengal were accomplished more by means of a focus on "the expansion of the productive forces" than was acknowledged by its Communist government.

The land reforms were meant to have a positive impact on small-scale production, but their results were primarily political. The upheaval in rural society through the successful establishment of the *panchayati raj*, or system of elected village councils, breached the tenuous hold of landlords and rich peasants. The formalization of democratically elected panchayats was the key factor that is thought to have changed the rural society in Burdwan, by putting a reasonably democratic institution in place. This also changed the nature of the public space by enabling the lower-caste people to enter the domain previously occupied by the bhadraloks. Everyday corruption, such as the routine "leakage" of government loans (such as those under the Integrated Rural Development Programme, or IRDP) from the lower castes and marginal farmers into the hands of the richer and upper-caste people, had diminished to a great extent (Lieten 1994: 517–518).

Besides the redivision of land, the redistribution of political power and access to benefits from public works programs were critical factors that changed the fabric of the regional rural society and economy. Bose (1999: 54–55) says that the key to rural prosperity and capitalization lay in private investments in tube-well irrigation and the rapid development of a water market. This water market was primarily based on accessing groundwater, often by comparatively richer farmers who could afford to borrow from rural banks. As groundwater assumed greater importance, the river, its water, and people making a living from the water receded from public vision. Therefore, the increasing prosperity of mainlands across embankments was responsible for further marginalization of chars. The relationship between chars and mainlands is slightly more complex than just this. It is incorrect to suggest that farming systems on chars have not been influenced by developments on mainlands. People living on chars have observed these new developments and adopted what they could on their own initiative, such as making use of groundwater to cultivate crops during winters when the riverbed is more or less dry. A few households have borrowed money to buy shallow tube wells to pump up groundwater. This development of tube-well irrigation has brought agricultural prosperity to chars. As can be expected, the use of groundwater in char farming has further marginalized the poorer farming households.

From the beginning of postindependence rural developments, chars were being settled on first by the Biharis and then by Bangladeshi Hindu migrants in several phases. As more and more people began settling on chars, they remained largely untouched by the economic and societal changes affecting the mainland in Burdwan. One can argue that the peopling of chars in Damodar was uninterrupted and remained largely unnoticed because state attention was focused solely on the mainlands. At the same time, one can also argue that those settling on chars saw an opportunity in the rising prosperity of the rural economy of Burdwan and decided that settling here was worth the risks posed by the fragility and unpredictability of the char environment. As shown later in this book, for a large proportion of char dwellers originating from Bangladesh, chars were the second or third step of their migration process. Therefore, at this stage, it can be readily assumed that for migrants to settle down on them, chars must have represented preferred environments and offered more and possibly better resources than other rural areas of West Bengal.

The following sections trace the social and economic changes in the region by drawing a sketch of the major forces of change affecting the mainland around the Damodar chars. These changes initiated a greater flow of resources into rural areas and reduced the rural-urban disparities in income and social and economic opportunities. Four critical elements of rural development relevant to Burdwan are outlined: land reforms; agricultural development; poverty alleviation; and improvements in infrastructure and services.

Land Reforms and the Chars

At the time of independence, Burdwan inherited a multilayered, feudal agrarian structure that was characterized by a highly skewed distribution of land and widespread sharecropping and tenancy. It is not surprising, therefore, that the earliest attempts to redistribute land were made, among other places in India, in rural Burdwan by the Communist Party of India (CPI) as early as the 1950s. For example, rural Burdwan saw the formation of one of the region's earliest agricultural cooperatives that followed the Soviet model of collective farms. In Shodya village, not too far from the chars and Burdwan town, when the maharajas were still facing an uncertain future in independent India, the first agricultural collective was built by a group of farmers. Heavily influenced by Marxist ideology, these farmers built a cooperative that purchased its own tractors and other heavy machinery to introduce technology into what was overwhelmingly plow-based agriculture. It was in Shodya village that *aal*s (raised demarcations bounding farm plots) were demolished by farmers to create the first "modern" machine tractor station of India. Although the cooperatives remained a "failed experiment" (because they were unable to bear the heavy taxes imposed by the state government, which was then led by the Indian National Congress), it provided inspiration to *jami-dakhal* movements led by the powerful Krishak Sabha (literally, "the platform for farmers") under the Communist banner during the 1960s. These initiatives attempted to forcibly harvest crops and occupy productive lands of *jotedar*s, or rich farmers, and often resulted in bloodshed. Consequently, when the Communist Party of India (Marxist) (CPI[M]) came to power in West Bengal in 1977, they put land reforms as a top priority in their agenda for meaningful agrarian reform. Land reforms in West Bengal took the shape of redistribution of land holdings and reforming the land tenure systems.[8]

The history of land reforms in West Bengal has even deeper roots: It goes back to at least 1885, when the Bengal Tenancy Act (BTA) was passed by the colonial British government. The BTA was a response to a series of peasant uprisings in the middle of the nineteenth century. The Permanent Settlement had given so much power into the hands of zamindars that the colonial government soon became aware of the need to control the greed and cruelty of zamindars in order to protect the tenants. The BTA defined "tenant" broadly, and some colonial administrators used the legal instrument to give a better deal to the peasant-cultivators than they had received from the zamindars. In Jalpaiguri district in north Bengal, for example, *adhiar*s (farmers who received a half share of crops) who had their own plow and cattle were recorded as ryots (farmers). In other districts of Bengal, settlement officers also began to give tenancy rights to a large number of *bhagchasi*, *bargadar*, and *dhnayakarari praja* (sharecroppers on different contracts). The landowners protested, and after the Tenancy Bill introduced in 1925 to assuage them had to be withdrawn, class and communal differences came out in the open. The chasm within Bengal society, initiated by the Permanent Settlement, had by now been established completely along the lines of those who owned and those who rented land, entrenching the owners' interests in the land. Sharecroppers had no right over the land they tilled. Sir Francis Floud and his colleagues at the Floud Commission attempted in 1939 to correct this imbalance by initiating the idea of Tebhaga, that is, that the bargadaar should receive two-thirds share of the harvest.[9] As the bhadralok landowners paid no attention to this (re)distribution of proceeds from farming the land, peasants rose against the exploitative practices. Interestingly, Burdwan was not one of the areas where the Tebhaga movement took root; Bandyopadhyay (2001) comments that this absence of protests illuminates the true nature of the leftist movements in Burdwan by revealing the close links between the interests of leftist leaders and the landed rural gentry.

After independence, however, this part of Bengal remained one of the pioneering regions in both land-reform initiatives and their implementation, where even during preindependence times the antifeudal movement was stronger here in comparison to the other states of India. A series of acts were passed on different aspects of landownership and tenure arrangements during this time. The most notable was based on the question of acquiring surplus land after imposing a ceiling on landownership and its distribution. In fact, during 1967–1970, more than one-fourth of the total surplus land distributed all over India belonged to the state of West Bengal. The jamidakhal movements in Burdwan were a direct result of the Land Ceiling Act, which was strongly opposed by several local landlords.

The most successful components of land reforms implemented in Burdwan were the redistribution of land and tenancy reforms. While the first was led by the central government, the latter was primarily led by the state government, largely dominated by the CPI(M). The first component of land reforms was the imposition of legal ceilings on the size of individual land holdings, including the vesting of land introduced in the late 1960s. The land that was vested above the ceiling was consequently redistributed among the rural poor. As compared to other states of India, the performance of West Bengal in this regard was much higher (Kar 1998). The second was Operation Barga, which gained the status of a movement in the countryside within a few months of its launch in October 1978, with the active support of a number of peasant organizations. Quick recording of the names of bargadars, preventing their eviction, and granting legal rights to cultivate land were considered as major incentives for marginal and small peasants to raise production (Sanyal et al. 1998). It is well known that farmer-owners are more likely to adopt new methods compared to sharecroppers. By 1984, about 1.2 million bargadars were recorded in West Bengal under Operation Barga, which fully consolidated the rural support base of the CPI(M) in the state. Among the various districts of West Bengal, Burdwan ranked third in terms of the number of bargadars recorded; as many as 104,000 bargadars were accorded legal rights to land that they had previously cultivated as tenant sharecroppers without legal rights, sometimes for several generations. A veteran Marxist leader of the Krishak Sabha, Harekrishna Konar, had led Operation Barga in Burdwan, leading to successful implementation of different aspects of land reform in the district. About 186,000 acres of ceiling surplus agricultural land have been vested in the district, of which 50,000 acres belong to the area we have described as the mainland. In areas lying around the chars, 1,190 acres of vested agricultural land were distributed among 89,393 landless poor, while 60,911 sharecroppers were registered with the land revenue department. The beneficiaries of the distribution of ceiling surplus land have been provided with legal landownership papers such as patta. According to a survey conducted by the district land revenue department, about 16 percent of the total vested nonagricultural land was also found fit for agriculture in the region around Burdwan town.

These measures triggered off other changes in the rural economy, resulting in net gains by agricultural laborers and poor peasants, and a consequent improvement in agrarian production (Lieten 1996). The registration of sharecroppers under Operation Barga created new rights for tenants, such as rent payments and access to credit from formal banking sectors, particularly nationalized banks, which began spreading their branches into rural areas at the time. Access to rural banks and institutional credit connected small sharecroppers and farmers to technological inputs. With the removal of tenurial insecurity, small operators started making viable production decisions (Sanyal et al. 1998). In Burdwan, the cropping pattern of even small farms changed from labor-intensive subsistence crops to commercial crops in response to market forces. Tenancy reforms also had effects on production; Ghatak (1995) notes that Operation Barga led to a higher rate of expansion of boro rice cultivation as well as output, adoption of High Yielding Variety (HYV) seeds, and encouragement of investments in private irrigation. Often, registered or recorded tenants were better off in terms of the proportional share of the harvest retained by the tenant than those who remained unrecorded.

Besides these reforms, Burdwan in particular made remarkable progress in fixing and enforcing minimum wages for agricultural laborers, resulting in a substantial increase in agricultural wages in the area since the 1980s.[10] Another important effort was supporting the assignees of surplus land and sharecroppers with provision for loans, inputs, and bullocks, with the help of the IRDP, implemented through a widely expanding network of commercial banks in rural areas. The district has forged ahead of others in the state in the implementation of land reforms. With successful decentralization of administration through the establishment of the panchayati raj, rural areas and rural social groups of Burdwan have assumed more political power than ever before.[11]

While these changes in agrarian society were taking place in rural Burdwan, chars remained largely invisible and untouched by government initiatives. This attracted more migrants: The more they were marginalized from mainland rural Burdwan, the more they were lured to settle on chars, where they were able to take advantage of, participate in, and contribute to the mainland economy. The nonlegal status of the chars allowed them a certain amount of invisibility since the central focus of peasant movements and land reforms was on mainland agricultural lands. The mainland rural economy began to flourish by the early 1970s, creating enough job opportunities for char dwellers located nearby as well as people from other areas of West Bengal and Bangladesh. Acquiring land that was less productive and less accessible and that provided comparatively less-secured incomes was not in the interest of any except the most wretched people. Charlands were initially uncultivable due to excessive sand and low silt. Migrants settled on these baze zameen and through their labor and skill converted them into fertile agricultural land, enough to sustain their fragile livelihoods.

Agriculture since the 1960s

Rural development can never be isolated from agricultural development, especially in India, where the rural sector still dominates the national economy. This applies to the region in this study as well, with its geographical advantages and long history of agricultural prosperity. As Burdwan received, in full measure, all postindependence initiatives for agricultural development—DVC canals, the "new" technology package from the IADP, and land reforms—much of its rural scenario was transformed as the economy diversified (Chandrasekhar 1993; Rawal 2001a, 2001b). The isolation of sleepy villages where farmers toiled for subsistence just as their ancestors had done for generations was broken.

Burdwan, with a cropping intensity of 169 percent, is the leading district of West Bengal in agricultural development. It has been known as the "rice bowl" and the "granary of West Bengal" because of its agricultural prosperity (Barman 1982). At present, the net cropped area occupies nearly 66 percent of the total area of the district. About 88 percent of the gross cropped area is irrigated annually, if the three seasons (*kharif*, *rabi*, and summer) are taken together. Considering the gross irrigated area (the total of irrigated areas during the three seasons), the rate of expansion of irrigated land between 1970–1971 and 1990–1991 nearly doubled (19,000 hectares per annum). As shown later, much of the credit for this indiscriminate extension of irrigation goes to the sinking of deep and shallow tube wells. Most tube wells are owned by individual farmers and the government's role is minimal, so the recent irrigation expansion in Burdwan has largely been the result of private investment, unlike the government-driven canal irrigation growth that took place during the 1960s. It is possible that the net cropped area of the district increased in response to the expansion of irrigation, as records show that over 100,000 hectares of crops were added during the postindependence period, particularly during the 1960s and the 1970s. The most remarkable expansion, however, took place in the double and multiple cropped land (12,000 hectares per annum), which is directly a consequence of the expansion of irrigation during the rabi and summer seasons.

Though rice is the most significant crop of Burdwan, potatoes have become the second major crop in recent years. Meanwhile, wheat and oilseeds are losing their importance in the district's agricultural economy in spite of their high yields. Wheat production has been replaced with the increased cultivation of potatoes, with production increasing by 18 percent per annum and productivity growing by 580 kilograms per hectare per annum. At present, Burdwan district is the second highest producer of potatoes among other districts of West Bengal. Consequent to this great demand for potatoes as a viable cash crop, char farmers have also begun farming potatoes in recent years. The sandy soils of chars provide ideal conditions for cultivation of potatoes during the winter season. Although the market price of potatoes varies widely from year to year, and farmers sometimes end up with only minimal profits, potato cropping provides adequate annual subsistence for a char family of three to four members.

Rural Poverty

Alleviation of poverty has been one of the components of rural development in the mainland areas of the region. In the early years of planning in India, rural development was viewed from an integrated perspective in which the objective of agricultural development was intertwined with goals of poverty eradication and the reduction of social and economic inequalities. In the First Five Year Plan, beginning in 1951, the major thrust was on programs of agricultural development. These programs were based on the view that a sustained process of agricultural growth could reduce rural poverty through significant changes in the production and labor markets in favor of the poor (M. Ghosh 1998). After ten to fifteen years, it was realized that the agricultural development programs had failed to make an impact on poverty. The rise in farm employment was slow in relation to the growth of agricultural output in the period, leading to insufficient percolation of benefits to the poor from agricultural growth (Rao 1994). To improve the situation, priority was given to a strategy popularly known as a "direct attack" on poverty through beneficiary-oriented programs. Several poverty alleviation programs were launched in the late 1970s through centrally sponsored schemes. These schemes have reduced rural poverty from around 56 percent of India's population in 1973–1974 to around 37 percent in 1993–1994 (this is discussed in greater detail in Lahiri-Dutt and Samanta 2002).

The schemes meant for poverty alleviation that had some impact on the rural economy were the IRDP, Training of Rural Youth for Self-Employment, Development of Women and Children in Rural Areas, and the more recent Swarnajayanti Gram Swarozgar Yojana (literally, the Golden Jubilee Village Self-Employment Project). The IRDP, introduced in 1978, was the single largest scheme for providing direct assistance to the poorest of the rural poor. Under this, those living below the defined poverty line in rural areas are identified and given assistance to acquire productive assets, such as appropriate skills for self-employment, which, in turn, should generate sufficient income to enable the beneficiaries to rise above the poverty line, as discussed in the Eighth Five Year Plan. Small and marginal farmers, Scheduled Castes (SCs), Scheduled Tribes (STs), Other Backward Castes (OBCs), rural artisans, landless agricultural and nonagricultural workers, and unemployed young people constitute the target groups of the IRDP. The Burdwan District Rural Development Agency (DRDA) has introduced several schemes, including forty-five principal schemes and eighty-two subsidiary assistance schemes under the IRDP. There are separate schemes for craftsmen, landless laborers, small and marginal farmers (farmers owning up to 1.25 acres of irrigated land), women and children, recorded bargadars and patta holders, the physically handicapped, SCs and STs, and other sections of the population with an annual income up to Rs. 11,000 (as per the Eighth Five Year Plan document).

Char dwellers did not benefit directly from these programs because of practical difficulties for them to produce verification of a residential address or the ration card or similar valid documents such as a record in the voter list as evidence of citizenship. But they benefited indirectly. As the attraction of the Damodar chars grew, more people settled there, many of the houses became more permanent in nature, many families became sedentary, and, above all, char dwellers benefited from transacting with a prosperous area nearby. Not only did they find small jobs on mainland farms and in various agricultural-processing industries that mushroomed in the area, they also began to cultivate the chars more intensively and to sell their produce in the burgeoning rural markets. This was made possible by the roads and other infrastructure that began to be established during this time.

Infrastructure and Services

Infrastructure is an essential component of socioeconomic development in rural areas. Mainstream economic research has consistently put great importance on infrastructure and public investment (for example, Aschawer 1989; Costa 1988; Costa et al. 1987; Lucas 1988; Porter 1990; Shah 1992); it shows that the impact of infrastructure on growth is substantial, and frequently greater than that of investment in other forms of capital in India. Infrastructure includes all things provided by the government that directly or indirectly promote productive activities (Kumar 1994). Depending on the nature of input services, infrastructure can be broadly divided into two types: physical and social (Ghosh and De 1998). The former consists of transport, electricity, irrigation, telecommunications, housing, and water supply; they work as direct, intermediate inputs to production and work for the improvement of these inputs in any geographical location that attracts flows of additional resources. Social infrastructure broadly includes education, health, nutrition, sanitation, child care, recreation, and banking and various forms of financial assistance and facilities; their contribution to improving productive activity, although indirect in some cases, is no less important.

In the chars, the provision of transport makes a crucial difference with regard to accessibility. Generally in rural areas, roads are the vital element among the different aspects of infrastructure. Farmers of the Damodar chars who can access efficient transport are in a better position to utilize their limited land resources than those with less mobility. For example, farmers living on Char Gaitanpur and Char Kasba have better access to urban markets where they sell their vegetables than farmers on other chars. The access to markets offers the residents of these two chars the potential for higher incomes. Owing to the physical uniformity of the region, a high population density, and relative agricultural prosperity, among other factors, chars have become somewhat better connected to the mainland region. Among the arterial roads, the most important is the G. T. Road running almost parallel to the Damodar at a distance of two to five kilometers from the northern bank of the river. Many smaller roads connect the larger settlements, giving rise to an integrated system of a town bus network (Lahiri-Dutt and Samanta 2004). Some of these town bus routes terminate at different points along the riverbank, making the nodal market points on the mainland accessible to char dwellers.

As discussed earlier, irrigation has been a prime factor in the development of agriculture, with the introduction of new technology; consequently, agricultural practices and cropping patterns changed to water-intensive multiple cropping. Privately owned deep tube wells and shallow submersible pumps radically modified the nature of the agricultural economy, not only of mainland Burdwan, but also of the chars since the 1970s. Extension of private irrigation—in the form of groundwater usage—has been such that even some farmers on chars have begun to use shallow pumps. The groundwater table in chars is high (only fifteen to twenty meters below the surface), which facilitates the installation of shallow pumps by reducing the cost to below US$500. As a result, even medium-scale farmers can afford to install a shallow pump, thereby enhancing their agricultural profit. Before the development of shallow pumps, char farmers could only grow one rain-fed crop during the summer, but it is now possible for them to produce three to four crops each year. The extension of private irrigation has seen the development of a water monopoly by submersible pump owners, who either sell water or rent others' land—mainly that of small and marginal farmers—in the command area on a *thika* contract. This is a typical example of how "waterlordism creeps onwards" (as noted by Webster 1999: 350). On chars, increased private control over groundwater has affected the distribution of benefits from agricultural production and eroded small producers' success.

Another significant factor in the development of agriculture is electricity. Approximately 95–98 percent of the mainland rural area is connected to the grid. Electricity has improved the quality of life and opened up a range of facilities for the development of minor irrigation, especially shallow and submersible private tube wells. Some chars, even those that are physically proximate to the mainland, still lack access to the grid. The supply of electricity is difficult to regularize because of difficulties in obtaining a legal connection. The want of electricity reduces livelihood opportunities since char farmers must bear higher costs to run their shallow tube wells on diesel instead of electricity.

The marketing of agricultural crops and the development of facilities for its improvement is an important component of rural infrastructure. With the successful introduction of "new technology" in agriculture, farmers have now recognized the importance of the market for selling increased surplus produce. Increased accessibility in the region has extended the marketability of agricultural products to a large extent. Marketing infrastructure, such as marketing cooperatives and government institutions that sell consumer goods, remains limited on chars, although Burdwan region in general has quite a large number of rural and wholesale markets that play considerable roles in providing marketing facilities. The periodic markets, popularly called *haats*, also play a significant role in providing numerous opportunities for marketing rural products and have facilitated the marketing of crops produced on chars. In response to improvements in the road network, vegetable cropping has increased in recent years. The vegetables are of high quality and remain fresh since they reach the market soon after being plucked from the fields. Farmers receive higher returns from these market-oriented vegetables than they do from staple food crops such as paddy or wheat.

Other elements of rural development in the mainland region include improved health and education facilities. Although not directly related to the rural economy, they indirectly impact the well-being of those living in rural areas. In mainland areas of Burdwan, the improvement of these two aspects of social development has played a significant role in bringing a new dynamism. A mass literacy program has extended educational awareness among the poor and illiterate of the region to a large extent. At present, a number of postliteracy Continuing Education Centers (CEC) are efficiently running the literacy program among the poor neoliterates of the mainland region. Chars, however, have remained marginal to the CECs.

Some basic educational services have now reached the chars; each char, except Char Bhasapur, now has a primary school. But that is the extent to which such services go, since none of the chars has a secondary school. Furthermore, in the island char of Majher Mana, which is surrounded by water throughout the year, boys and girls have to walk at least five kilometers each way and then cross the river by ferry to reach the nearest school. Therefore, the younger children who live on this char, particularly girls, find it difficult to pursue studies since parents avoid sending their daughters to schools that are located far away. One contribution of the CECs has been to develop a general awareness about issues such as health and environment, about the availability of various poverty alleviation programs run by the government, about legal assistance for women, about the awareness of health and hygiene, and, above all, about the understanding of the need to educate children at least up to a certain level among the poor and "backward" classes. Even without the CECs, educational awareness has generally been high among char dwellers, who consider educating their children as one of the means to protect them from extreme poverty.

Being located at the margins of the "mainland" and due to their uncertain legal status, chars are nowhere near the general development indicators that make Burdwan such an important district in eastern India. The lack of infrastructure and facilities has led to further marginalization. Whether in the case of public health facilities or educational infrastructure, the physical remoteness and difficulty of access mean that chars have remained outside the state's view. None of the chars have primary health workers or even visiting health extension workers nor do they have health centers. These chars thus witness loss of lives due to diseases such as diarrhea or gastroenteritis, or incidents such as snakebites, particularly during the monsoons. Since ferry services do not operate between chars and mainlands at night, in case of an emergency, the patient has to wait until morning for transportation to the hospital in the nearest town.

Remaining Outside

After independence, the Indian government continued to follow the principles of encouraging land-based wet farming that were initiated by the colonial government. Rural development initiatives, while benefiting the mainland farmers, have enhanced the effects of marginalization, isolation, and alienation of chars. One can say that rural development has changed the nature of the coexistence of land- and water-based communities. The two do not necessarily constitute "dual" or parallel existences that do not intersect each other; rather, the systems of chars and mainlands across embankments create a complex whole. While chars have remained physically and legally marginal, their economies and societies have not been entirely unconnected to the changes taking place elsewhere in the area.

The number of char dwellers has increased now as people are lured by the rural prosperity of the mainland. People living on chars interact on a daily basis with those on the mainland either to earn a livelihood or to access services or infrastructures. Because water levels in the river have tended to be lower since the construction of dams and the withdrawal of water for farming and industrial purposes, the level of interaction between those living on the riverbed and those living across embankments has increased. Char dwellers have constructed narrow fair-weather tracks that connect their lands to the embankments except when the river is full. Interactions between the char and mainland economy are many and varied. Char farmers sell their crops in wholesale markets located in Burdwan, while fisher folk sell their fish in mainland markets. They buy food and other necessities from retail markets. Those who are employed in nearby rice or other mills or work as domestic labor regularly commute to their places of work. Children go to schools, adults occasionally visit a fair or go to watch a movie in a hall or a video parlor. Paresh Ghosh, a char dweller, says:

> We live on the chars. The babus who live on danga don't even see us. But we see them all the time. Although we don't live on the *bhitarer jami* [inside land], how would we survive if it weren't there?

Paresh's view is not echoed by those living on the mainland. The people who live on the mainland today view those living on chars as illegal occupants. The interactions of mainland people with the char are generally limited to economic exchanges. Only those who do business with each other, such as those who collect agricultural produce from chars, visit chars on a more or less regular basis. Occasionally, the bigger farmers of the mainland employ labor from chars. Many of the individuals we spoke with, in spite of living in villages and towns located nearby, have never visited the chars. Even today the existence of char communities remains largely unknown, ill understood, and unexplored by those living across the embankments of the Damodar.

CHAPTER 5

Silent Footfalls

Peopling the Chars

The problem of illegal migration from Bangladesh into India . . . brings together all the skeins of the [issues] . . . to produce one gigantic brew of bitterness and conflict that is constantly churning and erupting and shows little or no sign of abatement.—SANJOY HAZARIKA (2000: 24)

The peopling of the Damodar chars took place primarily during the last one hundred years, but it is only since India's independence that these lands have become well settled. The need to "use" what was seen as "waste" land was the key factor in the earliest phase, when the Maharaja of Burdwan tried to populate the chars by designating them as baze zameen and then granting rights of ownership and access of these lands to certain communities. The chars, however, remained sparsely inhabited until around the early 1900s. In the second, post-Partition phase, chars have experienced waves of immigration of refugees who either directly or indirectly found their way into these lands. This was also the time when the flow of the river began to decrease and become irregular; the channel started to dry up and more chars arose as a result of the barrages and dams upstream. The two phases brought in two different ethnic communities, the Biharis and the Bangladeshis,[1] respectively. The Biharis arrived from northern Bihar, where repeated flooding and waterlogging had ravaged the local economy, and the exploitation by upper-caste landlords had driven the peasantry out of their villages. From across the border with Bangladesh came the Hindu refugees. Disregarding the shifting and flood-prone nature of the chars, they settled there in an effort to reestablish their homes and livelihoods. Both these communities were extremely poor and had to struggle to adjust to the char environment and make it more habitable. While the Bihari migrants largely depended on fishing, the Bangladeshis cleared the reeds and grasses growing on the chars not only to establish homesteads but also to transform them into productive agricultural lands. Even though some chars have stabilized over time and stay above the monsoon waters, their legal status as land remains uncertain and contested. For the Bangladeshis, no other place could offer such invisibility along with proximity to one of the richest agricultural areas on the Indian side of the border and also provide a livelihood that they were familiar with.

This chapter outlines the processes of migration into the Damodar chars, placing the movements in the contemporary social and political context of West Bengal and Bangladesh. It also explores the questions of legitimacy of cross-border movement of Bangladeshi Hindus and places these questions in the context of the history of the Partition of Bengal. No written history or official records exist about how these lands were first occupied by different communities. Yet popular tales and some popular literature in Bengali vividly describe the peopling process.[2] To reconstruct the peopling of chars in the past, in the absence of written records, we approached the few older people who still live there and recorded their stories. We also searched the archives of local newspapers for stories and images, if any, of the "refugee influx" that occurred after the Partition of Bengal. And indeed, there were a very few references to the "indescribable hardships" in the Nayanagar refugee camp in local news papers such as *Dainik Damodar*.[3] These reports told of not just the living conditions of refugees but also the assistance that was given by local residents.[4] Scanty pictures emerge from scattered words; for example, the refugees were accommodated in tents (*tanbu*) and temporary shelters (*chalaghar*) in the Kanchannagar and Udaypalli areas of Burdwan town, areas that were near the river and were sparsely populated because of the fall of the local ironworks industries. One newspaper report recorded that the refugees were provided with rice, clothes, and cash every Sunday. Another report noted that around one hundred thousand people were rehabilitated by government agencies in the eastern part of Burdwan district alone, but there was no mention of who they were or how they lived.[5] About chars and those settling on them, the newspapers were largely silent.

State Interventions and Conflicts

Lengthy conversations revealed old and long-forgotten stories of state intervention in trying to settle at least some refugees on the chars. One of the elderly villagers remembered that a number of families were settled by the government in the Kalimohanpur-Satyanandapur chars under the initiatives of the Refugee Rehabilitation department of the West Bengal government and the district administration of Burdwan. When we made inquiries in the government departments, it appeared that no one remembered about such "official" settlement. In 2004, we interviewed the Block Land Revenue Officer (BLRO) of Sonamukhi block under Bankura district, who since 1989 has been responsible for patta, or lease deeds, distribution and disputes resolution. Before this time, the Junior Land Reforms Officer (JLRO) undertook these functions. The BLRO remembered that during the Partition, chars were still owned as khas land by the Maharaja of Burdwan. These lands were taken over after the West Bengal Land Reforms Act of 1955 (popularly known as the Zamindari Abolition Act) and turned into "vested land." Land that is vested by the government is redistributed among the landless. The BLRO described this as an "ongoing process," accomplished in collaboration with the Refugee Rehabilitation department of the state government. This means that land distribution to refugees and char settlers is still taking place. Land is also constantly acquired by the state government. For example, if an area of *ryoti* (farming) land, which is recorded in someone's name but is lying fallow for some time, is squatted upon by the refugees, it can be purchased by the government at a low price and redistributed with patta to the refugees if they appeal for land. At block level, a *samiti*, or local committee, called Ban o Bhumi Sanskar Sthayi Samiti, comprising the BLRO, the forest ranger, the head of the forest department, and the local panchayat *pradhan* (elected village head), examines these applications and makes decisions. The BLRO thought that the Bangladeshis came to Kasba Mana of their own volition and cleared land, set up houses, and began farming. Soon they appealed to the Refugee Rehabilitation department for patta. The department requested that the JLRO "query" the status of this land, and ultimately the former took over the ownership right of land in Kasba Mana. The land pattas that were given during the 1970s were converted into "refugee deeds" in 1995. By 2003–2004, a number of villagers in Kasba Mana received such refugee deeds. These were not full ownership papers because the land could not be mortgaged to the bank; still, the papers were adequate to proclaim a kind of de facto user right over these lands. On the strength of these papers, the land can even be sold after eight to twelve years, and, during a sale, the government receives revenue for the transaction. The villagers in Kasba Mana appealed to get *parcha*, implying that their names should be registered in government record books. By 2004, a number of villagers in Kasba Mana received parcha, which does not mention them as refugees and accepts char dwellers as legal owners of these lands.

Not all char dwellers were as lucky as those in Kasba Mana, although, in general, the process of occupation of the Damodar chars was not as violent or bloody as the processes in more remote areas in Bangladesh. Yet the local *goala* castes (the cattle herders and milkmen community) in the mainland fought bitterly with the Bangladeshis to establish rights over lands that they used only for cattle grazing. The newcomers were not allowed to use the tracks trodden by goalas. As in Bangladesh, people labored hard to claim new chars rising on the riverbeds and to keep old lands under control. Up to the 1970s, the "rule of capture"[6]—whoever is the first to find and establish claim by clearing the land gets to keep the land—applied to the chars. In certain chars, for example, on Char Kasba Mana, occupation took place after several violent skirmishes during which one of the Bangladeshis was killed by a "local man," that is, a villager from the mainland. People who settled on Char Kasba Mana were from the Faridpur and Gopalganj districts of Bangladesh, and were well known as *lethel* (people who are skilled in pole fighting). Once a week or so, they displayed these skills on open ground to arouse fear among those who gathered there from the mainlands.[7]

Char dwellers say: "*Banchbar tagidei amra oikyabadhho chhilam*" (We were united due to the sheer need to survive). The remoteness of chars is such that the arm of the law often does not reach there or, even if it does, arrives too late. Moreover, the river demarcates two districts, Burdwan and Bankura, and the chars lie in the middle of the riverbed. Neither Burdwan nor Bankura police stations see them as part of their jurisdiction. The police stations refuse to record complaints made by char dwellers who themselves do not possess legal citizenship papers. The conflicts were not always to establish and retain control over existing chars; they were also to get to a newly rising char first and then claim it. The conflicts over chars are rooted also in the fact that the Damodar, while giving rise to a char in one part of its bed, erodes its banks and destroys old lands on another side.

The conflicts in Damodar chars were between different groups; initially there were conflicts between the Biharis, who were the older char dwellers, and the Bangladeshis, who were trying to settle into an established community. The other set of conflicts took place between char dwellers and local residents who lived across the embankment of the river on the mainland. Although the villagers living on the mainland did not see these lands as prospective agricultural land, they used them at times for grazing cattle. As new settlements came up in these areas, the inconvenience of reduced access to what was previously uninhabited and common property land annoyed the villagers. Naturally, the more powerful landed families would not tolerate this sudden loss of access to the new (and often illegal) immigrants who were settling on the Damodar chars. Desperate Bangladeshi refugees fought back, seeking permanent claim to chars by setting up houses and clearing land for farming and livestock grazing. During conflicts with mainland villagers, people from one char supported those from another. Chars are physically separated from each other; to communicate, they planted bamboo poles at intervals that were visible from quite a distance. When a fight built up in an area, the Bangladeshis raised a flag on a pole for others in nearby chars to see and immediately run to the spot. Women blew conch shells to alert those working in distant fields. Ultimately the Bangladeshi migrants succeeded in establishing and retaining their control over the chars through their social network, unified struggle with the other groups (the Bihari migrant and local mainland communities), and sheer desperation to hold on to agricultural land. Let us briefly explore the contemporary views on migration.

People on the Move

Migration is commonly understood to involve the voluntary movement of persons within or across borders, be it legally or illegally, in search of a better means of livelihood or just because people want to move. A view of migration as a flight from poverty is simplistic. For those who move across the borders in South Asia, a politically correct name is difficult to find. Although Ramachandran (2005) uses the term "transnational" to imply the migration of the Bangladeshis in India, "transborder" and "cross-border" are more common and familiar terms in the region. As people move across national boundaries to inhabit diasporic locations, home and belonging assume different meanings and are experienced in different ways. The ease of movement and the numbers and diversity of people who move today have led to a significant rethinking of what consitutes "home" and how one "belongs" to the home. Ahmed et al. (2003: 1–2), for example, note that migration does not necessarily involve complete freedom from places, that mobility and placement are interdependent, and that even grounded homes may be considered as sites of change, relocation, or uprooting. As will be shown later in this chapter, this is the case for the Bangladeshis who rebuilt their lives on chars. The complexity of history and contemporary politics of border crossings in Bengal is such that any complete separation of homing and migrating yields a simplistic image of the fluid movements of people that characterize char communities.

In spite of the many cultural similarities between their source and their destination, the Bangladeshi migrants on chars could be identified as transnational. For example, although the primary language on both sides of the border is Bangla, the dialect and pronunciation are different. The Biharis brought with them a new language, Bhojpuri (or Magdhi Hindi), into the predominantly Bangla-speaking area. Both groups of migrants needed to reconstruct their lives in the unfamiliar environment of the chars based on what they left behind. While they shared a common habitat on chars, maintaining their individual cultural identities was important. So when the Bihari Hindus followed Chhat Puja, the Bangladeshi Hindus celebrated Durga Puja or Kali Puja. Both groups, however, maintained fine cultural boundaries with the other group. It was also not uncommon to hear one community berating the other. The Bangladeshis feel that by clearing the land for farming, they have improved the cultural landscape of the chars, which the Biharis had not been able to use to the fullest capacity, as recounted by Prasanta Mondal, a leader of the Bangladeshi immigrant community on Char Gaitanpur. He also elaborated on the sense of their cultural superiority over the Biharis:

> When we first arrived here, Biharis were uncivilized. They did not know how to plough the land. They used to wear dirty clothes, used to leave their houses unclean, and did not wear slippers. They did not even use a khatia [a cot made of coconut string] to lie on. Sometimes they slept on a mattress made of grass and covered their bodies during the winter with used jute sacks. After coming in contact with our culture, they have now become refined.

The two communities have never integrated with each other. The Bihari community is discussed next—how they were brought, when they were brought, what brought them to the Damodar chars, and where they stand now.

Internal Migration from Bihar

Both groups of migrants—Biharis and Bangladeshis—who live on the Damodar chars have a tradition of outmigration from their own lands. A rich literature points to the relationships between poverty and migration in Bihar (Akbar 2003; Karan 2003; Sahay 2004). These authors have shown that migration from Bihar dates back to the nineteenth century when indentured laborers from Bihar and eastern Uttar Pradesh were being sent to overseas British colonies such as Fiji and the West Indies, as well as to other parts of the country such as the jute mills of West Bengal and the tea plantations of Assam.[8] Thus, Akbar's (2003) observation that the Biharis have been India's foremost "economic refugees" for many generations perhaps holds true. Bihar is one of the poorer states of the country, where poverty-induced migration is high even after five decades of independence and planned development. According to newspaper sources, there are 1.0, 0.5, 0.6, and 0.3 million Biharis in Delhi, Punjab, Kolkata, and Mumbai, respectively.[9] The high percentage of migration from Bihar is related to the overall poor socioeconomic condition of the state.

The rate of outmigration is also higher among the Bihari Muslims than among the Hindus because Bihari Muslims are poorer than their Hindu counterparts. As per ADRI (2004), about sixty-three people migrate for every one hundred Muslim households in rural Bihar. The report mentions that 50 percent of rural Muslims and 45 percent of urban Muslims live below the poverty line as compared to the national average of 34 percent (*India News* 2004). It also states that two out of every three Muslim households in rural Bihar send at least one family member of working age away to either Punjab or West Bengal to earn cash.

Our survey indicated that migration from Bihar to the chars took place mainly because of poverty. Some of those living currently on chars came from the poorer districts of south Bihar that now make up the separate state of Jharkhand because they provided them with the two scarce resources of land and water. Some landless Biharis also hail from northern districts such as Patna, Darbhanga, and Purnia, where there are limited jobs for wage laborers in the highly flood-prone and poorly developed agricultural area.

Cross-Border Migration from Bangladesh

Like the Biharis, the Bangladeshis have also featured significantly in recent migration discussions. Innumerable Bangladeshis now live in more developed countries as well as in west Asia and work as unskilled laborers. The choice of destination and levels of benefits and risks taken for the purpose of migration vary significantly according to the economic and social resources available to a Bangladeshi migrant. Siddiqui (2003) blames population pressure and extreme poverty for the peripatetic nature of Bangladeshis.[10] The size of the population, fixed amount of arable land, low level of incomes, and large number of poor people looking for avenues to earn a livelihood encourage both legal and unauthorized migration from Bangladesh.

Samaddar (1999) describes the Bangladeshis in general as composing an "immigrant niche," but contests the "population pressure leading to migration" thesis. He shows that migration from Bangladesh might be rooted in complex reasons, such as ever-increasing economic pressure, rapid population growth, disease, unemployment, starvation, and a constant threat of natural disasters. The continued population movement from Bangladesh to India is due to this variety of factors, which have multiple dimensions and are interrelated, and which include religious, political, ethnic, economic, and environmental reasons. For example Samaddar (1999: 156) discusses, although briefly, how poor water-management practices and recent water-control measures in the floodplains of Bangladesh have led to an agrarian impasse that reveals a "deep connection between water and migration."[11] Indeed, the wetlands and floodplains in Bangladesh have been vital for fish production and livelihoods. The customary rights around these water bodies were lost as the official "tackling of wetlands" spelled disaster for the subsistence strategy of the peasants, the fishermen, and particularly the Bangladeshi women. Bangladesh is more prone to environmental disasters—floods, droughts, tropical cyclones, and tidal surges—which tend to cause more harm to people and livelihoods due to the density of the rural population. Alam (2003) has also blamed environmental crises for emigration, in particular, the crises of land and water caused by rapid population growth, environmental change, politics over resource distribution, and low levels of economic development in rural Bangladesh. He believes that the fact that environmental conditions are worsening is manifested in the society in increasing landlessness, unemployment, declining wages and income, and in growing income disparities.[12]

Another contributing factor for Bangladeshi migration is the growing political turmoil, excessive corruption, and poor law and order situation. Increased radicalization of Islamic rural communities and the rise of religious groups in recent years have created a turbulent sociopolitical milieu in which minority communities have increasingly felt insecure in Bangladesh. This complex combination of environmental fragility, excessive population pressure on productive land, political instability, extreme poverty, and rampant corruption has encouraged Bangladeshis to migrate more than any other nationality. The persecution of religious minorities, primarily the Hindus, the Christians, and a few "tribal" groups such as the Chakmas who live in the Chittagong Hill Tracts, has become a common occurrence and some such reports have surfaced even in international media. At about 6 percent of the population, the Hindus continue to form the largest religious minority in Bangladesh and their migration to India to escape religious persecution, ever increasing since the Partition in 1947 and Bangladesh's independence in 1971 (see Samad 2004), has emerged as a sensitive issue.

Several Bangladeshi migrants participating in this study narrated their personal experiences of persecution in rural Bangladesh. Whereas some families were forced to leave their villages and others were threatened with dreadful consequences, some left on their own. Those Hindus who decided to (or had to) stay on in East Pakistan after the Partition found themselves increasingly trapped as the newly founded nation of Bangladesh, originally secular, adopted Islam as the state religion and religious fundamentalism gained momentum among peasant classes (*Human Rights Features* 2001; Mohsin 1997). In rural Bangladesh, the targets have generally been men and women from poorer and more disadvantaged groups.[13] Iqbal (2010: 4–5) argues that the deterioration of Bengal's ecology has intensified Hindu-Muslim communal antagonisms.

Until recently, geographical studies of the Partition had remained focused on "available data"; for example, the detailed cartographical exercises based on census data to clearly show the distribution of Hindu and Muslim populations of Bengal as undertaken by Professor S. P. Chatterjee (1947). Attempts to correct this gap are under way; recently Deb Sarkar (2009) has presented multiple voices of geographical contemplations on this major event. This way, the dearth of other material that historians lament is being slowly corrected (Rahman and van Schendel 2003). Unlike in the divided Punjab, population migration across the border in divided Bengal took place slowly. Also, in the initial years, the refugee influx, or at least its historical documentation, was primarily focused on the Bengali upper castes, the bhadraloks. As communal violence and riots escalated in post-Partition years, many more Hindus began to leave then East Pakistan. The stream of migrants after 1947 is thought (by Chatterjee 1995) to have brought about ten million Bengalis in the following decades. Most of these migrants took shelter in the neighboring Indian states of West Bengal and Assam due to political and religious suppression (Alam 2003).[14] These undocumented, unsung migrants—*bastutyagis* (those who left their homes), *bastuharas* (those who lost their homes), and *sharonarthis* (those seeking refuge)—literally are "midnight's orphans."[15] The 1990s saw a hardening of allegiances that conflated religion and nation in South Asia; the rise of the Bharatiya Janata Party (BJP) to power in New Delhi and the Bangladesh Nationalist Party (BNP) in 2002 in Bangladesh was critical. Datta (2004: 337) estimates that between five thousand and twenty thousand Bangladeshi Hindus and other minorities fled to escape violence. Each violent act against the Muslim community in India led to retaliatory attacks on the Hindus in rural Bangladesh, leading many of them to leave with their families in order to disperse within the Indian population (Bose 2000).

Unfriendly Neighbors: Bangladesh and India

Transborder movements of people have stirred bitter political debates around the world. One strand of the debate at the international level views the traffic of outsiders as posing a threat to national security and the moral and social economies of the receiving countries. Transborder movements without legal documents—"illegal" or "unauthorized" migration—have been turned into a "cottage industry" for their newsworthiness. People throughout the Asian region continually move across the political borders in this way (Battistella and Maruja 2003: 11–13), so the discourse of "trafficking" must be challenged by putting forth a corrective in understanding such movements. Van Schendel and Abraham offer a strong critique of the cartographic divisions of culturally linked communities and the state efforts to criminalize certain forms of human mobility. Their invitation to "look beyond the discourses that equate state organizations with law, order and bureaucratic probity" (2005: 9) forms the basis of the way we explain licit and illicit flows, identities, and place-making on chars.

In South Asia, political boundaries established during the colonial times are often obscured in long-standing disputes (Chakraborty et al. 1997). Yet these borders remain porous in spite of the official barbed wire, and a large number of people move across them, albeit illegally. In the absence of data, it is difficult to estimate the extent of unauthorized migration between the two countries. India-Bangladesh relations, in particular, have been strained over the sharing of river waters, particularly on the construction of the Farakka Barrage over the Ganga in West Bengal, and by the difficulties of drawing a clear-cut border, as in the case of Tin Bigha[16] or New Moore Island[17] (for more details on border disputes, see Ahmad 1997 and Jacques 2001).

The two-nation theory, which created Pakistan as the homeland of the Muslim community by partition from India in 1947, was based on religion and racism. The intermigration of the Hindus and the Muslims between India and Pakistan immediately following the Partition was productive for the rich. For the poor, who were the overwhelming majority on both sides, it turned out to be a disaster. India remained a secular country, whereas Pakistan declared itself as Islamic. Here lies the source of continuous conflict and the resultant unfriendly borders. Bangladesh won independence from Pakistan in 1971 and emerged as a secular polity with a continuous embargo on religion in politics. Between 1972 and 1975, during the regime of Sheikh Mujibur Rahman, the first president of Bangladesh, the state retained its secular constitutional provision. At the same time, there was an increasing government trend toward the Islamic attitudes of the majority Muslim population (Samad 1998).

In 1975, the government of Mustaque Ahmed declared that the People's Republic of Bangladesh was to be known as the Islamic Republic of Bangladesh, which was then recognized by Saudi Arabia, Libya, and China. The process of using Islam for leadership legitimation purposes gathered momentum during the military regimes of General Zia ur Rahman (1975–1981) and General H. M. Ershad (1982–1990). During the regime of the former, the constitution was changed and the principle of secularism was replaced by the words "Absolute trust and faith in the Almighty Allah shall be the basis of all action." General Ershad added the eighth amendment to the constitution, declaring Islam the state religion, and took the nation toward "Islamic Nationalism." During both military regimes, there was no room for accommodating minorities within the new state discourse (Mohsin 1997).

The subsequent regimes of Khaleda Zia (leader of the Bangladesh Nationalist Party), Sheikh Hasina (Awami League), and again Khaleda Zia came to power through free and fair election processes under neutral governments in 1991, 1996, and 2001, respectively. Each of these governments, which defined Ershad's regime as undemocratic and autocratic, continued the policy and dichotomy of his regime and did not try to reject Ershad's Islamization measures. Bangladesh still retains its Islamic status, which places stress on the minority communities living there.

Between 1947 and 1992, a number of incidents involving religious violence broke out, encouraging migration. The religious violence of December 1992 was the worst in terms of damage and destruction (State of Human Rights 1992, cited in Samad 1998). Incidents of looting, arson, rape, and demolition of temples by the majority community were not condemned by the government of Khaleda Zia. Low-intensity violence against the Hindu religious minority is not even recorded in Bangladesh, which makes the Hindus vulnerable. In addition, two discriminatory laws of 1974—the Enemy Property (Continuance and Emergency Provisions) Act and the Vested and Non-Resident Property (Administration) Act—contributed significantly to driving Hindus out of their lands in Bangladesh and ultimately pushing them beyond the border. Many Hindus in Bangladesh have to face great insecurity as their lives, property, and peace are threatened by the lack of police protection and by state policies and public action, which thereby force migration to other countries. The Hindus in Bangladesh have been described as "stateless" and "the marginal men" in the post-Partition Indian subcontinent (Chakrabarti 1990).

Cross-border migration in this part of South Asia has been a subject of intense political debate in recent years. In India, people coming from the "outside," mostly from Bangladesh but also from Nepal, are seen as constituting a threat to national security.[18] Some even believe that the "outsiders" will, in the long run, "take over" the economy (at least in the form of cheap labor), society, and culture of the insiders, even though today's insiders were all originally from within the modern state concerned (see Samaddar 1999 for an elaborate critique of this view). The question of illegal migration has been complex also because it is difficult to provide accurate numbers of illegal migrants, and estimates are often based on indirect observations.[19] Unfortunately, there is no accurate data for India; only some guesstimates are available. These vary wildly; the "official" government estimate, presented in the 2001 Census of India report, suggests that there were around three million Bangladeshis living without papers in India (GoI 2001: 19). Datta (2004), however, suggests that this figure is fifteen million. Another report, by Pathania (2003), suggests that the number is far greater—over five million in West Bengal alone.[20] The sheer weight of Bangladeshi migration has stirred nationalist sentiments; pernicious accusations have led to counteraccusations and evoked fear on both sides of the border. So sensitive is migration research in South Asia as a subject that battle lines are clearly drawn, and objectivity is difficult to achieve for a researcher. Populist views claim that the very idea of West Bengal, created as a non-Muslim majority state, is at stake due to the mass influx of the Bangladeshi Muslims into West Bengal (Ray 2009), and that on a number of occasions (such as in 1964, 1990, 1992, and, most recently, in 2002), pogroms have deliberately targeted the Hindus in rural Bangladesh (Roy 2001).

Rethinking the Illegality of Cross-Border Mobility

Two authoritative works (Samaddar's and Banerjee's, discussed below) have posed a critique of the conceptualization of borders as absolute and as key political instruments of statecraft and nation-building projects in South Asia. Both agree that border formation was a colonial project; subsequently, these borders as boundary lines were internalized by postcolonial states. Samaddar's early work (1999) on transborder migration from Bangladesh shows how such borders have become the markers of statehood in South Asia. Yet, he argues, these borders are unstable and contingent, and produce even more partitions by marking out the separateness of various solidarities. Questions of the illegality of transborder flows then get conflated with those of national security and acquire politically explosive dimensions. The transborder migrants who cross artificial political borders to maintain historical and social affinities or in the pursuit of economic objectives facilitated by geographic contiguity thus constitute a "marginal nation." Those who cross the border are "nowhere people"—those who are left stranded without valid papers on the no-man's-land between two countries (Achariya et al. 2003). More recently, Banerjee's (2010: xxxiv) suggestion that "it was the partition which changed them [the frontiers] into borders" is most relevant in understanding the cross-border mobility of the Bangladeshi Hindus into the char (and other) lands. Such mobility challenges the prevalent systems of power and theories of sovereignty that assume these borders as static lines. The presence of the Bangladeshi Hindus on the Damodar chars is proof that borders, though with different meanings and forms, are alive.

A landmark incident that triggered a rethinking of the illegitimacy of migration from Bangladesh and a greater understanding of borders in South Asia took place in Bengal in the late 1970s. Described as the Marichjhapi massacre, it marks one of the darkest incidents relating to population mobility in postcolonial Bengal. Marichjhapi, a small island in the Sundarbans in West Bengal, bore witness to a massacre of lower-caste Bangladeshi Hindus in 1979. The incident raised complex questions about the legitimacy of the claims of the Bangladeshi Hindus over livelihoods in India. Political parties in India have remained largely ambivalent to their plight, reasserting the illegality of their existence in West Bengal or other border states such as Assam. The reasons for this massacre go back to the post-Partition times when the Bangladeshi refugees pouring into West Bengal were sent to resettlement colonies and camps in faraway Andaman and the Nicobar Islands located in the Bay of Bengal. Some were resettled in the Dandakaranya areas of Madhya Pradesh in the central Indian uplands, which belonged to indigenous groups who resented the entry of Bengalis into their territories. These refugees usually belonged to lower castes such as the Namashudra; they belonged to lower economic classes and were accustomed to working only at flooded rice farming for their livelihood. They could not accept the new life in resettlement camps and, in particular, were incapable of rebuilding livelihoods in the rugged forest tracts of the Dandakaranya area. When the Left Front came to power in West Bengal in 1977, these communities were hopeful that with the support of the new "people's government," they would rebuild their lives in a land where they were familiar with the local environment and culture. Indeed, the Leftist parties, particularly the CPI(M), had been a pillar of support for Bangladeshi refugees. Nearly fifteen thousand families left central India for West Bengal and settled in the Sundarbans, where they began to clear forests to set up villages. The state government retaliated, objecting to the clearing of what was deemed to be an environmentally sensitive area, containing protected forest, and when

> persuasion failed to make the refugees abandon their settlement, the Left Front West Bengal government started, on January 26, 1979, an economic blockade of the settlement with thirty police launches. The community was tear-gassed, huts were razed, and fisheries and

> tubewells were destroyed, in an attempt to deprive refugees of food and water. At least several hundred men, women, and children were said to have been killed in the operation and their bodies dumped in the river. (Mallick 1999: 105)

Based on Biswas's (1982: 19) report, Mallick (1999: 104) calculates that over four thousand perished.[21] Although the Marichjhapi massacre did not stanch the slow but steady stream of refugees coming into West Bengal, the cruel treatment of the Bangladeshi Hindus made it apparent that the state government, no matter what political color, would not accommodate migrants officially. The incident provided an incentive for making the flow illegal, for the Bangladeshi Hindus to steal into India through kinship or other networks, and then try to obtain valid citizenship documentation. Settling in the no-man's-lands of the Damodar chars provided an excellent opportunity for such illicit flows.

The intricacies of power and social status achieved through caste played a significant role in Partition stories of eastern India. Pal's (2010) authoritative work shows that besides the economic strength of migrants, caste largely determined who got where, who lived in the metropolis, and who were able to rebuild their lives. During the Partition, political bargaining and power play were limited to the high-caste Hindus and upper-class Muslims. Jalais (2005: 1758) notes that the growing polarization of West Bengal and East Bengal as separate "homelands" for Hindus and Muslims, respectively, "affected most the lower caste, poor, rural population, especially of lower Bengal who were not divided so much along religious lines as along the cultural and economic divide of bhadralok/nimnobarner or 'nimnoborger lok.'" The *nimnobarno* communities (lower castes) became politically marginalized minorities in both countries. During or right after the Partition, it was the upper-class, upper-caste, better-off elite Hindus who left East Pakistan, leaving behind rural, poorer farming castes. According to Mallick,

> [w]ith the partition of India it was the upper-caste landed elite who were the most threatened by their tenants and who had wherewithal in education and assets to migrate to India. Even those not as well off had the connections to make a fairly rapid adjustment in India. The first wave of refugees was traditional upper-caste elite. Those who lacked town houses and property in India squatted on public and private land in Calcutta and other areas, and resisted all attempts to evict them. (1999: 105)

Immediately after the Partition, a Congress government ruled West Bengal. It failed to grant refugees patta for the squatter land. With the ruling state trying to evict them, the refugees turned to the Communist opposition party for support. In exchange for their support for the refugee cause, the Communists gained a ready following among the refugees, who gradually came to be organized by Communist-front organizations. Mallick also writes that the near-total departure of the Hindu upper-caste landed elite and urban middle classes from Bangladesh meant that communal anger was directed against the Hindu lower castes who were left behind. It is therefore understandable that the later refugees from Bangladesh were from the lower classes; therefore, they lacked the means to survive on their own and became dependent on government assistance. Since they lacked the family and caste connections of the previous wave of largely middle-class refugees, the namashudras (again, lower castes) had to accept the government policy of resettling them wherever land was made available in other states, claiming that there was not enough vacant land in West Bengal to settle these refugees.

Jalais observes that the subsequent migrants were "rural middle class cultivators and artisans. If the richest amongst them found a niche amongst relatives and friends in Kolkata and its outskirts, the poorer amongst them squatted on public and private land and tried to resist eviction" (2005: 1757). Clearly, although they seemed isolated, the peopling of the Damodar chars was intimately connected with the history of the region. The larger political processes that were shaping Bengal during these decades were also leaving their imprints on the chars. Even the social history of Bengal and the social characteristics of regional politics shaped the social milieu of the chars. From this perspective, chars begin to assume a symbolic meaning as a microcosm of Bengal.

Migration to the Damodar Chars

It was shown earlier that fertile land was easily available in the mainland areas of Burdwan district until the mid-twentieth century, and that consequently most chars of the Damodar had remained largely uninhabited until that time. The Biharis and the Bangladeshis who live here have different cultural traditions, came for different reasons, and have different livelihoods. A few chars were settled during the 1920s by small groups of Biharis (as noted by Bhattacharyya 1998). Immediately following independence and the Partition (1947–1949), another group of Bihari boatmen came to these chars; they had lost their traditional occupations because the river-borne trade between Bangladesh and the north Indian plain through the Ganga-Padma river had ceased. Their numbers were small in relation to the area of uninhabited chars. Although the peopling of chars started with the Biharis, they are now a tiny segment of the char dwellers.

At present, the majority of char dwellers belong to the Bangladeshi Hindu community. As has already been described, these refugees were granted patta to settle on chars by the district government of Burdwan after the Partition. Shifting river courses made these areas highly insecure: Considerable stretches of chars have since reverted to riverbed, whereas some new lands have emerged from the riverbed and considerable stretches of the river channel have been converted into seasonal croplands.

Another group of refugees were those who fled from government-sponsored camps and colonies such as most of the settlers on Char Kasba and Char Bhasapur. Together with those categorized as illegal migrants, they often preferred to remain invisible and opted for a location away from the mainland rural areas of Burdwan. Physical isolation from the mainstream community and locational disadvantages were therefore considered to be favorable factors for development of new settlements in the Damodar chars.

These chars attracted only those Bangladeshi migrants who were unable to garner a great deal of support for resettlement from either the Indian or the West Bengal government, or those who migrated later without papers and were in search of lands that suited their skills in agriculture. The Refugee Rehabilitation department of the West Bengal government divided refugees from temporary refugee camps located in different areas of the state into two groups for their rehabilitation. These two groups were categorized on the basis of their choice of livelihood options of either agriculture or business. The migrants who opted for agriculture were mostly allotted land in either Dandakaranya in Madhya Pradesh or the Andamans. Others chose "business" as their livelihood option. To avoid being exiled far away, many people, like Surath Mondal of Kasba Mana, changed their livelihood option from agriculture to business. Surath told the story of his long journey beginning in 1952, when he arrived in West Bengal from Bangladesh, and ending in 1962, when he bought some land in Kasba Mana and permanently settled there. After arriving in

West Bengal from Bangladesh, he spent several months in two transition camps in south Bengal. Then he found some wage work as a laborer at DVC canal construction sites. As he was weary of living in resettlement colonies outside Bengal, he paid someone to help him change the label of his refugee card to say that his original occupation in East Bengal had not been agriculture, but trade. Once he succeeded in altering this fact, he came to Burdwan to receive four kathas of land from the government to build a house and a grant of Rs. 750 for setting up a small business along with other families. But, he says:

> I was always looking for land that is suitable for agriculture. One day I heard from a relative that some land is available on Char Kasba. I immediately came to buy it from a Bihari. I bought eleven acres of land for Rs. 900 in 1962. Since then I have been living here. I received the patta of these lands in 1995.

Like Surath, many others did not accept the physical relocation to unknown lands with the potential of isolation from their family relations and village friends. Many were apprehensive of the difficulties that might befall them in an environment that was totally different from the familiar alluvial floodplains of Bangladesh. Naren Sarkar of Bhasapur Char comments:

> We had no skills except farming. We didn't even know how to ride a bicycle. So how could we make our livelihoods in any other areas except in the cultivable land such as these chars? We had the skill of making land more fertile and productive. Therefore, we preferred these chars for our resettlement and converted them into fertile cropland without any support from the government.

The settlement process in the chars intensified after the 1970s, when the Bangladesh Liberation Movement led to a significant increase in the flow of illegal migrants into southern West Bengal across the Bangladesh border. The last group of migrants to settle on chars began to arrive in 1971, following Bangladesh's independence from Pakistan. Streams of such people continue to enter India even today. The earlier settlers in these chars often purchased land for their relatives and neighbors, who then crossed the border illegally into India and settled in these chars. Kinship relations, at the village level as well as the extended clan level, had a strong influence on the shaping of these new settlements. The inflow of migrants and their settling here are a continuing process. Our field survey revealed that on Char Gaitanpur, twelve such families arrived between June 2003 and May 2004. Religious persecution and the increasing insecurity faced as minority Hindus in Bangladesh, together with poverty and lack of work, were cited by these people as the underlying reasons for their immigration.

At present, Bangladeshi immigrants are the dominant group in all Damodar chars, while Bihari settlers are gradually reducing. For example, of 199 families on Char Gaitanpur, 58 are Bihari fishermen-turned-laborers, whereas 141 families are of Bangladeshi origin. The Bihari fishermen no longer catch fish for their livelihood due to the reduction in water levels following the construction of DVC dams, and because of water pollution by the industrial and urban liquid wastes of western Burdwan district. Because the Biharis were unable to develop their agricultural skills and turn into farmers, they gradually sold whatever cultivable land they owned to the Bangladeshis. Younger generations of the Bihari settlers have left the chars in search of work in the nearest towns. Those who are still living on the chars make their livelihoods either by working as daily wage laborers in local agricultural lands or by digging and carrying sand from the riverbed.

The population composition of the chars is highly changeable because the char dwellers are fully aware of the vulnerability and uncertainty of these lands. Some spend only a short time, as a stop on their way to safer locations, trying to get away and settle on the mainland as soon as they can afford to do so. The ease of entry into chars due to their relative isolation always attracts fresh migrants, especially those who cross the border illegally. This dynamism of social composition is a distinctive characteristic of human habitation on chars.

The process of occupancy on chars is still not clearly understood; it is conceptually isolated and sparsely studied because of the remoteness of the chars. Settling on a char occurs through personal and social linkages, but the physical environment, local administration, and migrants act in tacit consonance. Char dwellers are prey to natural hazards as well as to locally powerful men who offer them a place to live and accept their existence. Chars, with their potentially fertile soil and inaccessibility from the mainland society and environment, provide ideal spaces for unauthorized migrants to settle down. With their expertise in farming and soil management, the Bangladeshi migrants have by now converted nearly all the chars of Damodar into fertile agricultural lands.

Migration Pathways

Migration pathways into chars are complex because migrant families and individuals may or may not move directly from their homes to the chars; their movements make up intricate systems of circulation between two or more destinations and take place through a network rather than as individual cases. Since the beginning, integrated networks of family, kin, and community on chars have provided access for most of the migrants. Migrants who arrived directly at the chars often had strong kin relations already settled in the area who helped them find work and arranged for their shelter. In most cases, the migrants left home after establishing a connection with at least one contact person, such as a neighbor or villager who had previously left the source region and who then provided them with shelter in West Bengal.

On average, approximately less than half of the Bangladeshi migrants on each char came directly from Bangladesh. For example, on Char Gaitanpur 43 percent and on Char Majher Mana 53 percent of Bangladeshi migrants came directly from Bangladesh. The rest arrived after initially staying in border districts such as Nadia and 24 Parganas (North and South) with contacts or close relations, and then arriving on the Damodar chars. Thus, most step migrants[22] arrived at the chars after spending between six months to five years in different places, with the highest proportion coming via 24 Parganas. It is not uncommon for these migrants to have changed residence three or four times in a year. Some had in the past visited India several times, used family or other connections to search for economic opportunities or prospects of land, and then returned to Bangladesh before finally settling on the chars.

Migrants living in the Damodar chars are mostly from the Khulna, Jessore, Dhaka, Faridpur, and Barishal districts of Bangladesh. Figure 5.1 shows the origins of Bangladeshis living on Damodar chars. Except for those who migrated directly, all crossed the border at different points of North and South 24 Parganas and originally lived there for at least some time. Towns on the Indian side such as Basirhat, Hijalganj, Chaital, Itinda, and Habra are the main entry points for migrants entering West Bengal. In a few cases, migrants returned to Bangladesh because they had been unable to arrange for papers, work, or shelter in West Bengal. In most cases, migrants made arrangements through close relatives already living in the chars.

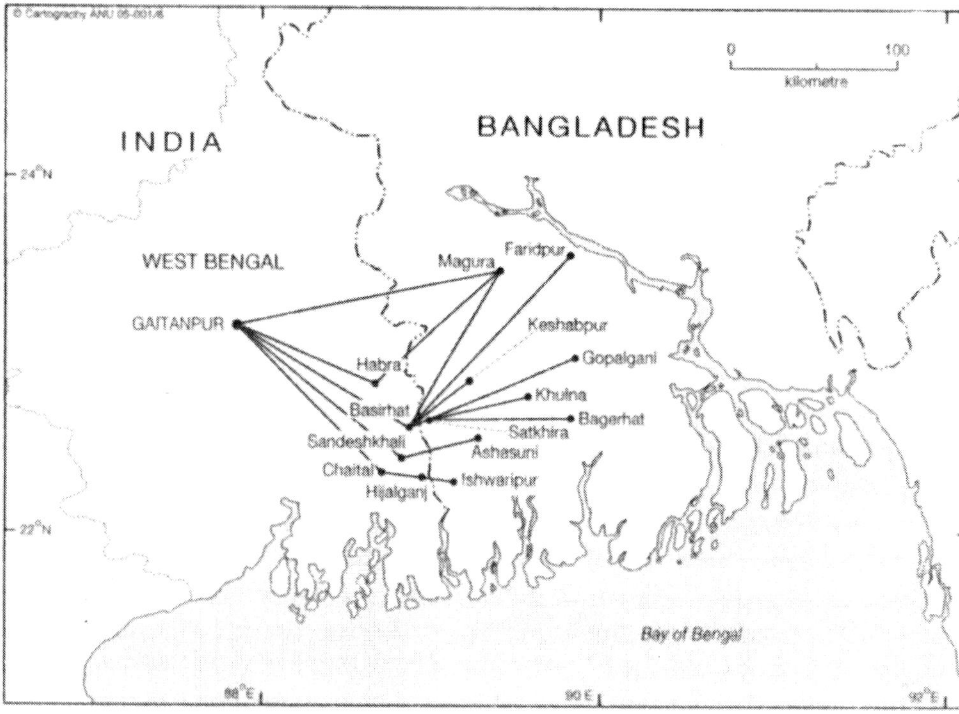

5.1 Migration Routes to Chars
Source: Field surveys.

Social networks are a major source of support and play a key role in the migration of char dwellers. Some immigrants, such as Prasanta Mondal of Char Gaitanpur (locally known as the "doctor" because he performs the role of a physician besides being a farmer) and Mahadeb Sarkar of Char Kasba, have played key roles in the char-migration network. These men were early settlers on individual chars and have served as contact persons who arrange livelihoods for their relatives and village men. This might give them a sense of power in rebuilding the social networks they left behind. The influence of kin and neighbor networks during the occupancy process has resulted in concentrations of Bangladeshi migrants from different districts in different chars. For example, on Char Gaitanpur the majority of migrants are from the Khulna district of Bangladesh; on Char Kasba they are mostly from the Gopalganj subdivision of Faridpur district; on Char Majher Mana they are from Barishal; on Char Kalimohanpur they are from

Jessore; and on Chars Lakshmipur, Bhasapur, and Bikrampur most of the migrants are from Dhaka.

Different Histories: Peopling of Some Chars

In choosing to settle on the chars, the new settlers did not ignore the minor disparities in the profile of the land surface. Even on the flat surface of the chars, tiny variations in relief determine how that land is utilized. Relatively higher grounds are occupied by houses, whereas the marginal lower lands are used for cultivation. In most cases, agricultural lands adjacent to a home are "owned" by the householder. Vast stretches of sand deposits are still found on the river channel side of the chars. The topsoil, though a few inches thick, is fertile for the production of several crops. Sand fields are gradually converted into croplands by biomanuring and the hard labor of the char people. During the field survey, we saw the reclamation of at least two acres of sandy land for crop production in a single char within a ten-month period. The sandy soil drains rapidly and requires large quantities of water for the production of any crop; the water requirement is even higher for paddy and only those owning shallow and submersible pumps can tap the groundwater. Farmers often keep their lands fallow during the kharif, or monsoonal main cropping season (July to October), since during this time of high evaporation, it is impossible to cultivate without irrigation. During this season, a number of vegetables are produced that can be sold in nearby urban markets. The better-off farmers can afford to invest in a second crop of rice (*borodhan*). The farmers who produce vegetables engage the women of their families to provide the extra attention that these crops need. Poorer people usually work in others' fields when their own lands are fallow during kharif. The fallow land during kharif provides an opportunity for the rearing of animals, especially cows, goats, and pigs, to supplement the family income. Kharif occurs during the wet season, when there is a good yield of local grass; therefore, the livestock needs to be fed only once a day. Farming is small and extremely labor-intensive in nature. Labor is, as a result, in high demand in the chars and wage work on farms is one of the main sources of income for new migrants.

Population densities are understandably greater in the higher or more permanent chars that are less liable to flood. For example, the population density of Char Gaitanpur is 388 persons per square kilometer (according to the 2001 census).[23] Population density is increasing rapidly in almost all the chars in this area with the continuous influx of unauthorized migrants from Bangladesh. Joint families[24] are uncommon on chars. Families have been uprooted and regrounded; the "new" nature of establishment and settlement never ages here. Similarly, the pieces of land owned by char dwellers are also tiny; farmers owning only 5 bighas (0.5 hectare) of agricultural land or more could be designated "big" landowners in the char.

The following section analyzes the peopling process in some chars in more detail, and is based entirely on the oral history provided by early settlers of these chars. These histories are more focused on Bangladeshi settlements, since there are more early settlers within the community from whose narratives we could reconstruct the history of those chars. The Bihari settlements are much older on these chars, so there were only a few early settlers from whom we could learn about their history. To reconstruct the history of each char, we separately talked to all early settlers who are still alive and thereafter sat together to have a group discussion to resolve any confusion about the dates or inconsistencies arising from individual interviews. We observed that although they had a clear memory of early days and some of the incidents are etched in their memories, they did not remember the exact years. Hence, we note that the years are only approximate.

Char Gaitanpur

The story of the peopling of Char Gaitanpur largely draws upon the memories of Rambali Mahato, Saraju Chowdhuri, and Sumaria Rajbhar, the three elderly early settlers from the Bihari community still alive today. The others who narrated their story of the early days were Gopal Mondal, the first Bangladeshi to settle on this char, and Prasanta Mondal, the *morol*, or headman, for the Bangladeshis. Rambali Mahato was the morol from 1978 to 1988, after which Saraju Chowdhuri took over from 1988 to 1993. These individuals have extensive knowledge about each person who settled on this char during the recent period.

According to Rambali, the first settlement wave occurred between 1947 and 1954, when several groups of Bihari boatmen[25] landed on this char and colonized the land by clearing bush and jungles. Being quite old, they were not able to recall the exact year. Bhattacharyya's (1998) study gives the year of first settlement as 1952. Judging from the age of their children when they came here and from what they remembered about the old times, it does appear that settlement started here immediately after independence. As Rambali recollects:

> We came here immediately after the Partition. This was when river-borne trade in this region came to an end. The competition with land-based surface transport through trucks also caused decline in river-trade. We came here in a number of groups starting from 1947 and continued to come till 1954 or so. When we came here, chars were still owned by the Burdwan Rajas. But no one lived here or used these lands. The char was covered by forest and bushes. We cleared those and started building our houses.

These communities used to sail boats, large barges, in the Ganga-Padma rivers, carrying goods between the north Indian plains and places in the east of undivided Bengal. This river-borne trade was cut off due to the Partition of Bengal, and the Bihari boatmen lost their livelihoods. Later, the construction of roads provided a faster mode of transport, and rendered these boatmen redundant in the economy of eastern India. Without their traditional occupation and in search of new lands, they came across the uninhabited bush-covered land of Char Gaitanpur. The proximity to the river was an additional attraction for them. Saraju Chowdhury, a seventy-eight-year-old man who arrived on Char Gaitanpur as a child with his father, tried to explain this choice of a riverine location made by his father:

> We are majhhi-malla lok [boatmen] originally. We are accustomed to rivers and living on water. This is how we found chars suitable for us to live on. Another reason was the free access to land for cultivation. Since there was plenty of fertile soil in the mainland of Burdwan, these chars remained uninhabited for a long time before we came here.

The two reasons, the search for a "suitable" place and free availability of land, appear to have driven the settling of the Biharis in the chars.

As the Bihari community made the land livable, news of it spread through word of mouth among kin, neighborhoods, and village friends, resulting in more landless peasants moving there. This settlement process continued until around 1954, by which time the initial occupancy of land on Char Gaitanpur was complete. This period was marked by a long struggle between the Bihari settlers and a local group of ex-servicemen of the Burdwan Raj—*munsis* and *tahasildars*—who visited from Burdwan town and claimed the land as their own property. The Biharis stood firm and said that they would leave the char only if the munsis and tahasildars could produce evidence of their ownership of the land in the records of Burdwan Raj's register. The munsis and tahasildars then filed a number of cases against the Biharis, and the local police used to come frequently to this char to arrest the Biharis and lock them up. The ex-servicemen were unable to prove their legal ownership of the lands in a court of law because, according to local custom, all of Char Gaitanpur was the property of the Raj family. In the meantime, the official process of surveying land and recording it for revenue purposes began in 1954–1955. By giving a small amount to the munsis and tahasildars (Rs. 100–150 against an acre of land), the Bihari settlers got those lands recorded in their own names and received legal rights to this char. During our survey, there were fifty-eight Bihari families living on this char.

Since the completion of the revenue survey, many Bihari families have left Char Gaitanpur and others have entered it in order to make a living. Talking about the reasons people might have for leaving the char, Rambali Mahato says:

> After arranging to buy a piece of land on Char Gaitanpur, some people brought their families over here from Bihar. But within a few months, the hard life, especially the difficulties during the rainy season, forced them to leave the char. Only those people who are like me—extremely poor and have no other choice—continued to stay here and are still struggling with poverty.

It appears that Rambali and others remained on the char because they could not find an easier alternative to build a livelihood.

This lack of choice is echoed by some Bangladeshi immigrants living on chars. The history of Bangladeshi migration to Char Gaitanpur began in 1988 when Gopal Mondal, the first Bangladeshi settler, purchased a large plot of thirteen acres there. Gopal had come to India in 1972 after the Bangladesh war of independence, and settled temporarily in 24 Parganas. From his new base, he was always looking out for cheap land. In his own words:

> I was a farmer in Bangladesh and sold my fertile land at a negligible price before I moved to India. I saved that money for purchasing land in West Bengal. I frequently visited different places in West Bengal wherever I had the slightest contacts, searching for cheap land. I know farming better than any other work and I have the confidence of making

> any land productive by using methods such as manuring, the knowledge of which was passed on to me by my forefathers. I had a relative in Udaypalli [the part of Burdwan town across the riverbank near Char Gaitanpur] who told me that land in this char was available. Then I purchased a large plot of thirteen acres at the cost of Rs. 39,000.

Since the char was eroding on the southern side, he purchased a more stable parcel of four acres on the northern side the following year and sold his previously held land to some Bangladeshi relatives, who immediately moved to India and built their houses. Gopal and his relatives came from the Khulna district of Bangladesh. Since the 1990s, many more Bangladeshis have come to live on this char, usually from his district in Bangladesh, but a small number also came from other parts of the country. Many of those who had originally migrated to other parts of West Bengal have now come to live on the chars through their network of kin and village folk. This steady immigration has resulted in a significant rise in the proportion of Bangladeshis on this small char.

Char Bhasapur

The name of Bhasapur is derived from the Bangla term *bhasa* (float), so it literally means "the settlement that floats." The history of settlement on Char Bhasapur was narrated by Sachindranath Biswas, one of the early settlers from Bangladesh. Supplementary information was also collected from Naren Sarkar, who has been living on this char over the last four decades. Sachindranath Biswas narrates:

> When we, two families, came to this place in 1949 it was not habitable. It was an imposing and vast riverbed covered by bushes and jungles. The jungle was full of snakes, fox, banberal [wild cat], wild pigs, and monkeys. There was not a soul living on these sands. To avoid ending up in the refugee camp, we were moving around in search of land and finally arrived here. The Damodar was a narrow channel flowing through the southern part of the island. The width of the river was no way comparable to what it is now. The change that you are seeing now is a result of continuous bank erosion since the formation of the DVC. Bhasapur became a char because of the DVC scheme. Earlier it was part of the mainland. It is true that even at that time it was marginal due to its location on the riverbank. Once the construction of embankments by the

DVC took place, it got completely separated from the mainland areas of Garamba, Mithapur, and Sonda mouzas and became a river char.

Based on Sachindranath's recollection of the early history of Char Bhasapur, it appears that the original owner of the land was the Maharaja of Burdwan, who gifted the land to one of his priests. The priest later sold this land to Dinabandhu Tewari, a local landed man, who claimed to be the zamindar. Dinabandhu then distributed the lands among his *praja* (subjects), but did not receive any revenue because the land remained unused for agriculture. Two families, Kirtania and Poddar from Nadia district, who had arrived earlier from Bangladesh, bought the entire land of 586 acres at the rate of Rs. 15 per acre from Dinabandhu Tewari. During that time, it was difficult for the two families to live in the middle of the jungle, which was full of animals and located far away from the other villages. Due to the isolation of this char, both the Kirtania and Poddar families started to sell the lands to other Bangladeshi refugees at the rate of Rs. 21 per acre, a rate that refugees could easily afford. Sachindranath is one of the early refugees who bought his land from the Poddars, built his house and cattle shed, and prepared farming land by clearing the jungle. Naren Sarkar lamented that not all Bangladeshis bought the land from Dinabandhu Tiwari. Often, they just squatted on the land and occupied it if it had been lying unused.

During the process of occupancy, Bangladeshi migrants took initiative to avoid confrontation with the local people from the mainland community, who used those lands for grazing their animals. In the initial phase, the immigrants began to construct their houses on the riverbank, keeping a stretch of jungle between the houses on the char and those on the mainland. Therefore, the development of the settlement went on unnoticed by the mainland community. When these people eventually noticed the settlement, it was already a sizeable one, making it difficult for the locals to fight against the Bangladeshis.

The locals did not readily accept this occupation of nearby lands by Bangladeshi refugees. They particularly resented the fact that these lands were being transformed into fertile agricultural lands. They came in groups, armed with indigenous weapons such as *barsha* and *ballam* (sharp, pointed weapons made of wood and iron) to attack the Bangladeshi settlers. Naren Sarkar describes the battles:

> Physical violence was frequent in those days. All the fights were centered on the issue of land and on the question of who will have its control.

> The weapon was only lathi [bamboo stick], but the fights were more or less organized, the date and time being set beforehand. The armed forces of the two groups used to gather on the land over which there was a dispute and used to start fighting with each and every one of the other group. The group that won the fight used to get the right to the land. Several people from both sides died in those violent conflicts.

People living on the mainland tried their best to evict the migrants by creating a number of other difficulties on an everyday basis. Sachindranath Biswas described the various means by which they tried to keep the migrants off the chars. He reminisces:

> Sometimes they used to let their cattle loose to ruin our crops. They designated us as socially outcast and as bangal [a derogatory term for people from Bangladesh]. They became uncooperative in all aspects of life and made our day-to-day living difficult. At that time, no farmer from the mainland community would give us work as laborers; no businessman would buy agricultural products from or sell consumer goods to us. We used to drink water from the Damodar, but in the dry season when the riverbed was dry, we needed drinking water from other sources. But the mainland people would not allow us to fetch water from their village wells and tube wells. It became really difficult for us to carry on living here.
>
> Unable to continue this way, one day we decided to arrange a meeting with the mainland people. Our objective was to have a dialog, but they did not listen to us. Rather, they set fire to a few houses in the char and took some people from the char and kept them tied in their *goalghar* [cowshed].

After this incident, the Bangladeshis went to the Galsi police station and filed a complaint against a few people including Dr. Sudarshan, who was leading the mainland community against them. The then police officer was also Bangladeshi in origin. He helped the poor by arresting a few people from the mainland community and by allowing the Bangladeshis to lodge a case against the mainland community members. This case lasted a few years. At last the case was resolved through mutual agreement and the long fight came to an end. Since then the Bangladeshi settlers have been living peacefully on this char. Some of them even received land patta in 1990–1992.

Char Kasba

We have reconstructed the history of settlement of Char Kasba through repeated and rigorous individual and group interviews with Mahadeb Sarkar, Parswanath Mondal, and Sushil Ray, who are the only remaining early settlers of this char. Since this char is dominated by Bangladeshis—only a few Bihari families still live here—we tried to focus on the peopling process of Bangladeshis only. This char was largely uninhabited up to 1950 and the entire area was khas land. It was covered by high bushes and was the habitat of snakes and wild pigs. After the Partition, when Hindus in Bangladesh began to face some discrimination, Mahadeb Sarkar, a school teacher in Bangladesh, who is still known as *mastermasai*, assumed the responsibility of shifting the entire community to India. He sent someone to inquire if land was available anywhere on the Indian side of the border. This person returned with the news that Char Kasba was an option. Immediately, Mahadeb, along with Parswanath Mondal and a few others, arrived to claim this land. They initially made improvised huts in which to stay while clearing the rest of the land and gradually transformed it into agricultural land.

At that time, these khas lands were under the control of two local *izaradars* (leaseholders), Bholanath Hazra and Shankar Singh, who used to lease out these lands to the local mainland farmers for a short term to grow grasses for grazing their cattle. When they found out that some Bangladeshi people were using their land, they called for a meeting with them. Mahadeb recollects:

> One day, four or five of us went to see the izaradars. They asked: "Who has allowed you to settle on those lands?" We lied that a powerful man from the Congress Party [the ruling political party at the time] had instructed us to settle here. We also said that he has told us to avoid the government camps as that would only increase the pressure on the government to give us land. Then those izaradars allowed us to settle here peacefully.

Following that incident, Mahadeb sent information to his contacts to come over from Bangladesh along with their families. Within one to two months, hundreds of Bangladeshi families arrived on the char. The village morol formed a committee to distribute the lands equally among them. Each family received five acres. By 1954–1955, almost 350 Bangladeshi families settled here to form the Char Kasba colony. The process did not come to an end with this settlement. Even after they had built the colony, the community faced a number of obstacles from the government department, local goalas, and the few Bangladeshi Biharis, who also arrived here at a later date.

In 1955–1956, a large part of the char was acquired by the milk commissioner of the West Bengal government based in Haringhata for developing a dairy farm there. To avoid eviction, Mahadeb immediately went to meet the then refugee rehabilitation minister of West Bengal, Renuka Ray, with a request to save the land for the 350 families living on the char at that time. In response, the minister organized a team of soil scientists to visit the char. These experts tested the soil quality to decide what the land should be used for, cultivation or dairying. After testing soil samples from a number of places, the scientists reported that the land was better suited for agriculture. The milk commissioner was then advised by the Government of West Bengal to release the land that had been acquired for dairy farming.

The next challenge came from the local goala community that had used these lands for grazing their cattle before the Bangladeshis arrived. The conflicts with them reached a peak around 1958–1959 when the goalas began to destroy the maturing crops by grazing their cattle. Bangladeshis responded by fighting back, resulting in violent riots following each incursion by the goalas. The only weapon they used were bamboo sticks, so there were no life-threatening casualties. Ultimately the Bangladeshis filed a case against this mainland milkman community for causing loss of their crops and fighting with them, which they finally won. The mainland community had to give a *muchlekha* (a written statement) that they would never fight with the refugees and would live peacefully with them.

Around 1960, a few Muslim families came from Bangladesh to live on this char. Some of them were boatmen and others were either farmers or laborers. As soon as they settled on this char, confrontation over the possession of land became regular again. These people were Bihari Muslims. Some Bangladeshis were arrested when one of them was murdered. The police would frequently come to arrest the suspected murderers, after which they would beat them as well as search and demolish their houses. The local teacher, Mahadeb Sarkar, was the leader of the Bangladeshi group. When the police started searching for him, he fled to a refugee camp located about ten kilometers away along with many others. He tells us:

> I then asked some powerful political leaders [of the Congress Party] located in the nearby areas to stand beside me and to protect the colony that we had built over a period of eight to ten years. They, three party leaders, were kind enough to help us and arranged a meeting and accompanied me to meet the then chief minister. That was a memorable day in my life; I requested him to protect our community from being displaced again. He [the chief minister] then ordered the district magistrate to resettle the refugee families from the camp on this char within a day and to give them police protection. The colony was by this time almost deserted and had been nearly destroyed by the police. My eyes filled up with tears when I saw the colony after about six months. After that, many people came back and many also left the area permanently. A new wave of migrants came to settle here and occupied the lands left by others.

These histories give us an idea of the difficulties these people faced in the early phase of occupancy of the Damodar chars. The question of legality and illegality of migration, the complex sociopolitical context of the Partition in Bengal, identity as lower or upper caste, legal rights over land, rights over common property resources—all these issues were brought to the fore as the chars were being occupied. On other chars, too, one can find more or less similar stories of fights between Bangladeshis and mainland communities, or between Bangladeshi and Bihari migrants, to take control of land. Almost all chars house both these ethnic communities. Only rarely, such as in the case of a char called Bikrampur, does one find a group of tribals. Members of this Santhal tribal community came from Puruliya and Bankura, the two poorest districts of West Bengal. These people used to come every year to work as daily wage laborers during the peak cropping seasons in rural Burdwan. Around the late 1970s, they began to settle on the char. Unlike the Bangladeshi and Bihari communities, who occupied uninhabited lands, they bought the land on which their homes stand today.

"Birds of Passage Are Also Women"

Siddiqui (2001, 2003) notes that since 1976, about thirty thousand women officially emigrated from Bangladesh for employment reasons in spite of that country's ban; however, the actual number of female migrants is likely to be substantially higher than this estimate.[26] Similarly, according to official government statistics, over 60 percent of all newly hired laborers from the Philippines were female. In the increasing stream of women labor migrants, the scale of domestic workers is impressive and growing, overtaking professionals as the dominant group in many parts of the world (Gulati 1997). This burgeoning phenomenon has been described as the "maid-trade" (Hayzer and Wee 1994). In the early 1990s, 1.7 million domestic workers were thought to have left the Philippines, Sri Lanka, Indonesia, and Bangladesh, bound for destinations in West Asian countries (Yeoh et al. 1999).

International migration of women in Asia has three main components—labor migration; marriage migration and family migration; and trafficking. In the Damodar chars, most women accompanied the male member of their families, usually either their husband or father. The few women who came alone were mostly widows and depended on the relatives with whom they moved to the chars. In family migration, women are generally considered to be passive agents who silently follow migration decisions made by male family members. This was reflected in some chars we surveyed. Gandhari says:

> I did not want to leave Bangladesh because all of my father's family is still living there. But my husband did not listen to me. I feel lonely and miss my family and friends, who are still in Bangladesh. I feel uprooted from home. I cannot yet think of this land as my own home.

Khukumani was in a similar situation:

> I tried to stop my husband from coming to India then because I had two little children. When we migrated, we often spent days without food. With two small kids, we were looking for a *matha gonjar thain* [shelter]. It was tough for me because the children would cry for food. We moved from one place to another for two years before coming here. Although life was not easy, this char has given me at least a permanent shelter.

It is possible that as women become used to changing their place of residence frequently, they begin to perceive the establishment of a home on the char as relatively permanent. In the next section, we look at the burden of a family's subsistence that women like Gandhari and Khukumani have to bear.

Migrant women living on the chars belong to different class backgrounds in their places of origin and char environment. This is indicated by their family's economic location; women tend to receive the status of their male family members. The postmigration work of making a living has fallen mostly on the women, who have faced increased burdens in the absence of familiar contacts established back home. Except in Partition studies, the literature on Bangladeshi migration to India has commonly been silent on the question of gender (see Datta 2004; Kabeer 1991; Kabeer and Subrahmaniam 1996; Ramachandran 2003).

After crossing the border with their families, some of the women we interviewed faced significant difficulties in gaining a foothold in India. Their families sometimes waited for months or even years to obtain legal documents such as ration cards, which are the only proof of residence for migrants. Debirani narrates her family's experience when they were without a ration card and other resources in the following words:

> It was June in 1984, the first time when I came to live here with my husband and four children. We spent three months of the rainy season in a makeshift arrangement made of coarse polythene sheets, under a banyan tree. When it rained, we took shelter in a veranda of someone else's house. That time we could not manage to get the ration cards and went back to Bangladesh at the end of September. After two years we again left Bangladesh. This time we came here directly as my elder son, who came here earlier, had been able to establish some contacts and procure some resources like a hut on this char. Since then we have been living here.

Renu Das's story echoes a similar struggle. For two months after crossing the border, she could not provide her children with more than one meal a day. The hope of a better life kept Renu and her family going even during these difficult times. These experiences represent the true transitional phases of these women's lives. In contrast, some women gained access to chars easily with the assistance of kin already settled there, like Debirani, whose elder son acquired a hut for them. Some women spent ten to fifteen days with relatives before constructing their own house and establishing the arrangements for work. A few migrants were able to send a sufficient amount of money to purchase land in the chars through their kin even before leaving Bangladesh. Although the migration process affected the lives of each woman differently, one thing is clear: Whatever the pathways and steps of migration, all women participated actively to sustain their families both before and after migration. The critical role that the char environment played in their struggle to survive cannot be overemphasized.

To conclude, we note the artificiality of borders in the Indian subcontinent. The migrants come not only in search of better economic opportunities on the other side or to avoid religious persecution, but often a sense of belonging in both places pervades their existence. This is particularly true of migrant women, who repeatedly mentioned in the interviews that they were better off in Bangladesh, where family and support networks were wider. Although migrant women may be part of the family that moves from one place to another, our reconstruction of char lives shows that not only is migration work gendered, but the burden of survival in a fragile environment offering few resources often falls on women.

Although this section focuses on the life experiences of a limited number of women, it highlights the processes of migration as gendered. The survival techniques the women adopt to eke out a living in the new homes in the face of many kinds of vulnerability are also highlighted. Women have to perform all the domestic chores, including cooking three times a day, looking after children and domestic animals, washing, and cleaning. At the same time, they work either as family labor on their own cultivation plots or as laborers on others' plots to earn cash. Women, thus, are overburdened with physical labor from dawn to dusk. They receive and give more kin help than the men: Men give money to kin, women give time or contacts. Apart from material exchanges, women also maintain kin connections as emotional resources. On the whole, women on chars work harder than men to secure their families' well-being after migration.

The char dwellers live in a hostile environment, coping with floods, using skills and resources they have learned over years of experience with this phenomenon either in Bangladesh or in India. It is difficult to measure precisely the value of the work put in by char women. Our study brought to light variations in life experiences and workloads, as well as seasonal variations in women's work on chars. The social construction of the char environment through the eyes of women was a particularly interesting exercise. The embeddedness of migration in social relations suggests that the social position of a woman shapes the range, meaning, and content of migration work. Women negotiate to get resources for the family and these are shaped by their social class positions. Women living on chars perceive their work burdens and lives differently. Although fragile and vulnerable, chars offer a more secure environment for the migrants than their former environment in Bangladesh. Thus, the specificity of the environment and its social construction by women assume significant roles.

Crossing the Border: Regrounding and Place-Making

As the fragmented experiences narrated above tell us, the mobile subjects on chars pose important questions relating to legitimacy of borders through their ceaseless search for home. In retaliation against the state-sponsored and homogenized identity of the citizen, char dwellers re-create and reinvent themselves. As uprooted subjects reground themselves, they contest the hegemonic view of citizenship. The fluid nature of chars and the uncertainties of life and livelihood provide yet another border to be negotiated. In the process, conflicts with those living on the mainland as well as internal struggles and strife, ethnicity, caste, and gender all make important differences. The roles played by ethnicity, caste, and gender appear most significant in the ways people "settle in" or make their homes on chars. Privileging women's experiences is the critical element in understanding place-making and reinvention of citizenship. In critiquing the universal notion of citizenship, Banerjee notes that "the ideological constructions of the state are weighted against women who remain on the borders of democracy" (2010: 138). Located between belonging and nonbelonging, women are also forced to negotiate their difference with the state, which denies space to differences based on either ethnicity or gender.

The complexities involved in this negotiation become most apparent in the actual and physical border crossings by women and men. Crossing the border is complicated by many bureaucratic requirements, which contribute to unauthorized movement. Although it is not strictly a line on the ground, the border between West Bengal and Bangladesh also has a physical presence—the barbed wire fences and the stretch of "no-man's-land" meant to keep people off the border. Crossing it physically is an experience that char dwellers neither cherish nor forget. Many mention it as a "nightmare" with superlatives such as "dreadful" and say, "never again." The policing at, and of, the border is meant to show overt physical force; the display of power is meant to create insecurities and arouse fear, to prevent transborder mobility. Therefore, it is not uncommon for women to encounter physical harassment along the border during the time of crossing. During the interview, Renubala lamented that her golden bangles were taken by the border security force. Pulling at earlobes to grab gold earrings and touching private body parts in the name of physical searches are also not unusual. Families migrating together are often separated, and so are the members of one family. Ganesh Sarkar left twenty-eight bighas of land in Bangladesh.

On the way to India, his three daughters were separated from him and his wife. He was detained for days, a situation he escaped only after the payment of bribes.

The mobility of char dwellers and the history of settlement on chars, therefore, are complex areas that evoke important questions. Clearly, one cannot talk about it as a simple matter of cross-border migration due to economic reasons or a physical relocation, following classical migration literature. Bangladeshi Hindu migration into West Bengal cannot be simply defined as labor migration or migration brought about by poverty; its roots are deep and are spread in the history, politics, culture, and economy of South Asia, as well as the special geographical environment offered by chars as places for new homes. The mobility of those settling in the micro world of chars is connected to the history and in particular the Partition of Bengal. The stories and claims narrated in this chapter "challenge the historiography of post-partition migration" (Rahman and van Schendel 2003: 576). We begin to see that the bhadralok migration, which has dominated the narratives of displacement, cannot be used as the model for the large and complex forms of migration. The "licit-illicit" debate that stirs nationalist imaginations reflects the "innocent and totalising belief in the neoclassical explanation" (Samaddar 1999: 160). Edward Said described the Partition as "a parting gift of the empire" (van Schendel 2005). Char dwellers are evidence that in South Asia people on either side of the border have not yet been able to surmount the philosophical problem of "the other," of learning how to live with, rather than despite, the other. They also show that the other is not a remote alien; it is always with them as one of us.

How the peasant classes move around and where they settle are still not well understood. Chars could be only one area where the lower castes settled on the Indian side of the border. There is a need to connect chars with the histories of other marginal places with fluid histories and geographies. To break the current mode of populist and nationalist style of research on cross-border flows, there is a need to go beyond simplistic licit-illicit dichotomies. We also need to explore the areas where silence has prevailed—for example, the experiences of women in cross-border migration throw new light on gender in the Bengali community.

Geography and history come together in exploring twentieth-century legacies of colonial rule and in viewing divisions such as the Partition as political "solutions." The process that began with the separation of land and water now turned into the splitting-up of a single geographical piece of land into homes for people who were thought to be distinctly different from each other. The way Bengal was divided may be equated to the way land and water were partitioned earlier. To de-essentialize such partitions, we need to move beyond binaries of not only land and water but also Hindu and Muslim and legal and illegal, and explore what social sciences define as the borderlands. When the border is territorial, it also produces internal boundaries, which, as Samaddar (1999) has shown, remain not merely physical but also spiritual and metaphorical.

CHAPTER 6

Living with Risk

Beyond Vulnerability/Security

We are like the drifting grains of sand, rolling from one place to another. In one place today, in another tomorrow, but always with the river's flow.—NAREN SARKAR, ONE OF THE RESIDENTS OF THE CHARS

The silty and sandy chars lie literally on the margins of land and water worlds, at "edges" where earth and water ecologies and cultures meet on the fringe of human habitation. The human use of these borderline lands throws up a rich reservoir of metaphors (the "edge effect" of "the bringing together of people, ideas and institutions" as described by McCay 2000), unique questions of environmental dynamics and management (EGIS 2000; Sarker et al. 2003), and debates around resilience and adaptation. We are particularly interested in examining poor people's resilience in marginal and vulnerable environments. The fragility inherent in the physical characteristics of the ecology of char formation leads to persistent poverty in these chars, which in turn allows us to acquire deeper insights into what we mean by terms such as "vulnerability," "resilience," and "adaptation." The studies of Chambers and Conway (1992) and Ashley et al. (2003) conclude that although the nature and causes of poverty are complex and interlinked, the root causes of poverty and vulnerability are often identical, and these usually overlap.

The violent confrontations concerning re-demarcation of land freshly covered by sand and alluvium after each flood do not necessarily characterize the Damodar chars. Consequently, the boundaries of property are somewhat permanent, offering the residents a somewhat secure livelihood. Floods that do occur, such as those in 1978 and in 2000, are more devastating in nature, and the waters stay longer than they did before. Floods have become variable in nature in the lower Damodar valley, and the ways in which local people traditionally have dealt with them have become complex, too. Increased flood damage now accompanies the increased controls on the river. Above all, bank erosion is a physical process that is part of the char ecology, making human habitation uncertain.

This continual adjustment—"rising above" the traumatic experiences and difficult circumstances posed by a hostile environment—brings us to a rethinking of the concepts of the "adaptation" and "resilience" of human communities.[1] The ability of char dwellers to adjust to what is commonly seen as an insecure environment offers a problem worth investigating. The inquiry reported in this chapter began with a set of questions about the perceptions people might have of chars as a secure place of residence. These questions are: Why do people live on chars in spite of immense insecurity? How much choice do they have in selecting a place to live in? Do char dwellers view chars as a permanent location or do they use them as a stepping-stone to move on to other places? What insights can be gained on the perceptions of char dwellers on their environment? And, above all, what lessons does one learn from the chars and the communities living on them? In attempting to seek answers to these questions, our local-level case study helped us redefine the concepts of "vulnerability" and "resilience" according to the perceptions of, and meanings derived by, local residents.

Many years ago, a geographer asked, "[W]hy do people live on flood plains?" (Kates 1962). Similar questioning continues even today,[2] though the theoretical standpoint has changed over time with greater insights into human behavior. How individuals sort through a maze of environmental constraints and opportunities to make decisions is now better understood through the lens of subjective perceptions and choices rather than within a framework of rigid group behavior. Consequently, the perceptions of environmental security were examined through the looking glass of the individual life histories of some char dwellers in the Damodar chars. The specific and complex geography of place that forms the context of livelihoods, and the specific cultural backgrounds of two main communities living there, gave new insights on popularly debated concepts such as adjustment, adaptation, and resilience.

Long before Kates (1962: 1) attempted to explain why people live in vulnerable environments with an explicit acknowledgment that "the way men view the risks and opportunities of their uncertain environment plays an important role in their decisions as to resource management,"

Gilbert White offered some pioneering insights. White's work in 1945 advanced possible alternatives to engineering works on rivers to reduce flood damage, and differentiated between "common knowledge" among the community of resource users and the "technical knowledge" of the experts. Kates's explanation is that: "Rationality may be used to simply describe that ability to choose clearly and consistently those alternate courses of human behavior that are most appropriate toward attaining some end or goal. Among the difficulties in comparing interdisciplinary research in decision-making are the conflicting assumptions as to man's rationality" (1962: 13). His alternative approach is based on the principle of bounded rationality. The idea was that the capacity of the human mind for formulating and solving complex problems is small, compared with the size of the problems whose solutions are required for objectively rational behavior in the real world—or even for a reasonable approximation of such subjective rationality.

Perceptions of vulnerability and insecurity, however, may differ widely between different segments of people living on chars. Whereas some may feel more secure living on chars than living among hostile neighbors, others might perceive these areas as suitable lands for only a temporary stay. Yet others might consider chars to be entirely unfit for habitation and, hence, are nonexistent in their view. Some might try to build permanent structures and make plans for a long-term stay, while others, being fully aware of their vulnerability on chars, use them as a temporary place of residence and strive to form alternative living arrangements in mainland areas. The conditions under which people live in a certain environment throw new light on our understandings of environmental insecurity, vulnerability, and livelihoods.

The question that remains is how best to explain people's attitudes and feelings in a situation that lacks wide choices. Human perceptions of the environment, especially the conditions of vulnerability and security, are difficult to quantify. The issue-based individual interviews with twenty women and men living in different chars in the lower Damodar valley present a more complex picture than Kates's behavioral approach does.

Dimensions of Vulnerability

Wisner defines vulnerability as the "likelihood of injury, death, loss, disruption of livelihood or other harm in an extreme event, and/or unusual difficulties in recovering from such effects" (2003: 136). Vulnerability has multiple facets, external (or environmental) and internal (human), but remains a potentially detrimental social response to environmental changes. It covers a broad range of possible harms and consequences; it implies, too, relatively lengthy time periods, exceeding the time frame of the extreme event that triggered it. This interpretation of vulnerability is unavoidably related to resilience (Bogardi 2004a). According to Blaikie et al. (1994: 8–9), resilience can be measured by the capacity of a person or group to anticipate, cope with, resist, and recover from the impact of a particular natural hazard. Thus, vulnerability represents the interface between exposure to physical threats and the capacity of people and communities to cope with those threats. Threats may arise from a combination of social and physical processes. The most conspicuous and widely reported manifestation of this kind of vulnerability is when people are affected—suddenly and violently—by natural hazards. Over the years, the meaning of vulnerability has expanded to include the notions of risk, impact, adaptability, and environmental justice. The field continues to remain complex, one in which scientists from a number of disciplines are working simultaneously to determine the nature and extent of the problem, identify the consequences, and address it politically. Subjectivity is inherent in the interpretation of environmental elements because vulnerability can be both an end and a starting point. As an end point, vulnerability represents the net impacts of an environmental hazard, whereas, as a starting point, vulnerability is a characteristic or a state generated by multiple environmental and social processes, but exacerbated by gradual or sudden changes in the environment (O'Brien et al. 2004: 1).

Human exposure to environmental threats is not evenly distributed over the earth's surface. Thousands of people live in places that are seen as inherently risky, such as river islands and floodplains, slopes of volcanoes, earthquake zones, and low-lying coastal areas. Sometimes people are forced to live in such highly vulnerable environments because of social, economic, and political factors, including acute poverty and development or war-related displacement. But again, people may also deliberately choose to live in what might be seen by others as vulnerable and insecure environments. For example, floodplains have always been favored for settlement because of the fertile soil and the plentiful availability of flat land. As populations grow and there is more competition for limited land and its resources, areas of increasing vulnerability are settled by refugees, migrants, and other displaced groups. One would think that they make themselves vulnerable by living in areas where the potential for livelihood loss is high.

With vulnerability comes associated risk, defined as the expected losses (lives lost, persons injured, damage to property, and disruption of economic activity and livelihood) caused by a particular hazard (Blaikie et al. 1994). Thus, risk is a function of the probability of particular occurrences and the losses each might cause. Some people are clearly more prone than others to loss and suffering. Economically better-off people are more prepared and often insured against damage, and their homes are built at safe sites, making the process of recovery easier. The most vulnerable people are those who find it difficult to reconstruct their livelihoods.

All over the world, but especially in poorer countries, vulnerable people often suffer repeated, multiple, mutually reinforcing shocks to their lives, their settlements, and their livelihoods. For example, the IPCC (2001) notes that developing countries, particularly the least developed, are more vulnerable to environmental threats, and this handicap is extreme among the poorest people and disadvantaged groups, such as women and children. Thus, the importance of the human and social context can never be ignored. As Blaikie et al. (1994: 31) note, there is a general consensus among researchers that the *absolute* number of natural hazard events has not increased in recent decades, which indicates that there is a need to look at social factors that increase vulnerability to explain the *apparent* increases in the number of disasters, in the value of losses and numbers of victims.

Three specific approaches can be outlined in environmental security and vulnerability studies: (a) those dealing with the identification of conditions that make people or places vulnerable to extreme natural events; (b) those assuming that vulnerability is a social condition, a measure of societal resistance or resilience to hazards; and (c) those integrating potential exposures and societal resilience with a specific focus on particular places or regions. In this research we choose to follow the line of argument of the second approach to understand the social conditions, perceptions, and adjustment processes in the Damodar chars. The absence of long-term measures among the char people is noted, and an attempt has been made to differentiate between "adjustment"—that is, action on a contingent basis to cope with emergencies as they occur—and "adaptation"—that is, long-term strategies to reduce flood frequency or other environmental risks.

Vulnerabilities of Char People

Vulnerability affects poor households on chars in numerous ways. There may be natural calamities (such as flood and riverbank erosion), socioeconomic calamities (such as abrupt falls in market prices of agricultural products), or illness. In their study on the chars of Bangladesh, Brocklesby and Hobley (2003) note that multiple vulnerabilities experienced by char dwellers are the underlying cause of their chronic, persistent, and extreme poverty. In the Damodar chars, the situation is similar in respect to the vulnerability/poverty equation.

Physical vulnerability is rooted in the threat of seasonal flooding, shifting of river courses, and riverbank erosion (DFID 2002). Elahi and Rogge (1990) estimate that about one million people are displaced every year by floods and riverbank erosion in Bangladesh. No equivalent data are available for India, but Rudra (2002) shows in his analysis of changes in the course of the Ganga in recent times that in the district of Murshidabad alone no less than ten thousand people have been displaced by erosion. In turn, these physical vulnerabilities can make char people socially vulnerable and politically marginal. Often the land is not legally owned, its boundaries are in constant flux, and the remoteness and lack of accessibility mean a total lack of health care, sanitation, water, and electricity supplies. Aditya Ghosh (2004) reports that over seventy thousand people live on the "no-man's-land of these islands on the Ganga," people whose villages have been engulfed by the river. In the absence of any rehabilitation scheme, they rebuild their lives on the chars on the Ganga. Both West Bengal and Jharkhand state governments have disowned these "river people," with their functionaries remaining engaged in academic discussions about the demarcation of borders. The Damodar chars too have their difficulties with bank erosion and shifts in the river course. For example, the Damodar demarcates the boundary between the Burdwan and Bankura districts of West Bengal. Most of the stabilized chars were situated closer to the south bank and came under the administrative jurisdiction of Bankura district. As the river shifted toward the north bank, that is, toward Burdwan district, the physical distance increased between the chars and Bankura, where public services and government offices, panchayats, police stations, and health centers are located.

In terms of longer-term impacts on people's lives, vulnerability to erosion effects much more than vulnerability to floods. Erosion is a frequent but irregular danger and creates fundamental and catastrophic livelihood shocks through which households lose their land, shelter, and other assets. Flooding, by contrast, is not a regular seasonal phenomenon in the Damodar valley and is therefore not so traumatic. Moreover, char people now receive advance warning from the DVC via radio about releases of water from the barrage upstream at Durgapur. Long-term char residents with experience of major floods are able to predict with some accuracy the height the floodwaters are likely to reach in specific chars. Warnings and local experience allow the local people to move themselves and their assets to the safety of the higher ground of the north bank at short notice.

Ill health, especially of income-earning members of the community, brings vulnerability to char dwellers because of their extreme poverty, affecting both the expenditures and income of households. Women who work outside their homes cannot go to work if their children fall ill, which results in a decreased family income, while at the same time daily expenses increase because of medical treatment of the children. Households with only one income-earning member are especially at risk at these times. Illness among children, which is frequent in poorer households, is one of the major factors determining the level of well-being, and illness was generally considered a worst-case scenario by our informants.

Perceptions of Security and Vulnerability

Human perceptions and behavior under different environmental events, especially those related to the natural environment, have been extensively analyzed (Burton and Kates 1964; Burton et al. 1969; Lowenthal 1967; Mitchell 1974; Saarinen 1966; Saarinen et al. 1984). Regarding the different behavioral patterns noticed during adjustment with hazardous environments, Sonnenfeld (1967: 42) notes that individuals generally tend to differ in their responses to any environment. Some achieve more, some less; some adjust easily, others adjust only with difficulty to environmental extremes. The differential response may be a function of different abilities or of different perceptions of the environment. It is essential to understand the source of variance in environmental perception to appreciate variations in human behavior. Our understanding is that perceptions of security in the chars are closely linked to flood events and associated bank erosion. In the Damodar chars, most of the settlers have also experienced social insecurity in the form of political turmoil, religious persecution, and cross-border migration. The vulnerability associated with these social factors has ironically increased people's acceptance of natural calamities. From the detailed investigation of participants' perceptions of security in the chars, we identified some specific issues in relation to which people's perceptions about their living environments can be understood.

Physical Isolation

The migrants from Bangladesh who settle in the Damodar chars often arrive without legal entry papers. Over the course of time, valid papers, such as ration cards or voter identification cards, are obtained through an informal chain of local political leaders, panchayat members, and community development block officials. The chars, then, can be seen as an entry point to the mainland society and economy, making vulnerability a temporary or transient phenomenon. One of the choruas, Sadhan Mondal, has this to say:

> We are not planning to stay here for a long time. We are fully aware of the risks of these chars. I have seen acres of land being swallowed up by the river each year due to bank erosion in the rainy season. Any day during the next flood the river can erode my house. I have been here for four years and have got the citizenship documents for my wife and me. Still I am living here as I have yet to collect the citizenship documents for my two sons.

The poverty and vulnerability of char dwellers like Sadhan Mondal are not simple; rather, they are complex and interlinked outcomes of people's illegal immigration to India and their consequent exposure to floods and river erosion.

Not every char dweller is waiting for an opportunity to leave. Some residents, whether or not they obtain citizenship documents, prefer to live on chars because they see them as a secure location. Isolation, usually avoided in choosing a place to live, is in this case often a major recommendation. Sandhya Mondal, a thirty-five-year-old woman, said of her char environment:

> We are much better off here than we were in Bangladesh. Here we never feel the pain of hunger. We can find work in farming more or less throughout the year. Even if one day we do not get work, my husband and I go to the river to catch fish. Sometimes we can get up to five kilograms of fish a day [worth Rs. 250]. We can sell the fish to the neighbors.

> We have arranged our elder daughter's marriage with a boy who is also living here on the char. We have built a house for them with our own labor. We are happily living here with no dearth of food and we are not going anywhere, as we don't have any valid document of Indian citizenship.

Social Isolation

Curiously, the distance from social networks of relatives and friends is a factor that sometimes disposes people to living on chars. We came across several instances where choruas felt pleased about how little was known about their past lives either in Bangladesh or elsewhere in West Bengal. Dhiren Mondal, a fifty-year-old single man, has lived on Char Gaitanpur since his wife left him. He explains:

> I have left my house and land property in South 24 Paraganas to avoid the people who were known to me. My wife had left home with one of my friends, taking my four children with her. I could not cope with the way people taunted me, and left my home to avoid those living there. At that time I was in search of an isolated place where nobody knows my past life. I felt that this char could provide me with a new life.

Dhiren perceives his life in the char to be more secure than it would be in the mainland because of the relative isolation. Here he has a house and some land which he farms or leases out. The physical toll of doing all the work at home and in the field is quite heavy, yet he feels at peace with himself.

Tukurani's story also helps us to understand the social isolation of women in the chars. At thirty-two, she has been living on Char Gaitanpur for ten years. But her husband went back to Bangladesh, where he had another wife. Why did she leave Bangladesh and stay on the char? She says:

> When I went to my husband's house after marriage I fought continuously with his first wife. She offered me no food and sometimes beat me. After a year, on my husband's suggestion, we left. We took shelter in a neighbor's house. Within a few days my husband built the hut where we started living together. We bought some land, a few goats, and cattle. I now run the household and feel happier even if he is not with me all the time. I am content with what I have got here.

Tukurani has four children, including a newborn. She owns jointly with her absentee husband 0.6 acres of agricultural land, a house with brick walls and a corrugated tin roof, five goats, and one cow. Living and securing a livelihood alone is a heavy burden for her, yet she feels that she has a more secure life here than she would have had if she had remained in Bangladesh. Tukurani is aware of the vulnerability of living in the chars, as is demonstrated in her response to our question: What will you do if your land and house are lost to the river by erosion?

> I do not want to think of it. I can't stop the shifting of the river and erosion of land. In case it happens, I would see what other arrangements for us could be made. I trust my husband; he is a responsible man.

This statement exemplifies the fatalism of char dwellers, who follow this mantra: Put oneself at the mercy of nature and try to make the best of the present. This attitude develops over time, through daily struggle and learning to live with the river.

The security of the chars as perceived by people like Dhiren and Tukurani is difficult to explain using neutral, objective, and absolute human knowledge systems of the environment. To fully understand their mental maps, one must look into personal histories. Usually, chars pose difficulties for women in obtaining water, food, and other supplies, as well as in sanitation and access to medical care. The difficulty of access and poor transportation are noted by women, whether in Bangladesh or in India. A char woman of Bangladesh is quoted by Sarker et al. as saying: "The worst thing about char life is women dying at childbirth because they cannot get medical attention during the floods" (2003: 76). Yet, for at least one migrant woman in a Damodar char, living on the char is apparently preferable to living in Bangladesh. This brings us to the question of subjective perceptions of human/nature interactions. Purely personal circumstances make Tukurani prefer the char over her original home. The construction of one's own secure home in what is commonly seen as a highly vulnerable environment can also reflect the inherent power differentials in society.

Availability of Land

Until the 1970s, land was freely available on some of the Damodar chars. Although this is no longer the case, land is still cheap due to its susceptibility to flooding and river erosion. The availability of cheap land attracts people like Narayan Biswas, who has expertise in farming and has experimented with the production of unusual vegetables. Narayan came to the

Damodar chars after losing his small business, which he had set up after moving to a nearby town in India. He took land on lease and produced marketable vegetables like capsicum and broccoli for select urban consumers. He chose a particular char because of its nearness to the urban market of Burdwan town, where he could sell his produce at a fair price. His interest is more in the several prizes he has won in Burdwan district's agricultural competition than in money. He is still poor, but feels content with his work:

> I am quite happy here, as I have been able to prove my skill in producing high-priced vegetables in the sandy soil of chars. My wife helps me in my experiments, as there is no false sense of prestige, common among the middle classes, about women's work in the fields. Here, in all families, women can participate in farming the fields. Vegetable crops need constant care, which my wife does better than me or any other wage labor.

Narayan says that the vulnerability of the land is not a major issue for him, since he has only a few permanent assets.

"Lottery with Nature"

The influence of cultural adjustment over generations is evident in the different ways the Bangladeshi and Bihari migrants—both groups hailing from flood-prone areas—have adjusted to the chars of the Damodar. Flood is an annual phenomenon of the northern part of Bihar from where the Bihari settlers originated; this is also the case in Bangladesh. Therefore, one might expect the Damodar char dwellers to be well versed in coping with floods—to know how to utilize the floodplains in order to get the maximum benefit out of them. As the regular flow of water in the river has decreased over the years, the Biharis have found it harder to cope with the changing ecology and have tended to move out of the chars, whereas the Bangladeshis, arriving without legal papers, have flourished by expertly manipulating their land- and water-based livelihoods. Low-magnitude floods are often welcomed by char people, since they replenish the natural fertility of the land by depositing fresh silt. Leaf (1997) observes in a sample survey of rural people's attitudes to flood in Bangladesh that 86 percent of households were satisfied with the way they adjusted to normal inundation and did not want any change to that situation. In our survey of the chars of Damodar, some respondents testified that they saw flooding as a natural element—part of the natural rhythm of things. More than floods, they were apprehensive of erosion of the scarce cultivable and livable chars. Bogardi (2004b) observes that the intensifying use of the floodplains over many decades has proved the willingness of societies to accept this "lottery against nature," having in mind (most likely unconsciously) the trade-off between potential (but occasionally quite high) losses and fairly regular benefits. In these chars, people are also aware of the potential damage to their property caused by flooding, and use the land for both agriculture and the grazing of animals to improve the chances of survival.

Naren Sarkar of Char Bhasapur is one such person. Originally from Dhaka, he came to India with his parents in the late 1950s at the age of six. The family first took shelter on a char on the Hooghly where their relatives lived. After a few years, they moved to Char Bhasapur (an attached char of the Damodar) and have lived there ever since. Naren's first house and lands were destroyed during the 1978 flood. Undeterred, he paid for some more land and built another house farther away from the main water channel and closer to the northern embankment. Even so, because of the shift of the river channel toward the northern bank, Naren's new house remains on the margin, so far as secured settlement is concerned. Nevertheless, in our conversation with him, he expressed satisfaction with his situation, noting: "We are like the drifting grains of sand, rolling from one place to another. In one place today, in another tomorrow, but always with the river's flow."

We asked: Did you ever consider this life as dangerous? Do you plan to live away from the life on the char? He replied:

> I have no skills or experience of any work other than farming. My parents have taught me how to till the land to make it yield more for our families. I can only use my farming skills for living. Land is cheap on chars and we have no dearth of water for irrigating our lands. See, we were brought up in flood-prone areas of Bangladesh. In comparison, the frequency and magnitude of floods are less on these chars. We also know how to cope with flood and river erosion. We do not want to move away from the river. If the river does not let us stay here, then we shall go somewhere else. Until the river destroys our entire house and land and drowns this char, we will be here. We feel secure here, as we have enough to feed our families.

This statement not only conveys a sense of security, but also a feeling of confidence. The belief that they can protect themselves, their homes and families, and others in the community and, if necessary, reestablish their livelihoods is strong among char dwellers. Nor is this an unrealizable dream. Such people have established a rapport with their environment and a keen awareness of their surroundings: an acceptance of the river's moods. They are prepared for sudden change. Here we come to the crux of our argument, which is that char dwellers see their adjustment to the river as a contingent, short-term, undefined process unclarified temporally.

Some char dwellers even refuse to be described as Bangladeshis or as migrants. Biswanath Mondal, another resident of Char Gaitanpur, burst out in anger when we asked him if he was a Bangladeshi:

> *Na! Ami keno Bangladeshi habo?* [No! Why would I be a Bangladeshi?] We have been living in this country from before [the Partition]. For some time, my ancestors lived in Orissa, at other times in 24 Parganas. My grandfathers were three brothers. One of them lived in Khulna, and two lived in 24 Parganas. Just because *my* grandfather's house fell on the other side of the border, we become Bangladeshis? *Eta ki onnyay noy?* [Is this not injustice?]

Although his official identity is contested, for Biswanath, this char is home. He has a large family, and has now constructed a *pucca* house—brick with an asbestos roof—on the land reclaimed from the abandoned river channel with a loan taken from the local *mahajan* (local moneylender). He sees the house as an investment in the future, but is aware that this might be a gamble:

> I am living on a dried-up riverbed. It is a land that might be claimed again by the river. Right now, I do not have the money to leave the char and settle elsewhere. I am trying to save some money from my crop sales so that I can leave this godforsaken land in the future.

Clearly, he thinks of his stay in this char as temporary, although there is no indication that he intends to leave any time soon.

Lives Defined by the River

Understanding the conditions under which people live in an environment seen by most as marginal and risky illuminates our comprehension of environmental insecurity, vulnerability, and livelihood. It is clear from our study that the perceptions of security, insecurity, and vulnerability are subjective, and may differ widely between different segments of people, even locally. Whereas some evidently feel more secure living on chars than living among hostile neighbors, others might perceive these areas as suitable lands for a temporary stay, while others again consider the chars to be places unfit for habitation. Some try to build permanent structures and make plans for a long-term stay, while other char dwellers are more sensitive to the vulnerability of the chars and use them purely as a temporary refuge.

We have noted that the frequency and intensity of floods in the Damodar chars have decreased since the construction of DVC dams. The reduced flow of the river and the altered nature of floods have added to the char dwellers' sense of security, resulting in a more intense use of local resources. With increasing competition for scarce land, more intensive kinds of farming have been introduced. This brings up the question: Have the steady inflow of people into this fragile environment and the more intensive use of chars increased or decreased vulnerability? This is not a simple question; as we have noted, during recent decades the older, established Bihari fishing communities have gradually left the chars while even more Bangladeshis have moved in. It is clear that old occupational and cultural traditions and experiences can have a significant influence on the ways subjective perceptions operate. We must also note that adjustment is also dependent upon income levels. Those who can afford to, build their homes on relatively higher grounds with higher foundations to lessen the impact of flood damage. The poorer people on the chars live in homes situated on lower-lying land near the riverbanks or even on the dried-up river channels. Thus, it becomes clear that poverty intensifies insecurity on chars. There are also generational differences: awareness of the devastation that the Damodar floods can cause is relatively higher among the older men and women who personally experienced the massive flood of 1978.

Char dwellers have honed their adaptive capacity as an important strategy for coping with the fragile environment in which they live. For this, they have developed an intimate understanding of this unreliable environment. They know more or less accurately the level to which the river water will rise for the different volumes of water that are released from upstream reservoirs, and remain alert during the monsoons. Small boats are kept ready to transport their families to safety when the waters rise. It is not a simple matter of semantics to describe this ability as resilience, as competency, or as capacity to adapt. In our view, it is best to define the ability of char dwellers in lower Bengal as one of "adjustment"—as a day-to-day, continual but contingent set of strategic choices and decisions made by individuals and communities. Char dwellers are continually gambling with nature, "dancing" with the changeable moods of the river, trying to make the best of their vulnerable situation in a marginal environment. It would be foolhardy to generalize that all char dwellers either are living happily, peacefully, and permanently or, alternatively, are on their way out of the chars. As noted earlier, many are acutely aware of the vulnerability of their riverine environment, but have no choice but to stay due to their problematic legal status. The aspects of the physical environment that they are particularly concerned about are riverbank erosion and the altering of the main course of the river—these changes have the potential to destroy major parts of the char, including homes and cultivated lands. Even then, some char dwellers feel comfortable about taking risks. In a way, their social marginality has helped them to adjust to the multiple vulnerabilities they face.

We now return to our original question: Why do people live in the marginal environment of chars in spite of immense insecurity? This chapter broadly confirms that the root causes of poverty and vulnerability are largely identical and usually overlap. Delving deeper, however, it suggests that subjective perceptions about livelihood and choice of living space are often personal. At one level, these issues are rooted in culture. Traditional occupations, attitudes, and feelings with respect to the environment clearly play an important role in how people adjust to vulnerable conditions. Our point is that the concepts of "risk" and "vulnerability" as used in relation to day-to-day life, though valid generalizations, do not work so well in specialized contexts such as those provided by the char environment. Some choruas simply have no choice. Individuals continuously redefine risks and vulnerabilities associated with a place before moving on or staying put. By doing so, they illuminate this contextual dilemma of resilience and underline the part played by cultural or occupational traditions in survival strategies.

CHAPTER 7

Livelihoods Defined by Water

Nadir Sathe Baas

Here each home has fishing nets, but also the plough, kept next to one another. . . . The lifegod of these people, like the god of the sky, spreads his arms to opposite directions. On one side the river is crowded with fish, and on the other, the ground is smiling with crops. If one day an invisible devil undoes the knots of their nets, and looses the iron ties of the boats, they will not die. . . . They will not die.—ADWAITA MALLABARMAN (1956: 56), *Teetas Ekti Nadir Naam*

Konomate Benche Thaka (To Survive Somehow)

Char dwellers survive in an environment that is characterized by extreme resource constraints. In the earlier chapters, it was shown that floods and riverbank erosion affect their living conditions the most, constantly making them aware of the fragility of their daily lives. The exclusion from mainland services and poor availability of infrastructure also exacerbate their vulnerabilities. To live here means to survive somehow, "*konomate benche thaka*," as one char dweller put it. Such living requires that every bit of any local resource is put to use. Water from the river as well as from below the sand on the riverbed or the soil/sand on the land (groundwater); livestock such as poultry, cattle, and ducks; plants growing naturally and crops—all play significant roles in the maintenance of households. One might ask: How exactly do people make ends meet? What factors support their existence on chars? Do the Bihari and the Bangladeshi migrants adopt different livelihood strategies? If so, why? In this chapter, we show that what matters most in coping with the dynamic landscape of chars is the intimate knowledge of the environment. Some people bring this knowledge from their traditional occupations, whereas others develop it from their personal experience of living on chars. Based on both what the local environment has to offer and their cultural and acquired skills, char dwellers establish livelihood strategies that, just like the uncertain, vulnerable environment they inhabit, vary according to the season and situation, and are characterized by high levels of diversification of production and income baskets. Depending on the season, for example, members of one household may engage in wet or dry farming, rear livestock, fish, trade informally, work as itinerant wage laborers on other peoples' fields, or quarry sand from the riverbed. For the extreme poor, these strategies merely permit survival rather than the accumulation of sufficient assets to escape poverty.

To explore these questions, this chapter uses observation-based, micro perspectives on char individuals and households in their day-to-day lives. Individual perceptions of the use of chars as a permanent base or home vary, as do the ways individuals make a living. This chapter also explores the links among the relative asset base, relative geographical location, level of income, and nature of livelihood strategies and livelihood diversification. Finally, it shows that the strategies of sustaining livelihoods are gendered in nature.

Char dwellers are neither visible to, nor constitute a priority for, the local or state governments and, therefore, in their struggle for existence, they receive little or no external support. Their livelihood strategies are linked with the ability to diversify income and assets; thus, the strategies of the poor are more complex than the strategies of those who are somewhat better off. This is because the poor often have difficulty pursuing a single source of livelihood and must diversify their "livelihood basket" to survive the vagaries of seasons. Beck and Ghosh's (2000) and Ghosh's (1995) path-breaking research in seven villages in West Bengal has shown the importance of "commons" in the subsistence of the poor, and the chars can be viewed as commons. Robert Chambers (1989) pioneered the idea of sustainability of livelihoods as a key enabling factor with which the poor can offset risks, ease shocks, and meet contingencies. In the various ways that "livelihoods" have been conceived,[1] other than according to economic well-being, relatively more importance is placed upon the noneconomic dimensions of processes involved in ensuring survival (for example, Blaikie et al. 1994: 9). Others such as Ellis (2000: 10) have chosen to see it as a broad amalgamation of various elements—the assets (natural, physical, human, financial, and social), the activities (strategies of use), and the access to these (mediated by institution and social relations) that together determine the living gained by the individual or household. Although frameworks for livelihood analysis differ in their detail, the basic elements consider resources (what people have), strategies (what people do), and outcomes (the goals people pursue). Research and policy initiatives connecting livelihoods research with poverty-reduction objectives have received high emphasis in livelihood analysis, usually conducted by developmental agencies.

A number of studies in livelihood literature focus upon the role migration can play in the livelihoods of poor rural households (de Haan 1999, 2000, 2002; de Haan et al. 2000; McDowell and de Haan 1997). It is now generally recognized that migration is a part of the normal livelihood strategy of the poor (for work on Bangladesh, see Hossain et al. 2003; Siddiqui 2003). The rate of migration, both permanent and temporary, for improved livelihood opportunities increases at times of socioeconomic distress, political crisis, and natural disasters. Seasonal migrations from a poverty-stricken to a better-off rural area, or from the villages to urban areas, are now well recorded in the economically underdeveloped parts of developing countries (Deshingkar and Start 2003; Hampshire 2002).

Others explore the challenges of diversification of livelihood strategies as the critical element in creating better options for sustainability (Deb et al. 2002; Ellis 1998, 1999; Ginguld et al. 1997; Karnath and Ramaswamy 2004; Toulmin et al. 2000). Gender is also important because the different roles, chores, and vulnerabilities mean that women and men are affected differently; thus their responses differ. Women in poor communities may constitute an even poorer or weaker group, being responsible for taking care of children and the family. A number of studies (for example, Cleaver 1998; Francis 1998, 2002; Hapke and Ayyankeril 2004; Masika and Joekes 1996; Valdivia and Gilles 2001) look at livelihood as a gendered activity. Most of these studies have focused on the livelihood strategies of poor women as well as the management of scarce natural resources at their disposal. Francis analyzes the bargaining power of women and their access to household resources as a factor of their contribution toward household livelihoods. To examine the enhancement of women's power in the household management system, she asks: "[D]o women have greater bargaining power when their contribution to household livelihoods is mediated through markets?" (1998: 75). She shows that women struggle to earn a livelihood for the family and run the household, but do not necessarily enjoy significant additional power as a consequence of their involvement in livelihood-generating activities.

Setting Up a River-Based Life on the Chars

The people who arrived on the chars during the 1950s and the 1960s had only a few material resources to depend on. At that time, the elders recall, barter was the mode of exchange since the market used to be even more difficult to access than presently. Families survived on only one meal that they could scrape together. Many of them became emotional when telling us about the early days of settlement. Remembering those difficult times, Sumaria Rajbhar, one of the Biharis who came at the age of sixteen to the chars with her newly wedded husband, says she still remembers the hunger pangs from those early days, and life has changed so much that

> it is impossible for the present generation living on chars to even imagine how we lived, and what we faced here in those early days.

The settlers started with maize, mesta, and melons, which grow easily on sandy soil without much water. But these crops were seasonal and people had to look for supplementary income for other parts of the year. Mahadeb Sarkar of Char Kasba gives us an idea about other options for livelihoods there in those days. He says that men from Char Kasba used to go to Bankura district by crossing the river barefoot to buy paddy and used to come back to the nearest market in Budbud on this side to sell it: "This trade gave us a minuscule profit to run the household. Some people made rice or *chira* [flattened rice] at home from the paddy and sold it at a better price in the market."

While the early Bihari settlers had no traditional knowledge of farming and lived by catching fish, rearing cattle, or laboring in the nearby mainland areas, the Bangladeshi immigrants made these lands productive and have considerably changed the landscape of the chars by turning them into croplands under intensive use. Sushil Ray tells us that in the initial days he could plant only mesta jute in summer and mustard in winter with the help of rainfall as the only source of water. During the years of little or no rain, his family lacked food for days and managed to survive only with the flour made from mesta and jute seeds. Getting rice or *chapatti* (handmade bread) for either lunch or dinner was a rare experience in those days. He is pleased about the years of hard work

> to make this land fertile and suitable for farming: *kakhono asha chhari ni* [we never gave up, never lost hope]. *Ar kono upay chhilo na* [We had no other options], so we kept trying to make this land produce good crops.

The Bangladeshi migrants, who brought agricultural experience from their homeland, plowed the sandy land and on it spread cow dung, poultry waste, ash, paddy husk, and so on, during summers. The biomanures, mixed with sand, rotted during the rainy season and finally a thin layer of soil developed on which they began to produce some crops during winters. Over time a considerable layer of fertile soil developed and made the land highly productive. The time required for generating a three- to five-inch-thick layer of soil varied depending on the nature of the biomaterials. Cow dung takes less time for conversion of sand to soil, but was largely beyond the reach of the poor farmers due to its high cost (Rs. 24,000 per acre if only cow dung is used). By comparison, the cost of poultry waste was Rs. 16,000 and of ash Rs. 10,000; these were used by marginal farmers. The poor farmer used paddy husk, which is available free of cost from nearby rice mills and requires only the transport cost (around Rs. 5,000 for one acre of land). During our field survey, we observed the reclamation of at least two acres of sand into cropland within two years at Gaitanpur. At present, although chemical fertilizers are more in use now than previously, the use of biomanures is still higher here than in agriculture on the mainland.

Jibaner Dhan: Livelihood Assets?

For char people, livelihood assets are "jibaner dhan," although *dhan* in Bangla more accurately implies assets that may be more valuable in commercial terms. For academics, livelihood assets comprise a combination of natural, physical, social, human, and financial capital upon which a group or community develops its livelihoods. They are usually created where production leads to a surplus beyond immediate consumption requirements, and households use the surplus to invest in or to build physical stores. Assets form the main source of backup for the livelihoods of rural people. Yaro (2002) suggests that the sustainability of any community's livelihoods largely depends on that community's access to assets that can be exchanged or cashed in during a crisis. The extent to which an individual can generate livelihood assets depends on the access to productive resources and their ability to control and use resources effectively. This, in turn, depends on the ability to participate in a variety of social institutions as well as on material wealth and market transactions. In the chars of Damodar, the main livelihood assets are physical capital, including cultivable lands for cropping, pasture for livestock rearing, river water for fishing, shallow subsurface water for irrigation, and riverbed sands for quarrying.

Fertile silt that is still being deposited by floodwaters and the availability of groundwater that facilitates irrigation are the two prime natural capitals. As the river has been drying up, more attention has been diverted toward land-based assets. Social capital is represented by kin relations and strong community spirit. Human capital includes the farming skills that people brought with them, their ability to live with the changing moods of the river, and their physical labor. All these assets are used by char residents to generate financial capital, which rarely surpasses the needs of households to create sufficient surplus for further investment.

Few or No Resources

Chars originally were sandy barren "islands" with little or no soil, but occupancy was free and water was available in the surrounding rivers. With their labor, migrant communities transformed the chars into a productive land. There is hardly any portion of land lying unused; most of the land area is used for agriculture and the rest is used for cattle raising (the two main livelihood activities on chars).

The present vegetative cover of the chars is also perceived by char dwellers, mostly by women, as an important livelihood asset. The chars were initially covered by catkin grass, bushes, and wild plum trees. Catkin grass has an integrated root network that accelerates silt deposition on the chars during floods. These grasses have multiple uses for char dwellers; they are used as fodder, fuel, and thatching materials and the stem of the plant is sometimes used to make fences around the houses. When the chars were settled, such grasses and bushes almost disappeared. Wild plum has also been largely replaced by other trees that have more utility.

At present, the chars have a dense canopy of trees, mostly in and around homes, which makes them invisible to the mainland people from the embankment. These trees are usually planted surrounding the houses to provide privacy, since the houses usually have open courtyards and no boundary walls. The trees planted by the settlers include a variety of fruit and timber trees such as mango, jackfruit, guava, lychee, papaya, coconut, bamboo, *shimul* (cotton fiber tree), and other leafy trees. They yield both food (vegetables as well as fruit) and fodder. Char dwellers consider these trees as important livelihood assets. Sabitri Mondal has two jackfruit and three mango trees in her courtyard. She uses their fruit in summer, which is a lean season on the char. She says:

> During the hard times, we depend on these trees as one of the main sources of food. We use jackfruit and mango as vegetables when they are green and use them as fruit when they are ripe. We can even eat a full plate of rice with mango dal [lentil soup with mango] and jackfruit curry. The green leaves of trees also give us fodder for the cattle during the winter, when all the lands are occupied by crops and no space is left for grazing.

In our discussions with them, many char women could put a rough value on the annual contribution of these trees to their households. Clearly, if the concept of livelihood assets is accepted as those that can be mobilized during a period of livelihood crisis (as defined by Swift 1989), then they are right in considering the trees as livelihood assets. The perception of livelihood assets is also gendered; it is women who see fruit trees as important. In contrast, the men did not consider anything as a livelihood asset that could not be sold in the market.

Lending a Helping Hand

Human ingenuity and sheer hard work, coupled with experiential skills of living on meager resources, have helped in building suitable and sustainable livelihood strategies on the chars. The populations on the chars are characterized by dynamism in which people are more or less continuously moving out or moving in. The younger generations, especially of the Biharis, are moving out with nonfarm jobs that give more certain wage income. For example, according to Prasanta Mondal, there were seventy-five Bihari households on Char Gaitanpur in the early 1990s; the number fell to fifty-eight in 2006. Farming is expanding at the cost of other occupations. At the same time, new inhabitants are arriving, especially illegally from Bangladesh. Accumulation of sufficient surplus enables some to move out of the chars. This trend is visible in every char we studied. The population is increasing at a spectacular rate of 11 percent per annum as against the Indian national population growth rate of 2 percent per annum in the last decade. In 2001, the population of Char Gaitanpur was 797; by 2004 it had increased to 1,068. Young children (zero to six years) constitute 21 percent of the char population, revealing the overall youthfulness of the migrant families. Each household, on average, has five to six members. The joint family system is gradually disappearing; still, 30 percent of the households on the chars live in such an arrangement. The support from an extended family in the joint family system is the key to old-age security for the elderly on chars. In several instances, the elderly, even at the age of seventy or eighty, work willingly, if physically able, to contribute to their families. In response to our question as to why he works at his age, one elderly man, Chhidam Biswas, gave a simple answer:

> My entire life was full of hardship and so I wish a better life for my sons. I still can do light work such as sowing potato seeds and clearing weeds in the fields and there is no dearth of such work during the cropping season. I am happy to work to earn and not be a burden on the family.

Older women also contribute to the family's well-being, sometimes even more than the men, by providing care and other services. Recent years have seen an increase in the number of nuclear families on the chars, leaving some elderly people to fend for themselves. The number of such instances is still not significant, but those who are in that situation face extreme difficulty.

About 70 percent of the population belongs to lower-caste namashudras, who are also economically the most disadvantaged and who brought almost no assets with them. These hardworking people are not apprehensive about undertaking physical labor on the farm. Relative isolation from the mainland also creates a sense of freedom from the conventional markers of social status and allows even upper-caste people to undertake manual work without hesitation. All women work in the field on the chars. In fact, all the members in the family, including women and children, do farm work according to their capacity and skill. Women from landless families work for wages as farm laborers.

Although the composition of the communities is fluid, community spirit and the sense of belonging stand out even to a casual visitor. To call this social capital is not enough; in practical terms it is much more than just a reserve to tap into, because it appears more important for everyone to contribute to it than to cash it. Everyone builds the sense of community, participates in the affairs of the community, and ensures the well-being of others as best as possible. From migration to the process of occupancy, to building a home and making a livelihood, intangibles such as mutual trust, old contacts, and help play critical roles. Family relations and neighbors help with food and shelter when someone new moves in, and continue to contribute to help them establish a new life in various ways: by helping to purchase land or by arranging wage work; by providing food when someone is unable to work; by taking people to the hospital if someone is ill; or even by raising money to pay for emergencies such as medical treatment. During floods, char dwellers are forced to depend on help from each other. Even during a low-intensity flood, some take the initiative of transporting people, poultry, and cattle by boat to the embankment. This is how Minati Sarkar explains the community spirit:

> We always help each other on the chars, not only just our relatives, but also our neighbors. When we arrived, we initially spent a month with my uncle. He had arranged for our land before we left. He also helped us to build our house. If there is no food or money at home, we can borrow some from our neighbors. They give gifts to each other—vegetables grown on the farm or help with money when one is in genuine financial crisis. All this cash or in-kind help keeps us going on the chars.

The morol of the individual char mobilizes community help for the poor. Morols also help people to complete official paperwork to obtain citizenship documents and the ration card that not only secures cheaper foodstuff and other essentials, but also acts as an identity card. None of the chars, excepting Char Gaitanpur, has even a primary school. The one in Gaitanpur was started in 1978, but it did not have a building. The headman acquired some money, but it was insufficient. He raised some more funds from the community after a good harvest. With these, char dwellers constructed a concrete building as a school. In a similar manner, some attempts were made to build roads to access Gaitanpur. The headman instructed everyone to give a day's labor for free for five days of paid labor in building the road with only limited funds.

Community spirit, as it operates on the ground in the chars, is not necessarily always neutral and benign. Some people do not receive any assistance if they do not follow the dictates of the ruling political party. For example, the list of farmers to receive free seedlings and seeds from the local panchayat is prepared by the village headman, who selectively chooses the recipients, arguing that help should reach the "better farmers." This recommendation is often not bias-free and may be influenced by political party allegiance.

Banchbar Upay: Livelihood Strategies

Agriculture

As in many places in South Asia (see DFID 2002; World Bank 2000), agriculture now forms the mainstay of the economy in the chars of Damodar. About 73 percent of households have some farming land, although most are best described as either small-scale or marginal farmers. Char agriculture is characterized by the small size of land holdings and labor-intensive cropping methods. Double cropping is practiced in all the chars, but multiple cropping is limited to the lands owned by farmers with shallow pumps for irrigation. Such farmers are only 26 percent of farming households on average. The important crops are vegetables and paddy. The dry season (winter and early summer) is the main cropping season on the chars. A number of vegetables including eggplant, cauliflower, radish, cabbage, carrot, beans, peas, spinach, okra, garden pulse, and mustard are grown. Better-off farmers produce paddy for both kharif and boro seasons. The choice of crops and the cropping calendar of the Bangladeshi and Bihari communities differ noticeably. The two communities have very different family food habits; hence, their crop production—rice for the Bangladeshis and wheat for the Biharis—is also very different. Wheat requires less water than rice, reducing its production cost. A rough estimate given to us was that the amount of wheat produced on one bigha of land (yielding around five hundred to six hundred kilograms) is enough for one meal in a day for a family of five to six members for a year. Although rice is more water-intensive and, hence, involves greater cost, yield from one bigha of land can offer two square meals a day to support a similar family for a year. The culture of farming developed by the migrant on these chars has thus been influenced not only by survival needs, but by the traditional ethnic ethos as well.

In the 1960s, agricultural societies were developed in some chars through the initiatives of early leaders and, interestingly, sometimes the local Block Development Officer (BDO), the representative of the state at the lowest administrative unit, stepped in and assisted them. These societies used to give loans to the farmers, which had to be repaid after harvest. On Char Kasba, an agricultural society with 150 farmer members was developed in 1965. In the late 1960s and the early 1970s, these chars experienced a water crisis following a few years of drought. The farmers could not repay their loans; the society too faced a crisis of management. Using that excuse, the government liquidated the society. Choruas think the society was closed primarily due to the difficulties for the officer of making physical visits, despite their sincere efforts to access better agricultural practices.

Table 7.1 shows that there has been a considerable increase in the price of agricultural land. Land prices rose for various reasons, proximity to market on the mainland being the key. Agricultural land on the char that is closer to the urban market fetches a better price. Even residential land values are higher on chars that are attached to the bank than on island chars—an example of the real estate marketing slogan "location, location, location!" The price of land also varies according to the present vulnerability of the char: the higher the erosion, the lower the land price. On Char Bikrampur, where land is rapidly eroding every year during the monsoon, the price of land has been falling in anticipation of its submergence. Within a single char, land prices vary according to the location, with higher lands generally attracting better prices than lower-lying lands.

The price of agricultural land also varies on the basis of its legal status. Land with registered ownership documents is more expensive than land without legal records. When the recorded land price was Rs. 20,000 per bigha, the price of nonrecorded land was Rs. 7,000. To avoid going to the court, the transfer of nonrecorded land is made possible by an informal community sanction. The deed is called *dash dalil* (roughly translated as the "deed of ten") because, in this informal registration, all details of transaction, including the seller, buyer, and the rate of cost of the transaction, are written on a stamp paper of the value of Rs. 10, which is then witnessed by

TABLE 7.1 AVERAGE PRICE OF RELATIVELY STABLE AGRICULTURAL LAND PER BIGHA IN SURVEYED CHARS

Period	Price in Rupees
1950s	Mostly freely acquired
1960s	150–200
1970s	500–600
1980s	1,000–3,000
Early 1990s	10,000–12,000
2000	20,000–24,000
2010	35,000–40,000

Source: Field survey conducted in 2007–2008.
Note: A bigha is one-third of an acre. Indian Rs. 100 equals US$1.84 (September 2012).

ten people from the village. In the case of any dispute, which is common in the chars, the signatories sit with local leaders to solve the problem as amicably as possible. The process of land transfer on the chars is complicated because people often come, buy lands, farm them for a few years, and, after saving some money, go to a secure and more permanent place on the mainland. To avoid paying registration fees in view of their temporary holdings, they also tend to transfer lands recorded in government surveys through dash dalil.

Farmers with more than three acres of land are seen locally as "big farmers." They usually have their own irrigation means, such as tube wells, and can hire additional labor for farm work. Small-scale farmers own less than two acres of land and can at times have shallow pumps, but generally cannot afford to hire labor and rely on family members to work on the farm. Small farmers, with their limited capital, try to offer short-term lease of their land for one crop at a time. In contrast, bigger farmers lease in extra land. Small and marginal farmers prefer to produce their staple crop, paddy, and wheat, and lease out the land for a second crop for cash. Leasing out and leasing in of land are common practices in char farming. Women-headed households and those households with fewer family members tend to lease out more. The short-term lease is usually valid for a single crop (three months) or two crops (six months). Occasionally, farmers take land on a one-year lease to raise crops throughout the year. The lease period usually starts in mid-April, the start of the Bengali New Year. The cost of leasing varies according to the position and situation of land, between Rs. 2,000 and Rs. 4,000 per bigha. The rate also varies according to the type of crop and the price level of the previous year for that crop. For example, the rate for potato varies between Rs. 1,200 and Rs. 1,500 per bigha and for maize between Rs. 800 and Rs. 1,000. The rate roughly depends on the speculation of crop price in the year concerned. While collecting information on the rates of different crops in the lease contract system, we found that for paddy and wheat, nobody knows the rate in cash. Prasanta Mondal clarified why:

> Small farmers like us always care for food security. Therefore, in leasing out the land for paddy and wheat, we never ask for cash. We just take a share of the crop.

In this system of crop contract against lease, the rate varies on the condition of whether the owner shares the farming cost or not. If the landowner shares half of the total cost of that crop, he gets half of the total produce, and if the cost is borne by the lease contractor, the owner gets one-third of the produce.

Bandaki lease (lease on mortgage) is a type of lease in which the small landowner takes a lump sum against his land for a full year. The interest on the loan is compensated by the profit made from the harvest since the borrower retains the land for that period. If the borrower fails to repay the money at the end of the year, the ownership of that land goes to the lender. Many people lose their land permanently because they cannot repay the money. For bigger farmers, this can be a deliberate strategy to procure land at a much cheaper price. The rate of such a lease price is Rs. 8,000 to Rs. 10,000, when the market price is between Rs. 20,000 and Rs. 25,000.

Flood and price fluctuations are the two major risks farmers on chars face. Floods are natural occurrences that define the lives of char dwellers. Those working in the low-lying lands tend to leave their land fallow during the rainy season to cope with this risk. During winter, the river may at times receive water released from the upstream reservoir when there is heavy rainfall in upper catchments. Although this is rare, the sudden increase in the water level can ruin the winter crop in the land recovered from the abandoned river channel. In January 2002, when the water remained stagnant for several days, it almost destroyed the winter crop of a number of farmers on Char Gaitanpur, Char Kalimohanpur, and Char Majher Mana. The inundation risk is greater for island chars like Majher Mana because they are flat and low-lying. Even average amounts of monsoon rain and the consequent increase in the river's water level cause floods in the peripheral areas of these chars. To cope with frequent floods, relatively better-off households keep their own boats ready during the rainy season. Although leaving the land fallow reduces the potential earnings, choruas in these island chars refrain from cropping during the rainy months as an adaptive measure to cut financial losses from floods.

Fluctuating crop prices is the most significant risk to farmers. Potatoes are an important crop since they grow well on sandy soils; also, being a winter crop, the risk of ruin from flooding is low. Over the last ten years, the average price of potatoes has varied between Rs. 120 and Rs. 300 per hundred kilograms (table 7.2). Profit and loss both have varied accordingly. Price variations can be severe and can leave a farmer in heavy debt. Char farmers cannot hoard their produce to receive a better price later. Most farmers produce potatoes with loans from local moneylenders at a high interest rate; therefore, they need immediate cash to repay the loan, even if

TABLE 7.2 POTATOES: YIELDS, PRICES, AND PROFITS ON SURVEYED CHARS

Average Yield per Acre (in kg)	Price per 100 Kilograms	Total Price (in Rs.)	Total Expenditure per Acre (in Rs.)	Profit per Acre (in Rs.)	Loss per Acre (in Rs.)
15,000	300	45,000	21,000	24,000	—
15,000	150	22,500	21,000	1,500	—
15,000	120	18,000	21,000	—	3,000

Source: Field survey conducted in 2007–2008.

they must bear a loss. In spite of the high investment cost and high risk of price fluctuations, all farmers grow potatoes since this crop provides a high return, provided prices do not fall. Ganesh Halder describes why farmers take that risk:

> Since we left Bangladesh, we have been living with risk. Living in this char is itself a risk. We take risks also because we do not have any alternative. On this sandy soil, we cannot produce winter rice, as it requires a lot of water; but we can produce potatoes because the soil is suitable for it. We live in the hope that life will be better one day. We also believe in fate, destiny, and do not worry about taking a risk.

Ganesh's words might give the impression that the inability to control the market price makes the char dwellers fatalistic. But in reality, most of them can easily reconcile themselves with farming-related losses by living in hope of a better crop next year.

Marketing the Produce

The remote location of chars limits the farmers' access to the markets and makes them dependent on middlemen, particularly for perishable products such as vegetables. Big farmers transport the produce by tractors to the wholesale market and get a relatively better price than lesser producers. The price the farmers get thus varies according to their geographical location and distance to the market. Profits are never satisfactory, as there is always a gap between the retail price in the market and the wholesale price received by the farmers (table 7.3).

TABLE 7.3 GAP IN THE PRICE BETWEEN WHOLESALE AND RETAIL RATES FOR VEGETABLES ON SURVEYED CHARS

Vegetables	Wholesale Price (Rs. per kg)	Retail Price (Rs. per kg)
Green Peas	5	15
Brinjal/Eggplant	3	10
Spinach	2.5	10
Green Chilli	10	50
Cabbage	3	8
Cauliflower	5	10–12

Source: Field survey conducted in 2010.
Note: The rates are for a specific day, and were acquired from both the farmer and the market in December 2010.

Generally, small farmers prefer to sell vegetables to wholesale traders even at a low price because the wholesale traders pay immediately, which middlemen do not always do. This way, the farmers develop a personal relationship with the wholesalers, who even lend money if needed. Mutual trust and relationship building have significant practical value in the farmers' livelihood practices and have a strong impact on making livelihood sustainable.

Wage Labor

The livelihood of the landless in South Asia is characterized by the seasonality of activities (Makita 2003). The landless people on chars also earn their livelihood as wage laborers in agricultural fields or in sand quarries on the riverbed. The wage rate of an agricultural laborer is fixed per day, but sand quarrying is paid against the volume of work. Therefore, younger people prefer to work in sand quarries, as they can move more sand and earn more money per day. Agricultural laborers can only earn up to Rs. 100 per day, while those engaged in sand quarrying, whose arrangement is on a piece-rate contract, can earn between Rs. 150 and Rs. 200 per day, depending on the volume of work. Agricultural labor has a strong seasonality of job opportunities, since large tracts of land remain fallow in the summer season. The wage rate also goes down in the lean season since the supply of labor is much higher than the demand for work. These agricultural laborers also often work in sand quarries during the lean cropping season. Elderly people, unable to work in sand quarries because of the requirement of heavy physical labor, mostly rely on seasonal agricultural work.

A recent change in the nature of agricultural laboring on chars is the introduction of contract labor in addition to casual labor. In casual labor, laborers get a fixed amount of money (around Rs. 100) against their daily toil of eight hours; however, their income cannot increase even if they have the capacity to labor more in a day. Therefore, both farmers and laborers now prefer contract work to casual labor. Dhiren Mondal, a farmer, feels that contract labor has increased the productivity of wage laborers:

> When the laborer works on a casual basis, he often tries to work less and wastes time by sitting idle. So we need to be always in the field to supervise their work and to get the maximum labor output from within the fixed time. When we hire labor on contract, they do not waste time and accomplish a lot in a day to increase their daily income. We do not need to supervise them and can get the maximum work done per day. They also become more productive, as they are paid according to the volume of work they do. Therefore, contract labor is good for both laborers and farmers.

On the chars, it is not only the landless people who live by laboring, but also small and marginal farmers, as toiling on their own land is not sufficient for a year's livelihood income. There are many jobs on their own as well as on others' farms. We have observed that for small and marginal farmers, men usually work on other people's farms, whereas women work on their own farms. From various conversations, we gathered that women's labor and work choices are constrained by social norms. Even in a marginal society like the chars, women would work on others' farms only if they have no other choice. When the financial status of the family is better, women's work in public spaces shrinks, and their work becomes limited to the private space of their own lands or homes.

During the last two decades, sand quarrying has offered yet another attractive income option. Since the river remains dry for the greater part of the year, quarrying sand has become feasible almost year round, except during those few weeks of the rainy season when water from the upstream reservoir floods the river channel. The demand for sand for construction work has also increased immensely in the recent past along with the expansion of urban-industrial activities in the nearby mainland areas of Burdwan. The Bangladeshis are more involved in agriculture since many of them own pieces of agricultural land, even if small. The Biharis engage more in sand quarrying since they do not get jobs throughout the year in the farm sector, and most of them do have their own farms where they need to work.

Rearing Livestock

For all char people, the rearing of livestock—particularly goats, oxen, bullocks, cows, and pigs (the Biharis prefer to raise pigs)—is an important subsidiary livelihood activity. They use the fallow land as pasture for domestic cattle, and use agricultural land for grazing during the lean cropping season, that is, during summer and monsoons. During the lean season, the cost of rearing cattle is actually low since the animals only need to be fed at night and the rest of the time they can graze freely on the common lands. In comparison, during the peak season (October to March), when the better land is cropped, costs tend to increase. To deal with the need to feed the cattle, they are grazed along the sides of the embankments or tied to stakes in small fallow patches. Again, goat-rearing is cheaper and can sustain households; for dairy cattle, fodder usually has to be purchased, while goats can be fed with leaves.

Older women look after the animals to supplement family incomes; however, they usually do not determine how the profits are to be spent. Women prefer to rear both hens and cows because of the multiple contributions they make to their daily livelihood. The eggs are meant for home consumption as well as for the market. Fulmati Mondal, one of our women participants, explained:

> With a goat, I can earn some cash. If I rear an ox or a bullock, they are used for plowing the land, which ultimately helps men in their field jobs. The cows give us milk, which helps children. I can manage the family's daily meals with rice, some mashed potato, and milk.

Chorua women who cannot afford to purchase animals take them on rent on the condition that they rear them. They take newborn cows, goats, or pigs from the owner and raise them. When that animal gives birth, the young one is taken by the borrower and the animal taken on rent is returned to the owner. In this way, women increase their own livestock and supplement family livelihoods.

Ganesh Biswas of Char Bhasapur gave us an interesting insight into the concept of livestock resources. Livestock rearing is considered by academics and development practitioners as a direct contribution to livelihoods. However, for Ganesh, his domestic cats protect his paddy crop as well as the stored jute bags of paddy from rodents. The need to buy new jute bags or to repair them every year was a major problem for him earlier. He also feels that his cats alert him to oncoming floods, and, hence, he values them as important resources. This reveals that the very concept of what constitutes "a resource" is subjective and contextual.

Informal Trading

Informal trading is an important livelihood activity for some families in the chars (such as Gaitanpur located near Burdwan town) located near the urban center. The people engaged in such trading activities earn an average income between Rs. 40 and Rs. 50 per day, depending on the market price. This income is much less than the daily wage for agricultural labor, which is Rs. 100 at present. Still, people take up such livelihood options, as there is no lean season in this livelihood activity. Some households depend entirely on informal trading, which provides a supplementary income throughout the year. On Char Gaitanpur, fifty-three people (twenty males and thirty-three females) from 199 households are engaged in petty trading. Most of them sell vegetables in Burdwan town, and only two are engaged in fish trading.

Sachin Mondal shares his experience:

> We prefer to sell our vegetables to the wholesaler rather than to small traders. The smaller traders usually only buy small amounts of vegetables. We like to sell in large quantities at one time to avoid weighing small quantities. Sometimes it is difficult to get the payment from the petty traders. Getting cash on a daily basis is more helpful.

Such regular flow of money enhances the economic circuit and creates jobs for men, who are more involved in such trading than women. Although men are usually young, women are only allowed to go out to sell the vegetables when they are in their middle age. Child-care responsibilities also prevent younger women from leaving their homes for prolonged periods. Men prefer to sell vegetables, for it provides an income throughout the year, whereas women usually choose it to secure access to the outside world and to build contacts to improve their economic and social status.

Fishing

The availability of fish has declined remarkably with the reduction in river flows and rising levels of water pollution. Consequently, fishing has lost its significance as a major source of income for char dwellers. People still fish for household consumption or for subsidiary income. The catch varies from 250 grams to 10 kilograms per day; this usually increases in summer and decreases in winter. The price paid for fish varies from Rs. 40 to Rs. 100 per kilogram, depending on the type and size of the catch.

The interviewees often recollected the ease with which they earlier could find fish, which was the main source of livelihood. Due to the fall in the fish catch, many have opted for farming and even quarrying of sand from the riverbed. Those fishermen who did not want to or could not move on to farming have now left the chars. Just before our study, around the end of the 1980s, a reasonably large fishing community left Char Lakshmipur permanently due to the fall in the fish catch in the Damodar. At present, most families on chars switch between fishing and farming, depending on the season. Sandhya and Ratan Mondal work as agricultural laborers during the peak cropping season and during the monsoon take up fishing. They sell their catch on headloads—loads carried on the head—to individual households across the embankment at rates that are much lower than market rates.

Diversification of Livelihoods

Deb et al. (2002) observe that diversification across income sources helps households combat unstable incomes and thereby increase the probability of maintaining livelihood security. While agriculture remains the main source of income for the majority of the households, a degree of diversification in livelihood strategies has taken place over the last ten years. Proximity to urban centers and the development of transport infrastructure have facilitated this diversification.

Diversified livelihood strategies are more common among poorer people than the relatively better-off. The study carried out by Deb et al. in two villages of Andhra Pradesh, India, observes that "whilst there are a small number of cases where diversification has enabled households to lift themselves significantly above the poverty line, the overwhelming experience of diversification is as a coping strategy" (2002: vi). In the area under the scope of our study, diversification is taken up by landless households and small, marginal farmers as a common livelihood strategy. Large farmers occupying better land on higher ground usually produce three vegetable crops per year using their own minor irrigation systems. Members of these farming households are occupied with production and marketing activities throughout the year and do not have the scope or need for diversification of livelihood activities.

Household poverty is closely linked with the diversification of livelihoods. For someone like Durga Sarkar, with six family members, it becomes difficult to pull together adequate resources to run the household. In her family, everyone is assigned different tasks to enhance family incomes even during the lean season. Durga and her husband work together as agricultural wage labor, her elder son transports river sand in headloads, and her younger son works as contract labor in the telephone exchange in Burdwan town. She expects her aged in-laws to pitch in by collecting greens and small fish.

Livelihoods during the Lean Season

The lean agricultural season—April to September—is a hard time for most choruas, especially the landless agricultural laborers. The relatively better-off farmers can support themselves during this season with the profit they make out of winter crops. Farmers owning small irrigation systems can produce summer crops, especially rice, although on limited stretches of land. The rest keep their land fallow and try to find other forms of employment and income. Since most of the land remains fallow in this season, some agricultural workers go to the mainland to look for seasonal work, but women tend not to travel such long distances and instead stay back to look after the household.

An important livelihood strategy during the lean season is the farming of vegetables on a subsistence basis in the courtyard of their houses. Ashalata, a woman agricultural laborer, states that she buys rice and mustard oil for the whole year after the harvest:

> To meet our daily needs, we grow vegetables in our courtyard, rear hens for eggs, and sometimes catch fish from the river. Pulling all these together, we manage to survive during the lean season. As a result, we do not suffer from acute poverty and do not die without food. But we also do not have enough surplus. With some rice at home, we can eat it with salt and water. *Khidei amader tarkari* [Hunger is our curry].

To cope with the lean season, people often change their food habits to fill the gap between required and available food. The Bihari community, which normally prefers wheat, consumes rice during this time. Rambali Mahato explains why:

> Although we like chapattis more than rice, we take rice during the period of crisis. The cost of one kilogram of rice and one kilogram of wheat flour is the same [that is, Rs. 15]. We have six members in the family and can carry on with one kilogram of rice for one meal of the day, but not with one kilogram of wheat flour. Moreover, rice takes more time to digest than chapatti and we do not feel hungry for a longer time. Therefore, we convert our food habits to cope with the lean season crisis.

Choruas thus have ingenious ways of coping with financial crisis due to the lack of work during the lean season: They try to control their demand and reduce the expenditure to adjust to the limited available resources. They sometimes have to depend on local moneylenders for the minimum survival/maintenance cost of the household.

As mentioned earlier, some people use chars as places for temporary shelter before moving to the mainland. They wait for two or three consecutive good crops from which they can make enough money and then leave. The fluidity of human communities therefore characterizes char habitation. Prasanta Mondal says:

> We know that this land is highly vulnerable, as the bank erosion is happening fast and will soon erode the entire char. Any day our land and house can vanish. . . . To cope with that risk in the future, I want to buy a small piece of land in the mainland to keep it as an option just in case this char does not exist one day. We do not want to leave either the river or the chars, as our lives were and are always associated with the river, whether in Bangladesh or here. If the river turns out to be cruel and takes our land, making us refugees for the second time, we will be forced to leave. *Nadi na chharle amra nadike chharbo na* [We will not leave the river if the river does not leave us].

Instead of succumbing to hardships, char dwellers have adjusted to a marginal environment and resource constraints, and have developed livelihood strategies to ensure their survival. The cultural rootedness of people in specific places and occupations continues to play an important role, with the Bihari inhabitants being less able to cope with char dynamics than the Bangladeshis. The level of diversification of livelihood strategies is high, and while none of the occupations can individually provide a solid subsistence, the overall mix proves to be reasonably adequate for survival, even if on a temporary basis.

Living on Next to Nothing

To "subsist" in the midst of pressing poverty and insecurity is to live on a day-to-day basis and to cope with needs and situations as they arise: "*Din ani, din khai*" (Eat what we earn in a day), as many char dwellers say. Choruas have fine-tuned hand-to-mouth survival strategies to cope with the poverty situation. On a day when the cash income is insignificant or perhaps nothing, as it sometimes is, life still carries on. Money surely plays an important role in the well-being of any household, but on the chars both the Bihari and the Bangladeshi communities are "cash-poor" and have a high level of indebtedness (table 7.4). The question that then arises is how these poor char families manage their cash to run their households. The myriad ways people make both ends meet include borrowing from others including the shopkeepers, and nonreturnable assistance from other community members as well as relatives. This section explores how the poor survive on such a low amount of income and how they manage their finances in order to see what happens "inside" the household in terms of money. Money is the most important aspect of livelihood: How do poor

TABLE 7.4 HOUSEHOLD INDEBTEDNESS ON TWO CHARS

Amounts of Loan (in Rs.)	Char Gaitanpur		Char Majher Mana	
	Number of Households	Percentage of Households	Number of Households	Percentage of Households
Less than 3,000	42	32	24	30
3,001–5,000	25	19	10	13
5,001–10,000	23	17	23	30
10,001–20,000	39	30	8	10
More than 20,000	3	2	13	17
Total	**132**	**100**	**78**	**100**

Source: Field survey conducted in 2007–2008.

people survive without it and what are the roles of social trust and hope that come through in informal credit systems? We trace the informal credit sources and show how these are accessed by char people and the role of informal credits in their livelihoods and overall well-being.

This part of the research was undertaken at two levels: community and household. At the community level, we initially looked into indebtedness, sources of credit, and the reasons for debt of char dwellers. Overall, two-thirds of the families are indebted, although the proportion varies significantly across the chars we studied. The remoteness of individual chars and the length of occupation by their inhabitants seem to influence the level of indebtedness. Within a given char, the amount of debt varies widely between families. Indebtedness of about 45 percent of them is reasonably low, that is, less than Rs. 5,000, while 40 percent of families have medium-level debts varying between Rs. 5,000 and Rs. 20,000. The remaining 15 percent of families are heavily indebted with loans of more than Rs. 20,000. If we assess the average level of debt for the indebted households across the chars, then those on Gaitanpur, Bhasapur, and Kasba have borrowed the most.

We could carry out this evaluation only toward the end of the study, when we had earned a reasonable amount of trust within the community. The precarious legal situation of char dwellers also meant that we needed to exercise caution and ethical judgment. Only those who were willing to be transparent about their finances participated in the survey. Because of its personal nature, each family had the option of leaving the study at any time. We also asked the younger and school-educated women and men of local communities to act as researchers: They visited the families every evening to note down the day's activities that involved money.

To better understand how the choruas manage their meager financial resources, we first tried to look into the sources of credit available locally upon which poor people generally depend. This was followed by an assessment of the levels of their indebtedness and financial strategies adopted by them to deal with debt. These strategies and situations are different from each family to the other. We also tried to explore the coping strategies of choruas with emergency financial needs through in-depth, micro-level case studies of individual households; this was done through the method of keeping financial diaries. Ten households from each of the four chars were selected, totaling forty samples, to record and analyze understandings of the financial policies and economic behavior of the poor people.

Managing Money at the Community Level

Although poverty is one of the dimensions of the lives and livelihoods of char families, the financial situation of each and every household is specific and highly changeable over even a short period of time. While some can overcome pressing situations in the short run or in the long run, there are also cases of households that have sunk deeper into extreme poverty. Often vulnerabilities to physical emergencies (such as flood and riverbank erosion), financial emergencies (such as crop failure, family illnesses, or the sudden death of the male earning member), or social compulsions (such as daughters' marriage) worsened the family's well-being by compelling the sale of land. The char dwellers, therefore, often have to rely heavily on the different types of credit available locally. The availability of credit and the conditions attached to it play an important role in determining the livelihood strategies in the char environment. On Char Gaitanpur, only 14 percent of households have any kind of savings account—either in banks or in post offices. Households without any savings frequently borrow from different informal credit organizations. During the field survey, we observed that on average 56 percent of char households had existing loans of varying amounts. Table 7.5 lists the number of households that have taken loans from different sources. Table 7.6 lays out the reasons for borrowing at the household level.

TABLE 7.5 SOURCES OF LOANS ON TWO CHARS BY INDEBTED HOUSEHOLD

Loan Sources	Char Gaitanpur		Char Majher Mana	
	Number of Indebted Households	Percentage with Loan Source	Number of Indebted Households	Percentage with Loan Source
Bank	5	4	15	19
Mahajan	99	75	27	35
Kin/Relative	11	8	8	10
Neighbor	11	8	8	10
Shopkeeper	6	5	4	5
Credit Club	—	—	16	21
Total	132	100	78	100

Source: Field survey conducted in 2007–2008.

TABLE 7.6 REASONS FOR HOUSEHOLD BORROWING ON TWO CHARS

Reasons for Borrowing	Char Gaitanpur		Char Majher Mana	
	Number of Households	Percentage of Households	Number of Households	Percentage of Households
Cultivation	54	41	59	75
Buying Cattle	5	4	3	4
Purchasing Land	14	11	2	3
Petty Trading	5	4	3	4
Constructing House	11	8	1	1
Leasing Land	7	5	2	3
Running Household	20	15	8	10
Dowry for Daughter's Marriage	16	12	—	—
Total	**132**	**100**	78	**100**

Source: Field survey conducted in 2007–2008.

Role of the Mahajans

The most significant source of informal credit in the chars is the moneylender, locally called the mahajan. Even though people pay a high interest rate of Rs. 50 to Rs. 60 per Rs. 1,000 each month to the mahajans (equivalent to 60 percent or more per year), the poorer families depend on them. The obvious reason for this is that choruas have little or no access to formal credit from banks. The other reason is more psychological—a faith in the old system and the advantages of taking out a quickly repayable loan. The moneylenders also prefer short-term loans, as they believe that the poor cannot repay longer-term loans. It becomes difficult for the farmers to repay the loan if profit is low from a crop due to a fall in the price level or due to accidental damage of the crop by drought, flood, or pest attack. For this reason, the moneylenders selectively judge the repayment capacity of the borrower. Unfortunately, the poorest of the poor sometimes do not get a loan even from a moneylender. To ensure repayment from the poor, some businessmen-cum-moneylenders prefer special conditional loans called *dadan*.

Dadan on Chars

Dadan is a traditional advance-lending system that continues to play an important role in the subsistence economy of the chars. Here, the farmers borrow the total amount required to produce a certain crop in cash from the mahajans, who are also wholesale businessmen selling agricultural goods. Some portion of this loan may be in kind, as agricultural inputs. The interest rate is commonly set by the mahajan, depending on his personal relations with the client—his familiarity with and trust in him or her as a borrower. The essential condition of dadan is that the farmer is required to sell the crop only to the respective mahajan. As a result, in a year of low prices or crop loss, the farmer may have to give away the entire harvest to repay the loan. Some moneylenders may even buy the produce at a price lower than the market price. In spite of these exploitative preconditions, for a number of reasons choruas prefer dadan over the usual form of loan from moneylenders or mahajans. The latter generally try not to lend to the farmers whose repayment capacity is poor, whereas a dadan loan is accessible even to poor farmers. Another reason for preferring dadan is the possibility that the mahajans will be lenient and allow one more year for repayment if the farmer is in real distress. The mahajan may also waive the additional interest. This mutual faith and trust add a positive dimension to dadan.

Operation of Credit Groups

Informal credit groups are a relatively new addition to the sources and ways of credit mobilization in the chars of Damodar. The oldest group is the Bhasapur Gram Samiti, which was formed in 1999 by three or four early settlers. The Samiti now has four hundred shareholder members scattered over Char Bhasapur and six other adjoining chars. These societies are not registered and can therefore be considered extralegal. Few people are prepared to discuss these informal credit groups in public, and not everyone has a clear idea of how these groups operate.

Usually such societies are run by a core *parichalan samiti* (management committee) comprising six to ten members. The membership of the committee changes every three years. All monetary transactions (getting loans, repayments, and dispute resolutions) are carried out at monthly meetings in the presence of all members. Core members are also selected in those meetings to be the office-bearers for three years. In March 2011, this committee had a capital of Rs. 14 lakhs (1,400,000 rupees)—a substantial increase over the initial capital of Rs. 1.5 lakhs in 1999. This capital is kept in a nearby bank in an account jointly held by two or three founding members.

These credit groups operate much like an informal bank, and people living on the chars use them for both credit and savings. Informal credit is provided at interest rates about half those charged by local moneylenders, but still more than three times the rate charged by commercial banks. These groups flourish not only because char dwellers are unable to access the banks without citizenship papers; even those who could are reluctant to use banks. The reluctance is rooted in the large amount of paperwork required by banks, which is in English, and going to the bank is a daunting task for the illiterate poor. Those who use credit for cropping benefit from the shorter application and loan processing time of these informal institutions.

Effectiveness of Informal Credit Systems

When we asked individuals about the effectiveness of these informal credit mobilization systems, responses were varied. Families with more land usually benefit more from these credit groups: They can procure a short-term loan, especially just before a cropping season, more easily and can immediately repay with interest after the harvest. Some relatively better-off families also build up savings this way. The poorest families prefer this type of credit, as no assets are required to be mortgaged. There are also differences in reasons for taking out loans; often the poorer families borrow to meet their consumption needs, whereas the better-off families use loans for farming. Peer pressure to repay these debts is also great. Some families that are unable to repay debts experience extreme peer pressure from other villagers, as most of their money is also with this group as public shares. There are cases where extremely poor families have had to sell their cattle or part of their land to repay the loan and accumulated interest. The positive aspects of the system of informal credit are several: The poor can access cash when needed and they can do so reasonably quickly, and no longer have to depend on local moneylenders and be subject to their exploitation. The negative aspects, however, relate to the nature of the char communities and the purpose of the credit.

Managing Money at Home

In the academic discourse on poverty, debates center on the measurement yardsticks of poverty, poverty alleviation strategies, and financial help from donor agencies, government, and nongovernment institutions. The literature on what constitutes poverty tends to subsume the efforts to understand how poor people survive with such a low income as less than $2 a day of irregular income. Planners and policymakers, who design the schemes for poverty alleviation, also rarely recognize the importance of understanding the financial practices of the poor. The broad-based economic surveys do not cover the minute details of income and expenditure of the poor over a certain time period nor do anthropological studies, undertaken at the micro level, come up with quantitatively understandable details of the financial management of the poor. This gap in identifying viable methods of understanding cash management by the poor has recently been tackled by a group of scholars (Collins et al. 2009) who made families keep diaries to understand their financial policies for daily maintenance in the short and long terms. Their study covered 250 households' financial balance sheets and recorded how individual households managed their money. The analysis revealed that the poor do not consume their entire incomes immediately, but try to put their money in different places to minimize the risk of loss.

To understand the financial lives of the char people, we adopted the technique used by Collins et al. (2009) to record the financial balance sheets for forty households. The "financial diaries" were kept for two months during the last year of our study, that is, 2010, and we took one lean season month (during the monsoons) to balance one peak season month (during the cropping cycle). This gave us, we hoped, a better idea of financial management at times when plenty of work is available as well as when work opportunities are limited. Due to the limited literacy of char dwellers, we used research assistants to visit each household on every other day to note down the details of income and expenditure. For each individual household, we tried to understand both the short-term and the long-term financial management. When asking about the day's income and expenditure, we tried also to have informal discussions with the household members with the aim of understanding the long-term financial management. The resultant data revealed immense complexity in household financial behavior. Four selected cases that represent how different the micro-financial policies of the people on chars are and how each household negotiates the challenge of survival differently are offered below.

Household One: Landless Laborer

Gopinath Kirtania came to India from Bangladesh with his parents in 1957 at the age of four. After four years in a refugee camp they moved to the Damodar chars in 1961, where his father bought some land at the cost of Rs. 60 per bigha. Gopinath did not get the opportunity to go to school due to the isolation of the chars. At the age of twenty, he married Minati, a girl from the same village and had five sons and four daughters, three of whom are now married. Two of their older sons work, whereas the two other boys and one daughter go to school.

Gopinath's half an acre of land had to be put on bandaki (mortgaged) to marry off the eldest daughter five years ago, but he was unable to repay the loan and lost his land. He and his two grown-up sons work as agricultural laborers. At times, he gets casual laboring jobs at minimum wage or under the National Rural Employment Guarantee Scheme (NREGS). Minati supplements the cash income by raising animals for milk and meat. Gopinath sometimes earns by performing *kirtan* (devotional folk singing) during the lean season at small gatherings in other chars. Gopinath and Minati have a savings account in the bank where they deposit small amounts of extra income earned during the peak season.

Examination of their day-to-day income and expenditure pattern reveals that, in the peak season (November to March), the combined wages bring in on average Rs. 7,000 to Rs. 8,000 per month. During the peak season, they spend regularly on groceries and vegetables. They are able to afford protein with their meals and offer sweets to visiting relatives. Since rice is usually cheaper in the peak season, the family invests by buying rice to store for the lean season.

In the remaining months, their income comes down to Rs. 2,000 or less per month. To feed the family three meals a day, they must get additional incomes from other sources. Gopinath earns Rs. 250 per month from his performances. Problems occur when some extra expenditure becomes necessary; for instance, Minati had to sell a goat to feed five visitors who came to negotiate her youngest daughter's marriage.

On the expenditure side, they only bought groceries at a minimum level on a regular basis, often on credit. During the lean months the household made do with produce grown in their courtyard. They faced a critical situation during this time because of medical expenses.

With regard to their long-term financial management, they are not able to save money consistently. Besides meeting the family's regular expenditure, Gopinath had the added responsibility of getting his four daughters married. We saw that during the marriage of his first daughter, he lost his agricultural land on bandaki. For the marriage of his second daughter, Minati sold the few gold ornaments she had. They also sold some big trees in their courtyard for a little money. For the third daughter, they did not have any assets to sell, so Minati sold her only cow and they also borrowed some money from the local informal credit group. They have one daughter yet to get married and since they no longer have any reserves, they plan to arrange the money from different relatives as well as on credit from the local moneylenders and the informal credit society. One of their sons has recently started to work in the sand quarry on the riverbed, where wages are higher than those paid for agricultural laboring.

Household Two: Marginal Farmer and Sharecropper

Thirty-five-year-old Subhas Mondal is a marginal farmer who inherited two bighas of land from his father's original six bighas (two acres). Subhas came to the Damodar chars from Bangladesh in the 1950s and has lived here since. After primary school he began to work in the fields and when he was twenty, his marriage was arranged with Champa, a girl from the same district of Bangladesh. After the birth of their two daughters, Subhas built a bamboo-mud hut where he moved his family.

Subhas never leases his land, but labors to produce paddy, potato, and other vegetables. In 2009, he earned a profit of Rs. 16,000 from this land. He also cultivates other people's land on a crop-share basis. If he has a few free days in hand, he tries to find work as a day laborer.

Champa has a regular income of about Rs. 20 to Rs. 25 every day from making *bidis* (local cigarettes). She also raises goats and poultry from which she earns some money, though not regularly. Their two daughters attend school and are not expected to work to enhance the family income. Champa's income is used for the education of the children, whereas Subhas's is used for everyday expenditure and for savings.

Subhas and Champa have four types of savings: a savings account with a nationalized bank where they put some money whenever they can; a life insurance policy where they deposit an amount of Rs. 250 quarterly; a small amount of Champa's money goes into a group savings account under the Self Help Group (SHG) scheme of the government; and they are members of the informal credit society of their char with the hope of taking out a loan in the future.

During the peak season, their daily income varies between Rs. 100 and Rs. 125, or around Rs. 3,000 per month, although when Subhas works on his own farm, he does not earn any cash. He receives a lump sum after the crop is harvested. The consumption pattern in the Champa-Subhas household is characterized by low daily expenditure, but it actually increases during the lean season when Subhas earns cash every day from laboring.

The financial diaries of this household, in both the lean and peak seasons, did not show any expenditure on staple foods (such as rice and potato) or other storable consumption items (such as coal dust to prepare coal briquettes or kerosene for the cooking stove). They usually buy these nonperishable items immediately after harvest at the end of the winter. From their day-to-day financial diary, we observed that on a day when Subhas earns Rs. 100 from casual labor, he spends about Rs. 40 to 50 on groceries and vegetables. When he does not earn any cash, he uses the balance from the previous day's income. If he does not get any cash income for five or six consecutive days, Champa takes over this responsibility and spends her money to buy foodstuff. She keeps a record of the money she uses for this purpose and takes it back from Subhas.

The story of Subhas and Champa is consistent with other poor households, in that women put more emphasis on the future and savings than men, who are more focused on day-to-day income expenditure. Monies earned by the husband and wife are earmarked for different uses. When women like Champa earn even a small amount of money, they can be involved in household decisions to protect the family from destitution.

Household Three: Marginal Farmer and Agricultural Laborer

Haridas was born on Char Bhasapur to Bangladeshi migrant parents and has a ration card. Haridas started his own family, now consisting of five members, about fifteen years ago. Since his father was a landless laborer, he did not inherit any agricultural land and has worked in other people's fields from age thirteen. He married Namita, a local girl, at the age of eighteen. Namita allowed him to invest the proceeds of the sale of her jewelry, which she had received as a gift from her father during the wedding, to start a *mahajani karbar* (a moneylending business). Namita saves and records the transactions of the proceeds in her *boka bhanrh*, an earthen pot for saving cash. Eventually they bought one bigha of farmland. Namita's father helped them to build a house and also gifted a milch cow to his grandchildren. She sells the extra milk after feeding the family, and has invested in the purchase of another cow and a few goats. Namita also works as an agricultural laborer during winters, the potato-farming season, when demand for labor is high on all chars. Haridas bought another bigha of land from the income earned from his moneylending business, but he closed this business recently due to the uncertainty and hassles of getting money back from defaulters. At present, their assets include one *bhitabari* (residential house), two bighas of farming land, two milch cows, and six goats. Their eldest daughter has been married and the younger daughter and son are in schools. They put importance on the children's education with the hope that, with their SC certificate, there is some support for jobs for them in the future.

As with the other cases, there are seasonal variations in both income and expenditure. During the peak season, Haridas earned Rs. 20,000 profit from producing potatoes on his two bighas of land and worked as a day laborer for much of the time. In the peak season, they bought vegetables and groceries on every other day and bulk rice for the entire month. Some expenditure was incurred on private tuition fees for the children and for buying notebooks and other stationary items. They also purchased some pesticide to use on their own crop and some straw as fodder for their cows.

In the lean season Haridas earned Rs. 1,200 from the NREGS. He cut expenditure on vegetables during this month, as his income was low.

Long-term money management of this household depends on building assets, especially agricultural land and savings in the bank. The marriage of their eldest daughter required considerable expenditure, but they have kept money in the bank for the other daughter's marriage. Whenever Namita sells a cow or a goat, she saves the proceeds; when she earns income from farm work, she usually contributes the money for family expenditure. She intends to use the incomes made from livestock for major expenditures such as her daughter's marriage or the building of a house.

Household Four: Poorest of the Poor—Woman-Headed Household

The head of this family on Char Majher Mana is Aloka Mohali, who lives with her sister Nirmala and her eight-year-old son. The sisters were born on the Damodar char of Bangladeshi parents who arrived after a few years of living in a relief camp. Aloka's arranged marriage broke down after only six months, and she has been living in her parental home ever since. Nirmala was married to a farmer in the faraway province of Uttar Pradesh, but was thrown out after about five years along with her son. Her husband had a violent temper and beat her frequently and finally left her unconscious in a Howrah-bound train. She too came back to her parents. When Nirmala returned, her sad and destitute parents passed away; this is when Aloka, the elder sister, took charge of running the household. They have only a mud hut and one bigha of agricultural land.

The household is run solely on the basis of what they can produce in their small field. They hardly buy anything for consumption, except salt and kerosene; they do buy crop inputs such as fertilizer, water, and seeds. Their only other expenditure is on clothes, medication when required, and pencils and notebooks for the school-going child. Aloka is apprehensive about the continuation of her nephew's education after he completes the primary level because, in the lean season of monsoons, they have no income and, unbelievable but true, no cash expenditure. Aloka told us: "We cannot even buy oil for hair, we always wear torn clothes. How can we spend for his education?"

Aloka and Nirmala have never hired laborers to work on their land. They also work on others' land if they are asked to, but because Majher Mana is an island char, people cannot easily commute to other areas for daily wage work; however, they do find work for three to four months in the peak season, which has to provide for their household for the whole year. They produce rice, potato, mustard, and seasonal vegetables for their own consumption, and if they need to, they barter with their neighbors.

In comparison to the other households, Aloka's is exceptional and provides deep insights into the survival strategies of the poorest of the poor living in a perpetual state of risk and uncertainty. Char Majher Mana is being eroded gradually and they might lose their land and house any day. Questions about the future upset them; they requested not to be reminded of the future. Aloka said: "In our current predicament, we live for just the day and do not even want to think about tomorrow. We leave the future alone." The statement is not just fatalism, although most char dwellers follow the mantra of putting oneself at the mercy of nature in order to steal the best of it for the present. This attitude develops only over time, through daily struggle and learning to live with the river.

Insights from the Diaries

One needs to be familiar with the specific environment to understand the mental landscapes of char people, who must cope with their poverty in innovative ways. However, some general lessons emerge from these glimpses into their financial lives. We see that individuals take risks, but also work within communities to support each other. The collective strength of the community is a key pillar in maintaining livelihoods; people can depend on others in the community to lend small amounts when faced with a major family expenditure like a daughter's wedding. The financial success of some couples lies in their ability to generate surplus and build assets gradually: sales of gold jewelry to start a business or multiplying the number of cattle to earn more steady incomes. To generate surplus from a basic minimum, family members stick together. This allows the investments households make on their children's education. In some instances, the husband and the wife run the household based on mutual collaboration and expenditure sharing. Almost always, the couple makes sure that they have a varied basket of resources to fall back upon. People try to utilize a variety of skills to widen their income base and use different seasons' or household members' incomes for different purposes. Choruas manage their microscopic incomes with extreme caution and care, and maneuver through emergencies and family crises expertly. Those who earn seasonal incomes buy their annual supply of nonperishables when they are earning.

From our interviews with individuals, we found it possible to summarize the various financial strategies of the char poor under two headings, primary and secondary. They represent a combination of community- and household-level credit and money management systems. Figure 7.1 presents this schematically.

The relationship between the two sets of strategies is not linear and there are overlaps depending on the nature of the household and contingent situation. Household four, for example, lives on the bare minimum and adopts none of these strategies. Even then, one might describe their strategy

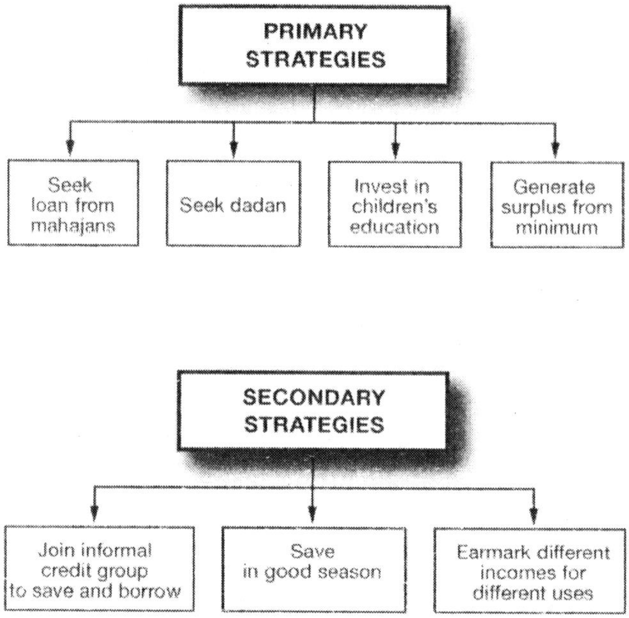

7.1 Coping Strategies of the Poor on Chars

as one of taking risk and seeing what the future holds for them. The case studies in this chapter demonstrate that unlike what is commonly expected, poor people can have significant financial skills. These skills are generally not depicted in quantitative measurements of formal system parameters. The informal systems of credit and household money management systems need further investigation to explore, for example, the mechanisms of capital accumulation, asset building, and factors that contribute to success and failure of individual households. The poor often have more faith in money-lenders than they do in banks, especially as they need quick access to money. They also value personal relationships, which often help them to survive through extreme crisis. These customary practices, state regulations, and market exchanges make up the hybrid economic landscape (Altman 2009a, 2009b; Gibson-Graham 2006). The diverse livelihood base developed through social relationships should not be beyond the understanding of policymakers in understanding what poor people do, what they need, and when they need it to sustain their livelihoods. Clearly, there is a need also to look at the specific contexts in which the poor live and manage money ingeniously through informal networks. Unfortunately—but perhaps not surprisingly—social factors such as the compulsion to marry off daughters are a significant reason for running into debt. The first household illustrates this and suggests that there is an urgent need to implement pro-poor policies to provide basic services like health, education, water, and sanitation, rather than focusing solely on financial inclusion. The implication of the study is that policy interventions that aim to tag the poor to the bottom rung of the formal monetary system as "micro partners" need rethinking.

The choruas manage their micro incomes with extreme caution and care, and maneuver through emergencies and family crises expertly. The collective strength of the community is also a key pillar to fall back upon; people can depend on others in the community to lend small amounts when faced with a major family expenditure. In summarizing the survival of people on the chars, we also see that the family comes first. Families stick together in the face of adversity and support each other. In some instances, the husband and wife in particular run the household based on mutual collaboration and expenditure sharing. The financial success of some households lies in their ability to generate surplus and build assets gradually: for example, the sales of gold jewelry to start a business that yields some income and to multiply the number of cattle to earn more steady income.

The diaries reveal day-to-day management of livelihood portfolios; as noted by Collins et al., "it is because of, not in spite of, their low and uncertain incomes that poor people are extremely active in financial intermediation, through whatever means are available to them" (2009: 176). But, our realization deviates somewhat from Collins et al. As we were going through the financial portfolios, we felt that a holistic approach would be essential if one ever considers assisting the char dwellers rather than just bringing in new institutions such as those for micro finance. Indeed, any support that people like Gopinath and Minati receive must also help to push forward improvements in other services. If the char dwellers are enabled, it should be through meeting their demands for health and better medical treatment, education for their children, and other support services rather than just providing access to banks and credit.

This study also illustrates the mental landscapes of choruas, undertaking what others would consider impossible risks. This psychology and courage of living every day as it comes throw new light on much-used terms like "resilience" and "risk." Glimpses into their ways of life allow us to ponder deeply how we should think about uncertainty and vulnerability.

Making a Living on Chars as a Woman

The char environment is not only a difficult one in which to survive, but also a new environment for women who have migrated either from Bihar or from Bangladesh. Regardless of their origin, almost all women in the chars work relentlessly from dawn to dusk to meet their households' minimum livelihood requirements. Although men too are engaged in a continual effort for survival, the struggle is more intensive for women than for men, as they also shoulder the entire responsibility of domestic chores. Women thus provide labor in productive activities—either in their own agricultural fields or as wage laborers—to supplement household incomes in addition to their domestic labor. It is common to come across women walking long distances with a basket of vegetables meant for sale in the town market. Combined with their domestic chores, this in general means that women face extreme hardships while living on the chars.

The gender-based variations in life experiences, workloads, and seasonal differences in generating livelihoods on the chars have been illuminated. These marked differences in the perceptions of the insecurity of life here between women and men are apparent in the following sections. Women are more concerned about homelessness caused by monsoonal inundations, floods, and riverbank erosion. Their inability to be a part of the mainland and their lack of legal citizenship that would allow them to obtain better, more secure, and wider livelihood options were mentioned repeatedly by Bangladeshi women.

Class and Caste: Continuing Roles

Women do not constitute a homogeneous group in char society. There are class differences as well as differences according to their place of origin and in their char environment. One section of these women was uprooted from Bihar and migrated to the Damodar chars due to extreme poverty. The other section comprises lower-caste Hindus who illegally migrated from Bangladesh. The cultural taboos of these two communities are totally different, the impact of which is visible in the social status and livelihood strategies of the women; however, differences in income levels are more pronounced in the families' socioeconomic locations. Caste differences are not much pronounced in the chars, since most households are from lower-caste and lower economic classes. Irrespective of differences in class and caste backgrounds, char women are placed at the bottom of society. They relentlessly struggle with poverty, flood, river erosion, and consequent homelessness, and, above all, with gender discrimination of various kinds. The poorest of the char women are those who are the heads of families without any adult male.

The class backgrounds of migrant women on the chars continue to play a significant role in the present status of these women in the family as well as in society. Societal inhibitions and family prestige imposed on women do not apply so much in the case of Bihari women, who are generally poor and lower-caste. In the case of Bangladeshi migrants, women are from different economic classes—some are from the landless working class, others from the land-owning cultivators' section. The social status and position of the family remain a dominant factor in the status of women. Therefore, although women's work participation rates are high in the chars, the participation rate of migrant women from Bangladesh generally in farming remains lower than that of women from the poorer labor classes. Thus, family status is the key to social prestige in the chars. In the interviews conducted during the study, some women expressed the view that as families become more settled, a social stigma is sometimes attached to their work. Neighbors see women from better-off households as not needing to work to earn money. For a woman to work is seen as a sign of poverty and a loss of prestige for middle-class families. This results in a continuous struggle for women to stay away from being "seen as working." Concerns about gender propriety are usually connected to family status among those who are better off (Salway et al. 2003). This concern does not seem so important for women in poorer households since, in cases of insecure and inadequate family incomes, gender propriety and norms take a back seat. Yet much of women's work on the chars remains socially unrecognized. They have little command over their income and assets, and little decision-making power within the household.

Although there are innumerable combinations, depending on family status, we observed five broad groups of char women: (a) women who work only within the household; (b) women who work on their own farms as family labor as well as managing domestic chores; (c) women who work as daily agricultural laborers on other farms as well as on their own farm and also manage the domestic chores; (d) women who are engaged in work other than agriculture—petty trading, giving private tuition, and bidi-making—as well as managing the household; and (e) women who are the sole breadwinner, that is, heads of women-headed households.

Irrespective of their roles within the household, the one common feature is the burden of survival and livelihood carried by women. Migration literature generally sees women as dependent migrants, yet they play major roles in providing livelihood support to families. Here, too, women's lives may have become more burdensome after migrating to the chars, which present a mismatch with the images they had of their future homes. The sheer pressure to survive ensures that there is no escape, and each woman we spoke to was expected to find ways to secure her family's survival.

Gender Roles in Livelihood Activities

Char women, as mentioned, make a significant contribution to managing the household. Gender-role differentiation is strong and women's work is identified with the private sphere of the household—all the domestic work is considered to be the responsibility of the women. In addition to these chores, women are burdened with heavy manual jobs that provide an uncertain income. In terms of their decision-making power, women are marginal both within the household and within society. With little or no security available through the state support system, women are forced to devise innovative ways of making a living in hostile circumstances.

As noted, the persistent social stigma attached to women's participation in the workforce is rooted in the perception of women's employment as a sign of poverty. Only poorer women (28 percent of the total women surveyed) earn a livelihood outside their home. Younger women in poorer households often take their children to their place of work. Working women who have other female household members (mothers-in-law, daughters, or daughters-in-law) to share the domestic burden with consider themselves lucky. Thus, despite the positive impact of women's labor force participation on human resource allocation and economic productivity, there are negative implications.

On the chars, poorer women work as wage laborers in agricultural fields, where they perform very similar tasks to men. Wage rates of agricultural laborers are more or less the same for women and men. Even during the potato-harvesting period in February and March, when there is huge demand for labor, ten- to fifteen-year-old girls working as laborers receive the same wages as men. Women work for seven to eight hours each day—from 7 AM to 5 or 6 PM, with a three-hour break for lunch between noon and 3 PM. Wage laboring requires great physical strength, and is difficult for those suffering from malnutrition.

Animal rearing is entirely the responsibility of women in almost all the households; it supplements family incomes, especially during the lean farming season. Although it is only carried out at a subsistence level, women generate sufficient livelihood resources to enable the household to cope during the lean farming season. Grazing is supervised by women and adds an extra burden to their already busy schedules. Like the chars themselves, the grazing fields are temporary in nature, as these lands are cropped during the peak farming season. With more and more people settling on chars, the fallow lands that can be used for community grazing are continuously shrinking due to the extension of agricultural land. This increases the domestic burden of women who collect fodder for domestic animals; collection of fodder is yet again women's responsibility, as their families cannot usually afford to purchase fodder from the market.

Women on the chars also make a significant livelihood contribution through another task—fishing. Although the Biharis as a community tend to fish, interestingly women from this community generally never go to fish in the river. On the contrary, while the Bangladeshis as a community tend to be farmers, fishing has traditionally been a woman's chore, so much so that some older women even catch fish by hand without using a net. Maya, an interviewee, recalls her experience:

> We go to fish in the river [the Damodar] whenever we want to eat fish curry or if there are no vegetables at home. Formerly, we never came back from the river without fish, but nowadays, there are fewer fish in the river.

Because of the construction of the DVC barrage upstream and the subsequent decrease in water, fishing for livelihood has changed over the past few decades. Now women with long, deep-water nets can carry out this activity with assistance from the male family members. The pollution of river water in the western part of the district where industrial sewage is drained directly into the river is another significant reason for the reduced fish catch. The decline in fishing as a source of livelihood in the Damodar chars has directly affected women's subsistence roles. Apart from supplementing the lack of vegetables in the house, women also sell their catch to others. Sandhya Das sells fish door-to-door and has a number of regular customers. Her husband never accompanies her because, as she explains:

> My husband . . . thinks it is below his dignity. He only goes to deliver to those houses who give us prior orders. But instead, he cooks in the evening when I sell the fish.

Thus, while jobs with low prestige are allotted to women, some husbands make it up by taking up household chores which they would not have undertaken under "normal" circumstances. Most women do not see the sexual division of labor unfavorably; Sandhya is happy because her husband does the cooking, which she might have to do otherwise, and comments how her travels introduce her to new people in the community.

As a rule, women are solely responsible for cooking at home; the collection and management of fuel is an important component of women's livelihoods on the charlands. Straw, crop residues, and cow dung are used as domestic fuel. All these fuel sources are stored for use during the rainy season. Poorer households with no agricultural land or cattle depend on wood, grasses, crop residues, dried weeds and bushes, rice bran, and so on for fuel throughout the year, which they collect from grazing land. Dried leaves and tree branches are also used as fuel. In times of crisis—for example, during the rainy season when there is no fuel available and stocks have been exhausted—women use tree branches from their own courtyards for fuel. Sometimes bushes on the fallow parts of chars are used for both fuel and fodder. With the increasing population on chars, people are forced to buy wood or jute straw to supplement their fuel requirements. Sadhana Mondal, a middle-aged housewife, says:

> We never bought fuel before. There was plenty of grass and bush, the collection of which was easy and enough for our annual consumption. Nowadays things have changed. Even the bit of the river channel that still exists is continuously being converted into farmland. We have to spend more time now to collect fuel and fodder from farther away. The supply is also decreasing as more of us are collecting these days.

It is clear that the shrinkage of common property resources has more negative impacts on the lives of char women than on the lives of men. Women from households where men earn by lifting sand from the riverbed have the additional burden of traveling substantial distances to deliver lunch to them every day in the sun. This task becomes unbearable especially during the summer months. The point made by Maloti, a twenty-five-year-old housewife, is illustrative:

> If you ask me what I dislike most to do, then I tell you that it is delivering lunch to my husband. The workplace of my husband is two-and-a-half kilometers from our house. In summer, it becomes difficult to walk on the hot sand for five kilometers.

Night is the only time for rest; longer winter nights are always precious to these women. Sandhya Sarker, an agricultural laborer, tells of her preference for the winter season:

> Our work as laborers increases in winter, as that is the busy cropping season in the chars. Still, we prefer winter, which gives us a longer night as well as a longer period of rest from our heavy physical burden. Nights are too short in the summer, which often does not allow us to recover from the physical stresses of the previous day. Because of that, I always look forward to the winter.

These women somehow manage to bear the burdensome life of the chars while wanting to leave the area permanently as soon as their husbands can afford to. They hope for a better life outside the char.

Power Relations within the Household

There is a general consensus among scholars (Agrawal 1994; Blumberg 1995; Engle 1995) that gender relations and relative power of women and men alter as incomes are redistributed and that asset-control pattern changes within the household facilitate women's capacity to improve their livelihoods. Women from poorer families living on the chars have less control over their incomes and over other kinds of power within the household. Women's position within the household depends upon the social value placed on them by their society and their consequent bargaining power. Sen (1990) believes that where women's acknowledged contribution to the household economy is greater than men's, particularly where women earn an income, they appear to have greater access to resources. In our study, mixed responses from women precluded a conclusive observation. In some cases, women obviously enjoyed power in the household due to the additional income they earned, but in other cases the relative power of men and women did not depend on the women's income. Only 38 percent of the working women can use their income, obviously for household expenditure. The remaining 62 percent did not even touch the money they earned: Their husbands took the income directly from the employer.

Do women have greater bargaining power when their contribution to household livelihoods is mediated through markets? The answer is: not always. Plenty of evidence suggested that char women often find it difficult to translate their income-earning power into real bargaining power within the family. On the chars, women find it difficult to enjoy the fruits of their income because the husbands assert their claim over the wives' earnings. Trying to argue with their husbands to have access to their wages can increase household conflict and result in domestic violence. Indrani Mondal, a thirty-six-year-old agricultural laborer, recounts the result of bargaining within her household:

> I have been earning as an agricultural laborer for at least ten years since the time we arrived from Bangladesh. My husband used to take my wages from the employer. Both of us earn; still, we cannot escape poverty. My husband spends money on alcohol every evening. In my younger days, I used to quarrel with him and ask for money every day. I ended up getting beaten by him. Nowadays I have given up. Who likes to be beaten after exhausting physical labor? Peace is more desirable than money. I just hope that my son will not follow his father's path. I try my best to train him well.

In a number of studies in Africa, Whitehead (1984, 1990) shows that women's incomes were appropriated by their husbands or were used to fulfill what are seen as women's responsibilities to provide for children. Similarly, on the chars of Damodar, some men not only utilize women's labor in the farms and control the incomes from the production of crops; they also try to take the wages earned by wives. Whatever access the women of the chars have to resources and income, it is used to increase welfare expenditure and the consequent well-being of the household. Our survey on the expenditure patterns of women who have access to household incomes revealed that women only use the money for food, medicine, children's education, and purchasing livestock as a future investment. Livestock assets generated by women can be sold and converted into ready cash in times of distress or emergency.

Perceiving the Char as "Home"

The char women try to reconstruct their lives in their new homes along the lines of what they had to leave behind; chars grow to become places with new environmental adjustments where gendered lives are interwoven with local realities and distant dreams. To our question "how do you feel about living here?" participants reacted in different ways. Gandhari, Ashalata, and Khukumani felt that they were living well. Gandhari said:

> I can get sufficient food and [we] have some cash in our hands. All of my family members give me patient hearing when decisions are made regarding any family matters.

Different generations and economic groupings of char women perceive their new home differently. While some younger women revealed discontent, women over forty with grown-up sons had more positive assessments. Older women do not need to work in the fields, as their families are now relatively better off; they are also less burdened with domestic chores, as daughters-in-law usually help with domestic chores. They can now afford to relax and do light household work and care for domestic animals. Some still feel that life in India is not as pleasant and contented as it was in Bangladesh. This is mainly because they do not have relatives or a wide support network with which to communicate and relate to. Sikha, who is younger than most interviewed wives, thinks that she was better off in Bangladesh. Not only did she work outside the home, she also was surrounded there by people whom she knew as part of the community:

> We never thought of this char as home. This area is not even what a real village is like. Here everybody is working from dawn to dusk to earn their basic livelihood. Nobody has any time to listen to others. We work, eat, and sleep. Is this a life?

Although many women thought that life in the chars is better than the violent persecution families faced in Bangladesh, when it comes to coping with a new environment such as the chars, much of the work burden falls on women. To others, it provides a foothold on Indian soil that offers relatively less competition from locals. The hierarchies migrant women bring with them from their original societies remain intact in making a new home in the chars. How long these will remain is not yet clear.

Women-Headed Households

Women-headed households on chars include divorced, deserted, or widowed women. Their greater vulnerability arises from the "activity burden" and a higher dependency ratio for being the single income earner. The proportion of these households in the chars is not high in comparison to both developed and developing countries' standards (that is, 20 percent and 33 percent, respectively) and these women are mostly circumstantial heads of households; for example, the number of women-headed households on Char Gaitanpur is only 11 out of a total of 199 households. They are mostly *de jure* women heads (widows and deserted women), that is, women who are legal and customary heads of their own households with full control over household incomes and expenditures. Sometimes de facto heads (married women heading their households in the absence of their husbands), though few in number, are also found on chars. In specific cases, we came across households where the husband permanently lived in Bangladesh with his first wife, leaving his second wife to run her own household in the chars. These men may visit the chars once or twice a year.

Women heads range in age between thirty-two and fifty-five years, averaging forty to forty-five years, which matches the findings by other scholars (Vecchio and Roy 1998). In some cases, the women had come to the char with their husbands, who later either died or left them. In other cases, they came as widows with their children and have close family ties nearby on the char. The average family size is four to five persons. Some women have lived on the chars for ten to fifteen years, whereas others are relatively new. Most women put great importance on children's education, although in some cases their education cannot continue beyond the primary level. Acute poverty means that women with grown-up children will encourage them to earn in order to supplement the household income. For a woman with an older son who can act as the income-generating adult male member in the household, it is slightly easier. This son gradually takes over as the head of the household as the earning capacity of the woman diminishes.

The choruas' livelihoods are greatly dependent on the number of earning household members. Women-headed households are even poorer because of the lack of adult male earning members. They are marginalized in char society in respect to income-generating activities, social status, health, and children's education. Their poverty also affects their ability to provide for adequate self-protection; as a result, they are less able to create safe conditions during floods and riverbank erosion. Network support and the social capital of kinship relations are the chief mechanisms that women-headed households use to mobilize resources and cope with contingencies.

Women heads of households are aware of their low status within the char social milieu and, hence, are engaged in a daily struggle to secure their means of survival by finding solutions to daily problems. This raises the issue of "belonging," of the attachments of a particular set of women to a particular place that forms a specific context. In the case of the Damodar chars, extreme poverty and, in some cases, noncitizen identity act as critical elements in increasing their vulnerability to reduced livelihood choices.

Vulnerabilities affect all char households, but lack of an adult male member makes it difficult for women-headed households. Children's illness due to malnutrition is a recurrent problem in the poorer households, affecting both the expenditure and income of the households negatively. Working women cannot carry on with their work if their children fall ill. When they stay at home, family income decreases, and daily expense increases because they have to purchase medicines. Illness of the sole earning woman member of a household engaged in day labor leads to extreme vulnerability. Women-headed households rarely have significant savings with which to run the household for a length of time without an income. In such periods of crisis, women usually seek help from their friends, relatives, and neighbors. Sometimes they borrow money or seek advance payments from the farmers on whose farms they work. This sort of advance payment often takes a heavy toll and sometimes leads to exploitation, as the women have to work at a lower wage to compensate the lender for the interest of the loan amount.

Making a Living

With little or no formal support from the state, women are forced to find the means to stay alive in these hostile circumstances in the chars. In addition to the enormous physical strain of carrying out domestic work, they endure high levels of mental stress arising out of the demand to meet their families' bare minimum needs. The women are marginal not only to the char society at large, but also sometimes within their own households. It is easy to exploit their labor at a low wage as they are forced to take loans or advance payments from farmers to cope with the lean-season crises. They are rarely invited to village meetings, which are mostly organized with the male members of each household. Inside the households, the women are usually the decision-makers. The situation is different for the women household heads whose grown-up sons take over the responsibility of decision-making for the household as soon as they begin to earn.

The casual and low-paid jobs, such as working as agricultural wage laborers, that women household heads are engaged in yield only uncertain incomes. Although women agricultural laborers may earn the same wages as men, the nature of the jobs offered is gender-coded. For example, women do not till the land with animal-driven plows or carry bundles of crops from the fields to courtyards. This restricts the scope of work and shrinks the household income. Job opportunities are seasonal and coping with seasonal employment is not as easy for women as it is for male agricultural laborers. Men have a range of wage labor to choose from; women do not. Men can also easily switch over to other off-farm seasonal laboring activities available locally outside the chars; women cannot. Lean seasons, therefore, are harder for women than they are for men, and they depend upon fishing in the river, growing vegetables in the courtyard for household subsistence, sharing livestock rearing, and selling livestock resources, especially poultry and goats. Only four women-headed households in the entire area have cultivated land that they lease out, which adds a significant income of Rs. 800 to Rs. 1,000 per crop per bigha to the household's overall earnings. Women who own small pieces of cultivable land usually lease these out for cash. Some women engage in petty trading of vegetables when their char is accessible to a nearby town, such as Burdwan. Dashania Mahato is one woman who has taken up such trading. Her economic status is relatively better in comparison to other women engaged in agricultural labor. Dashania laments:

> My husband passed away, leaving behind three children. I started petty trading then. I work for 365 days in a year. I do not have to depend on others. I have married off two daughters on my own. My son goes to school. I do not allow him to work to help me. I am looking forward to the future: when my son grows up and starts earning, I will give up this hard work.

Mobilizing Trust and Support

Financial, social, and physical support from either kin or neighbors plays an immensely important role in the livelihoods of women-headed households on chars. Help from kin often serves to meet daily livelihood needs during the lean season. For women, access to private loans from local moneylenders is restricted; hence, during emergencies they approach male neighbors to act as guarantors. Such help may take the form of borrowing rice, foodstuffs, or cash.

One of the main family needs is dealing with a daughter's marriage, which requires large amounts of money to pay the dowry and to give a feast to the neighbors. Dipa Sarkar points out that having relatives nearby helps because her father and brother arranged her daughter's marriage. Tulsi Barui recollects her daughter's wedding and how everyone helped her:

> I asked the community leader for help—he organized a meeting and asked every household to give something. Each family promised to help either in the form of cash or in kind. A list was made in that meeting, and everyone kept their word. I still needed some more cash, which I secured through a loan from my employer, a farmer. I paid off this loan by working for him over the years. Without the help of these people, I could not have married my daughter off.

Emergencies occurring during floods are also dealt with collectively. Men help by carrying the movable assets away to safer areas on the embankment and women organize for food. If the mud huts are washed away by floodwaters, both men and women are forced to seek shelter in the verandas (placed higher on the ground) of other's houses. When floodwaters recede, the huts are reconstructed quickly with the help of neighbors and other community members. Most of the women we spoke to acknowledged this assistance and put importance on social relations that ensure their survival. This is not uncommon for poor people in difficult situations, but in the chars the value of these networks cannot be overstated. The lack of citizenship makes such intracommunity social capital essential for the survival of Bangladeshi migrant women.

Both physical and mental stresses are higher for women who act as household heads. Our conversations with the women were often interrupted by deep sighs: long working days, short lunch breaks, lack of rest, excessive work, and poor nutrition characterize their lives. Vickery (1977) noted that the "double day" economic burden made all women-headed households time-poor—lacking in leisure time (Rosenhouse 1989)—causing the intergenerational transmission of disadvantage through nutritional deficiency, illiteracy, and children having to labor (Buvinic and Gupta 1997). All these characteristics of women-headed households are reflected in the Damodar chars.

Poverty also takes its toll on the health of women, who often do not get sufficient nutrition to compensate for their heavy physical labor. This makes some children weak and unwilling to take up physical labor. Apart from suffering from malnutrition, some children of women-headed households are also illiterate or have only a very low level of education. It is not easy to pay for the education of a child. Dipa can afford to send her daughter to the local primary school, but regrets that she cannot purchase textbooks or afford to arrange private tuition for her daughter, and laments:

> How will she be educated? She has to look after the house when I am at work. Getting an education is not possible for the children of poor people like us.

The relatively younger women with young children are usually burdened with more domestic responsibilities. If there is no other female member in the family, infants are often taken to the place of work. Tukurani Ray, the de facto household head on Char Gaitanpur, started working in the fields just five days after the birth of her fourth daughter. Since her husband lives in Bangladesh with his first wife and only occasionally visits the family in India, she had no family support when she gave birth to her youngest daughter:

> I had nobody to assist me except my little daughters. We did not have sufficient food for about a month. Soon, I had to start working even though my health had not fully recovered. Nowadays I feel weak—when working in the field with the strong sun over my head, I feel exhausted.

Though Tukurani has a husband, her livelihood stresses are no less than those of widowed or deserted women household heads.

Being illegal migrants, char women have neither legal rights over local resources nor access to the state support system for poor women, such as the schemes for poverty alleviation and widow's pension. The women household heads have strong perceptions and feelings about their lack of citizenship rights. Yet, some, like Dipa Sarkar, are not particularly concerned about their lack of citizenship. Dipa said:

> We are living on this char far away from mainland society because of the lack of citizenship. We are poor, illiterate people who can offer only our physical labor. To do manual work one does not need citizenship documents. That is why I am not interested in pursuing that piece of paper.

Not everyone feels this way; there are many who pursue local channels and become successful in obtaining valid papers for themselves and their families. Men are more successful in building networks with and getting access to people living across embankments. Unlike men, women heads of households experience difficulty accessing informal networks through which citizenship documents are obtained. A bitter Sumita Sarkar comments:

> We have neither money nor an adult male in the household who can do the rounds for obtaining Indian citizenship documents. Like me, my children will also remain illegal people.

Another group of women are eager to obtain Indian citizenship documents, but as women, they cannot access the informal networks necessary for this. They are aware of the problems related to their noncitizen status. Tulsi Barui clarifies:

> We do not get any economic support from the local panchayat, as we do not exist to the Indian government. Without legal citizenship, we cannot move out of this char. We are stuck here; I fear that my children will also suffer.

This statement brings us back to our characterization of char livelihoods as "beyond the state." We see that both Biharis and Bangladeshis living on chars are intimately connected to the land and the river, yet they are keenly aware of the vulnerabilities of living in a dynamic environment. The char location provides a unique setting—a risky environment with just about enough resources to somehow scrape together a living—providing a geographical context in understanding the livelihood strategies of women-headed households. Here, we see the importance of locality—the key characteristic of place—playing a major role in influencing the activities of two sets of translocal women. The focus of our attention remains on how, in the shifting sands of chars, choruas build a sense of community in securing livelihoods for themselves and their families. Chars are not deterritorialized in the process in which culture and power is enmeshed, even though in the chars neither locality nor community is rooted in "natural" identities. Char communities, through their complex and hybrid livelihood strategies, create new forms of economic citizenship that are beyond the state.

CHAPTER 8

Living on Chars, Drifting with Rivers

. . . from water was made available every living thing—THE HOLY QUR'AN

āpo vā idaṁ sarvaṁ viśvā bhūtānyāpā prāṇā vā āpaḥ paśava āpo 'nnam āpo 'mṛtam āpaḥ samrāḍ āpo virāḍ āpaḥ svarāḍ āpaś chandāṁsyāpo jyotīṁṣyāpo yajūṁṣyāpaḥ satyam āpaḥ sarvā devatā āpo bhūr bhuvaḥ suvar āpa aum [All this is indeed water. All beings are water. Breath is indeed water. Animals are water. Food is water. Nectar is water. Sovereignty is water. Splendour is water. Independence is water. The Vedic metres are water. The celestial bodies are water. The Vedic formulae are water. Truth is water. All the deities are water. *Bhūḥ bhuvaḥ* and *suvaḥ* are water. *Oṁ!*]—MAHĀNĀRĀYAṆA UPANIṢAD 29TH ANUVĀKA (translation by McComas Taylor, Australian National University, 2012)

Coming from two different ecological contexts, the first from the lands of sand and thirst and the second from the floodplains of the Ganga, which are one of the wetter parts of the world, the two epigraphs both reflect a passionate, age-old reverence and respect for and attachment to water. Of water in all its forms, rivers have probably been the most loved by humans. As the ancient Egyptians intuitively realized, water flowing in the rivers is one of the most powerful and awe-inspiring of all natural forces, and we are dependent on it. Other cultures have attributed primacy to water flowing in rivers as well: Strabo thought that rivers (and mountains) constitute one of the essential features in describing the world and in "geographizing" a place (mentioned in Brittain 1959: 204). The fourteenth-century Islamic traveler Ibn Battuta described rivers as "a double-edged sword" because they give as well as take human life. In almost all cultures, rivers evoke images of spiritual-intellectual energy that cascades through the manifold planes of life, linking the humans intimately with their source, nourishing and sustaining life, and flowing forth to connect one part of the landscape with the other. Rivers are always present in the collective consciousness of Bengal, not just as symbols or even as physical manifestations of cultural meanings, but forming the relations between places. We sometimes forget that rivers are much more than just conduits for water, that every day they not only frame people's lives and experiences, but also connect places and peoples. Rivers are not simply a source of water (and, hence, human life and society) or a sanctified element of nature; they are also an important part of the self-definition of communities and are an element in people's sense of place. Throughout history, human societies have interacted with rivers and each has changed the other. Such interactions have not stopped; local people who live on, near, or around rivers learn to intimately know the changing moods of the river. The riverine communities not only use the rivers; almost every aspect of their everyday lives is adjusted to the rivers' rise and fall. As the rivers influence their lives, they too learn to use the resources that the rivers offer them. The rivers of Bengal, carrying the fecund waters of life, therefore present potent symbols of the regenerative power that is inherent in nature. They are benevolent, forgiving, and giving. Even their beds are the "wombs" that provide life to riverine communities, their flow the surge of time itself. The rivers of Bengal are also powerful entities: When in spate, they are not docile, but have a tremendous fierceness, a brutality that reveals their destructive powers, which they unleash through floods.

As rivers descend from their sources and weave their way to the sea, they pick up sand and silt. At the delta, where land and water are joined and neither land nor water is independent of the other, "the land is a land of rivers, mixed up with water and mud" (Bandyopadhyay, quoted in Lahiri-Dutt 2006: 402). Here, at the delta, the innumerable rivers crisscrossing each other have captured a culture, and set in relief the imageries of riverine ways of life. This is where the rivers have carved out new lands and created new horizons for human communities whose lives are inextricably shaped by the rivers themselves. But humans have also left their imprints on the layers of silt through their interactions with nature. Speaking of the region, Rudra says that "the layers of silt of the Ganges delta hide history" (2008: 3). Even though we study hybrid environments, we can only trace a small part of the imprints left by the passage of time. As the rivers flow "dirty" with the fecundity of life, the tremendous amount of sand and biological life flows with them. Sands are important to us: As geographers, we are taught to see the cosmos in a grain of sand. A grain of sand has been on this earth from the beginning of its creation and has drifted along in the river to be deposited in the sea or in a depressed spot to form a piece of rock, only to be eroded again. This cycle has gone on and on from the beginning of this earth, and goes on through today. This is how we see land, made of grains of sand that have existed for much longer than us—probably for millions of years on this earth, since the beginning of Creation. Each insignificant grain of sand has experienced the breaking-up and rebuilding of lands. It has rolled and rolled, turned into a piece of land, and again flowed along with the waters. Together with innumerable other grains, it built lands, only to be turned into another grain and to submerge under water.

Elements of nature such as the rivers do not stand alone within a specific context; they are part of the interconnected ecological processes within which both plant and human communities live.[1] Rivers are complex systems that do complex ecological work. Ecologists Postel and Richter (2003) argue that rivers need to be valued for a host of reasons: some spiritual, some aesthetic, and some practical. Their interpretation starts with pointing out the central role rivers play in the global cycling of water between the sea, air, and land. A similar view is offered by Wohl (2011), who emphasizes that despite the fact that rivers offer a wealth of services and resources, throughout the world they have been impoverished, which has in turn impoverished all creatures that rely on them. One of the crucial tasks that rivers perform, and one that is often overlooked, is the transportation of not only waters but also silt and sediments, as mentioned in the previous paragraph. Descending from their sources, rivers carry sand and silt to deposit them on the mouth of their exit before "emptying themselves" into the sea. This silt is vital for supporting human and ecological systems.

Amitav Ghosh has written a memorable description of the occluded waters of the river near the delta mouth in *The Hungry Tide*, the "curtain of silt" that hangs to block and disorient light within a few centimeters below the water's surface. The young girl in the novel, a researcher, visiting the field to study dolphins that are rapidly becoming extinct in the Sundarbans, falls into the river and realizes that beneath the shimmering surface of the water

> lies a flowing stream of suspended matter in which visibility does not extend beyond an arm's length. With no lighted portal to point the way, top and bottom and up and down become very quickly confused. (2004: 54)

The "placental sac" that envelops her, the shroud that folds her in its cloudy wrappings, is not "pure water"; this water contains so much silt that it can be described only as part water and part mud. This is a hybrid material formed of both land and water. Made up of and built by rivers and their silt, the whole of the Bengal delta is a unique hybrid environment, a landscape where the boundaries of water and ground penetrate each other and where history is enmeshed within the physicality of its formation. It is no wonder, therefore, that this unstable land, formed as a colloidal system and worked and reworked continuously by hydraulic volatility, cannot be neatly placed within a single category. Consequently, D'Souza observes (2004: 241) about the delta that it "is an interstitial zone where land, river and sea collide and shape each other. The delta, as an ecological complex, does not fit clearly into most familiar tropes about nature in South Asia." In this book, we have spoken about only a minuscule part of the junction of land and water that the delta represents and have brought to life the ways the poor defy all conventional conceptions of vulnerability and security and adjust to the ways the rivers are. It is these microscopic pieces of chars that throw robust challenges to macro generalizations about the environment. We begin to see that the rivers and their waters are not without silt and realize that sands are part and parcel of the waters' flows and the lands that the rivers build. As human geographers, we come back to the core values of topophilia (Tuan 1974) and the close bond that it represents between people and place in the microcosmic setting of the chars. We have only provided a brief glimpse into the rivers and the lands through which they flow, creating a setting in which the boundaries between water and land are elusive and ever changing.

Another point made early in this book is that the rivers of tropical lands are different from those in temperate lands. Such differences have been noted, observed, and understood in different ways. For example, in their book *Varieties of Environmentalism*, Guha and Martinez-Alier (1997) have highlighted the geographical, cultural, and historical contexts within which different environmental movements have taken root. They begin with the story of the English writer Aldous Huxley's trip to Asia in the winter of 1925–1926. An essay on Huxley's Indian travels was published in 1929 with the intriguing title "Wordsworth in the Tropics," which, Guha and Martinez-Alier comment, exhibits the easy confidence of someone who has just experienced something entirely new, which expanded his range of understanding. In Huxley's view, the appreciation and love for nature could only flourish in benign temperate ecologies: It could scarcely be exported to the dark, forbidding, and dangerous tropics. The worship of nature can come easily to those "who live beneath a temperate sky and in the age of Henry Ford." This is because nature in the tropics is utterly different, not quite "enslaved to man"; "under a vertical sun, and nourished by the equatorial rains, [nature] is not at all like the chaste, mild deity who presides over the . . . prettiness, the cosy sublimities of the Lake District."

Yet, in spite of this acute understanding of difference, the modernist worldview initiated unprecedented and profound transformations of the rivers all over the world. The rivers in Bengal, with their constantly shifting and changing courses, were seen as inconvenient and in need of control. The long history of human life and living with water became invisible and was ignored by the modernist worldview that was in favor of engineering its control. Thus, engineering control of rivers came to be seen as fundamental to the economic and social advancement of communities living with the rivers and continues to dominate mainstream thinking about waters and rivers (Barrows 1948; Brammer 2004; Parker 1949). Indeed, while some societies have reaped substantial economic rewards from these modifications of rivers, we now know that changed river ecologies have also had far-reaching consequences to some communities. The worldview was expressed in the inaugural address of the American President Theodore Roosevelt when he said that "great storage works are necessary" to "equalize the flow of streams and to save the flood waters" (quoted in Postel and Richter 2003). This worldview encouraged much of the world to embark on a similar path (Boyce 1990), and also led to the control of the Damodar river. As the government engineers built dams and reservoirs and diked the banks to contain unruly floodwaters within its channel, the Damodar created a completely new world within it about which those living on solid land knew little. These dams and diversions have fundamentally altered the timing and volume of the natural flow regimes of the river, affected its health and the aquatic ecosystems within it. But the rivers have also nurtured the livelihoods of people, further nourishing the hybrid environments existing within the two banks of the river. Yet in many countries, engineers continue to devise plans to control rivers and view their shifting courses as deviant. Even today, we try to stabilize them by confining them in single, straight-line channels that do not spill across the banks into the floodplains or migrate from side to side across the valley bottom. We have yet to accept that this confinement diminishes the complexity and diversity of habitats that nourish the human communities. To make this point, a renowned river expert, Wohl (2011), selected ten of the world's largest rivers to illustrate how the changes humans impose can impoverish the rivers, and by extension impoverish all the innumerable creatures, including the humans, who rely on them. Water control reduces rivers to a stand-alone system—neglecting the holistic connections between nature, its various elements, and humans—leading to unintended consequences. Such consequences are at times disastrous for those living with the river; yet, as has been depicted in this book, people find a way to use and adapt to the changes wrought by river control.

Since we did not follow a linear manner of presenting research, this chapter is not exactly meant as a conclusion but can be treated more as a reflection on the research itself. Conclusions were partly presented in every chapter to retain their distinctiveness. As the char environments and livelihoods are distinctive from the mainland, they are also distinctive even from each other. Each char has its own history of settlement and its distinctive culture and social economy. If chars in general can be described as hybrid environments that defy the boundaries between land and water, each individual char presents, in a microcosm, real examples of the hybridity that we spoke of in the first chapter. Through this diversity and hybridity, chars pose a challenge to positivist ways of thinking about nature, lands, and waters, and also human lives and livelihoods. Increasingly, we begin to accept fragmentation of reality and multiple ways of seeing and understanding the world.

This book has been full of detail. To show how hybrid environments are coproduced by nature and culture, we delved into the colonial histories of the land revenue system and embankment construction, and into the postcolonial continuation of these systems of separation and control. We examined agrarian transition as well as the history of dam construction. We traced out hundreds of individuals' histories, told their stories in their voices as best we could, and tracked their livelihoods. Without a micro view, it would have been impossible to show how individuals survive by scavenging the diverse yet tiny resources offered by their environment. Seen from the top, and from a distance in the context of wider transition and diversification of livelihoods, that "basket" would appear quite small. But, as we have shown, particularly in chapter 7, the drive for survival pushes individuals and families to use the smallest resources, and enables them to manage these resources efficiently and expertly to achieve the best survival results. The grinding poverty of char dwellers is not something that we want to play down. Indeed, we do think that a holistic approach might be essential in helping them to secure a better livelihood. From that point, however, we also move into more subtle areas and issues of legality and illegality, moving beyond the state as the point of departure. We also bring the borderland debate into geography to present the chars as undocumented or extralegal and fluid spaces where the movement of people cannot be pinned down geographically to one specific site. Our microscopic study of char livelihoods not only illuminates the importance of specific geographic context in understanding special adjustment processes as well as illicit flows into what James Scott (2009: 22–32) described as "nonstate spaces," where resilient and resistant peoples seek refuge in response to statist consolidation of borders. The research also points to the need to rethink boundaries and borders, and the illegitimacies that are produced by these artificial boundaries. Indeed, any support that char people might receive must also help to push forward improvements in other services to enable them to improve on the assets they have created in the absence of basic supports and services. Any assistance should be through meeting their demands for health and better medical treatment, education for their children, and other support services, rather than just providing access to banks and credit. To live with the river and to make a living on the chars is not an easy task. The illegitimacy of existence, the lack of ownership of productive resources that ordinary citizens can claim, and the lack of access to services that many of us take for granted hide the many complexities in the ways that people seize minimal opportunities to build assets and livelihoods. Understanding this expertise has been a long journey for us, but one that we hope will illuminate a few gray areas or at least open up new ways of thinking about the environment and livelihood. In the context of India, where the two are being increasingly posed as antagonistic to each other, we conclude the book with the note that livelihoods linked to the hybrid hydraulic regimes of tropical rivers are also intrinsically hybrid. On chars, water remains the most important source of wealth as well as the biggest threat to a "secure" life. Water determines the production cycle, which determines the ups and downs in the well-being of families. No conventional ways of understanding security and vulnerability apply to the lives that are defined by water; people do the best they can on an everyday basis, either individually or collectively. They adopt tentative and micro-level strategies to adjust to the ever-changing environment and mobilize the intangible skills and assets that they have either brought into or developed through living on the chars. Things such as collective credit and mutual cooperation, trust and hope, family and community rules, and values and norms, all informal and often intangible things, assume key roles in producing this hybrid environment.

At the end, we come back to the wider question of how one might connect the hybrid environments and livelihoods of char people to wider theoretical issues within contemporary debates on environment livelihoods. French sociologist-historian Lucien Febvre observed in his review, published in 1923, of Paul Vidal de la Blache's work titled *Geography Textbook: A Geographical Introduction to History* that "nature does not drive man along a particular road, but it offers a number of opportunities from among which man is free to select" (1962 [1923]). This statement must be viewed with extreme caution; clearly, char dwellers have little autonomy over most parts of their lives and almost none over the environment within which they live. Yet, as we have shown in this book, they do not lack agency in using their experiential wisdom in making choices to shape certain other aspects of their lives. The livelihood of char people represents a break from sense empiricism, and is best expressed in Vidal de la Blache's words: where "[hu]man joins in nature's game." That human perception is not all, that human behavior is not fully controlled by culture, and that nature does shape human lives, among other such facts, are revealed through the present micro-regional study of the complex whole of how players play their individual hands. This way, our expository and intricately empirical study joins one end of that explanatory continuum of systematic methodological interpretation instead of falling into the exceptionalist trap.

Appendix

Full Census Data for Surveyed Chars

	Gaitanpur	Satyanandapur	Majher Mana	Namosonda	Bhasapur	Joykrishnapur	Lakshmipur	Chakpur	Gobcal	Bikrampur	Simisimi	Kasba	Total
Total Number of Households	199	100	148	29	137	86	13	27	64	74	35	400	1,312
Family Head													
Male	188	95	139	21	124	83	10	20	49	65	29	363	1,186
Female	11	5	9	8	13	3	3	7	15	9	6	37	126
Religion													
Hindu	199	100	148	29	137	86	13	27	64	60	35	400	1,298
Muslim	0	0	0	0	0	0	0	0	0	14	0	0	14
Caste													
General	0	0	0	15	8	85	13	27	28	16	9	40	241
SC	N/A	99	N/A	14	124	1	0	0	36	45	26	308	653
ST	0	1	0	0	0	0	0	0	0	11	0	0	12
OBC	0	0	0	0	5	0	0	0	0	2	0	52	59
Type of Family													
Single	52	90	95	28	99	56	9	16	32	66	18	345	906
Joint	147	10	53	1	38	30	4	11	32	8	17	55	406
Family Size													
1–2	9	7	8	2	9	4	0	4	5	7	2	24	81
3–4	61	37	87	15	52	27	8	4	13	19	7	150	480
5–6	72	43	33	10	50	30	4	19	32	31	25	163	512
7–8	35	7	15	2	16	13	1	0	13	10	1	52	165
9–10	17	5	5	0	3	9	0	0	1	5	0	7	52
> 10	4	2	0	0	7	3	0	0	0	2	0	4	22
Total Population													
Male	416	267	456	70	368	254	29	68	180	211	88	1,030	3,437
Female	421	225	404	54	353	224	29	54	156	183	79	958	3,140
Total	837	492	860	124	721	478	58	122	336	394	167	1,988	6,577
0–6 Age Group													
Male	121	34	132	7	40	19	2	1	10	23	3	110	502
Female	110	29	101	4	42	26	2	2	7	26	7	116	472

Literacy Level (Number of Persons)													
Illiterate	455	158	516	48	229	150	7	39	109	121	67	1,461	**3,360**
Literate	382	295	344	76	490	334	51	83	227	273	100	527	**3,182**
Up to Primary	214	96	283	48	283	135	11	21	83	242	50	439	**1,905**
Up to Secondary	159	185	55	19	178	186	38	60	135	23	49	879	**1,966**
Up to Higher Secondary	2	9	4	0	19	4	1	0	5	6	0	75	**125**
Graduate	6	4	2	2	12	9	1	1	4	1	1	62	**105**
Post Graduate	1	1	0	0	0	0	0	1	0	1	0	6	**10**
Number of Earning Members per Family													
1	70	40	66	4	60	24	5	11	15	28	9	253	**585**
2	84	39	63	19	40	33	5	11	23	32	15	84	**448**
3	38	14	5	3	21	21	2	3	19	7	5	40	**178**
4	5	4	5	2	16	6	1	2	3	4	6	14	**68**
> 4	2	3	9	1	0	2	0	0	4	3	0	9	**33**
Sex of the Earning Members Taken Together													
Male	282	146	222	43	176	153	20	45	119	110	59	563	**1,938**
Female	103	46	51	20	22	14	5	5	34	36	19	79	**434**
Size of Land Holdings (in Bighas)													
< 1	27	25	2	0	8	5	0	1	1	9	0	29	**107**
1–2	39	16	28	3	49	11	0	2	9	18	7	101	**283**
2.1–4	54	7	54	5	22	13	6	12	15	9	14	112	**323**
4.1–6	15	3	34	10	9	18	4	8	17	3	8	64	**193**
6.1–8	7	3	8	3	9	8	1	2	10	2	3	33	**89**
8.1–10	2	0	11	1	4	6	1	2	4	1	0	22	**54**
10.1–15	2	3	7	0	3	7	0	0	2	0	0	2	**26**
15.1–20	0	0	2	0	1	3	0	0	1	0	0	4	**11**
> 20	0	0	0	0	1	1	0	0	0	0	0	0	**2**
Cropping Type (Number of Households)													
Single	11	0	2	0	3	0	0	0	0	2	0	2	**20**
Double	97	25	93	19	77	51	12	25	52	23	32	114	**620**
Triple	38	32	51	3	26	21	0	2	7	17	0	251	**448**

Treatment of Diseases in Households													
Health Center	64	16	34	0	59	0	0	0	3	27	0	46	249
Private Clinic	82	72	85	29	73	86	13	27	61	26	35	292	881
Both	53	12	29	0	4	0	0	0	0	31	0	62	191
Television in Households													
Yes	20	8	13	17	14	23	4	10	22	1	8	86	226
No	179	92	135	12	123	63	9	17	42	73	27	314	1,086
Radio in Households													
Yes	78	36	81	24	53	53	12	24	53	20	32	187	653
No	121	64	67	5	84	33	1	3	11	54	3	213	659
Telephone in Households													
Yes	1	2	0	2	1	17	3	1	7	0	3	17	54
No	198	98	148	27	136	69	10	26	57	74	32	383	1,258
Newspaper Purchase (by Households)													
Yes	0	5	2	0	5	0	0	1	0	0	1	7	21
No	199	95	146	29	132	86	13	26	64	74	34	393	1,291
Bicycles in Household													
Yes	133	76	114	30	120	110	14	26	70	59	37	516	1,305
No	66	24	34	0	22	3	0	1	0	15	0	33	198
Motorcycles in Household													
Yes	2	4	0	6	9	29	4	5	18	2	7	24	110
No	197	96	148	23	128	57	9	22	46	72	28	376	1,202
Domestic Fuel Use in Households													
Cow Dung Cake	151	34	17	19	79	43	13	26	51	25	35	44	537
Wood	146	40	85	29	113	77	13	27	64	37	35	158	824
Twigs, etc., from the Jungle	0	27	17	0	0	0	0	0	0	33	0	150	227
Straw	102	12	28	0	24	1	0	0	0	11	0	196	374
Dry Leaves and Other Biomass	15	11	0	9	37	34	0	0	10	43	1	79	239
Coal	5	9	0	1	8	6	0	4	0	10	0	7	50
Pieces of Dried Bamboo	7	1	0	0	2	0	0	0	0	0	0	6	16
Liquefied Petroleum Gas	0	1	0	2	1	1	0	1	5	0	0	0	11
Kerosene Stove	2	0	0	0	5	0	0	0	0	0	0	12	19

Number of Meals Cooked Every Day in Households													
One	8	5	4	5	12	4	0	1	3	2	2	57	103
Two	162	87	129	24	123	82	13	26	61	71	33	330	1,141
Three	29	8	15	0	2	0	0	0	0	1	0	13	68
Type of Wall Material of Houses													
Mud	86	37	57	25	78	44	12	22	60	61	31	167	680
Brick	13	4	2	5	15	6	1	1	4	4	3	62	120
Woven Bamboo Slices (*Chanch*)	23	31	16	0	34	24	0	2	0	5	1	51	187
Tin	10	14	8	0	15	12	0	2	0	0	0	18	79
Bamboo	67	6	65	0	5	0	0	0	0	0	0	121	264
Catkin Grass	0	11	0	0	0	0	0	0	0	5	0	0	16
Roof Material Used in Houses													
Straw	123	16	72	4	39	8	2	9	12	44	13	123	465
Tin	27	79	70	20	90	78	10	17	44	33	22	209	699
Asbestos	18	7	4	2	4	0	1	0	3	2	0	24	65
Concrete	0	0	0	4	2	0	0	1	4	0	0	13	24
Tiles	31	1	2	0	2	0	0	0	0	0	0	24	60
Catkin Grass	0	0	0	0	0	0	0	0	0	3	0	51	54
Household Latrines													
Yes	104	35	56	17	37	29	5	19	44	47	11	128	532
No	95	65	92	12	100	57	8	8	20	27	24	272	780
Bathroom/ Shower/Washing Area													
Yes	44	15	26	17	26	26	3	16	38	7	6	103	327
No	155	85	122	12	111	60	10	11	26	67	29	297	985
Tube Well													
Yes	124	84	125	24	95	80	7	18	53	53	23	367	1,053
No	75	16	23	5	42	6	6	9	11	21	12	33	259
Domestic Animals													
Buffalo and Bull	218	38	0	37	100	104	20	44	78	43	44	290	1,016
Milk Cow	253	158	0	29	168	108	17	31	83	63	32	477	1,419
Goat	383	198	N/A	30	166	132	32	39	124	124	95	435	1,758
Poultry	475	45	0	43	69	0	69	33	219	105	141	620	1,819
Pig	40	0	0	0	4	0	0	0	0	0	0	4	48
Agricultural Equipment in Households													
Cart	1	9	0	8	10	13	6	7	28	1	13	2	98

Hoe	0	24	0	15	46	41	10	20	33	22	21	114	346
Shallow Pump	56	42	129	16	99	81	8	23	51	24	23	341	893
Savings													
Bank or Life Insurance Corporation	23	26	13	28	76	85	7	16	61	10	17	119	477
Post Office	4	2	0	0	3	0	0	0	0	1	0	4	14
Both	0	1	0	0	10	0	0	0	1	1	0	0	13
No Deposit	172	71	135	2	48	1	6	11	12	62	18	277	815
Loan to Repay													
Yes	132	65	78	5	85	39	5	0	17	42	4	306	778
No	67	35	70	24	52	47	8	27	0	32	31	94	487
Sources of Loan													
Bank	5	4	15	3	40	35	4	0	13	8	2	66	195
Moneylender /Mahajans	99	45	27	2	2	0	0	0	0	14	0	129	318
Big Farmers	0	0	0	0	0	0	0	0	0	16	0	0	16
Relatives	11	11	8	0	11	4	1	0	2	4	1	29	82
Cooperatives	0	0	16	0	18	0	0	0	0	1	0	29	64
SHGs	0	4	0	0	0	0	0	0	2	0	0	20	26
Moneylender & Cooperatives	0	0	0	0	7	0	0	0	0	0	0	11	18
Contacts in the Char	0	2	0	0	1	0	0	0	0	0	0	0	3
Neighbor	11	0	8	0	0	0	0	0	0	0	1	0	20
Shopkeepers	6	1	4	0	0	0	0	0	0	0	0	22	33
Reasons for Taking Loan													
Farming	68	41	66	3	61	32	3	0	17	16	2	184	493
Construction/ Repair of House	11	2	1	0	0	2	0	0	0	3	0	20	39
Family Maintenance	12	7	8	0	8	5	0	0	0	15	0	31	86
Daughter's Marriage	16	6	0	1	3	0	0	0	0	0	0	31	57
Business	5	5	3	0	7	0	2	0	0	3	1	2	28
Others	0	1	0	0	2	0	0	0	0	0	0	15	18
Women Work Outside of Home													
Yes	97	32	96	9	84	0	1	1	17	39	12	246	634
No	102	68	52	20	53	86	12	26	47	35	23	154	678
Location of Women's Work													
On Land Owned by the Family	32	22	74	3	80	0	1	1	11	22	12	242	500

On Land Owned by Others	53	10	22	6	4	0	0	0	6	17	0	4	122
Other Work	12	0	0	0	0	0	0	0	0	0	0	0	12
Household's Place of Origin													
Bangladesh	60	40	78	0	86	25	1	10	0	47	4	350	701
Bihar	58	0	0	0	0	0	0	0	0	0	0	6	64
Uttar Pradesh	6	1	0	0	0	0	0	0	0	0	0	2	9
Nadia	7	4	18	—*	1	0	0	0	0	0	0	0	30
Bankura	0	1	0	0	0	0	0	0	0	11	0	0	12
Purulia	0	0	0	0	0	0	0	0	0	13	0	0	13
24 Parganas	58	8	39	0	0	0	0	0	0	2	0	2	109
Medinipur	0	0	0	0	0	0	0	0	0	0	0	2	2
Hoogli	0	0	0	0	0	0	0	0	0	0	0	7	7
Murshidabad	0	0	0	0	2	0	0	0	0	0	0	2	4
Haora	0	0	0	0	0	0	0	0	0	0	0	2	2
Burdwan	10	3	13	0	0	0	0	0	0	0	0	0	26
Jalpaiguri	0	1	0	0	0	0	0	0	0	0	0	0	1
Bangladesh (2nd Generation)	0	30	0	0	0	0	0	0	0	0	0	0	30
Length of Stay in Chars													
< 1	10	0	15	0	0	0	0	0	0	0	0	2	27
1–2	18	2	23	0	0	0	0	0	0	0	0	6	49
3–5	23	7	18	0	0	0	0	0	0	0	0	11	59
6–10	39	7	30	0	0	0	0	0	0	2	0	13	91
11–15	51	8	12	0	0	0	0	0	0	1	0	18	90
16–20	12	15	7	0	2	0	0	0	0	6	0	17	59
21–40	28	20	13	0	11	3	0	2	0	32	1	103	213
41–50	10	5	18	0	23	3	0	4	0	30	0	112	205
> 50	8	4	12	0	53	19	1	4	0	0	3	70	174
Assistance in Settling in Char from:													
Relatives	92	42	62	0	15	8	1	2	0	30	0	127	379
Villagers	40	18	32	0	17	1	0	4	0	14	1	95	222
Personal Contacts	0	0	8	0	10	0	0	4	0	17	3	39	64
Self-Initiative	67	14	46	0	47	16	12	0	0	13	0	112	315
Type of Migration													
Step-by-Step	81	20	57	0	25	4	1	10	0	32	1	255	466
Direct	118	54	91	0	64	21	12	0	0	42	3	118	468
Farming Done by													
Self	132	53	140	22	95	71	0	27	56	41	32	316	985
Lessee	3	3	6	0	4	0	0	0	1	0	0	7	24
Shared between Self & Lessee	11	6	0	0	15	1	0	0	2	0	0	15	50

Work as Agricultural Laborer													
Yes	139	71	53	10	62	23	3	4	30	63	16	202	676
No	60	29	95	19	75	63	10	23	34	11	19	198	636
Livelihood Activities of Household													
Cultivation	29	22	81	19	50	54	8	21	37	6	17	136	480
Service	0	0	0	0	4	0	0	0	0	0	0	4	8
Business	0	8	0	1	5	0	0	0	0	1	1	15	31
Agricultural Laborer	24	24	2	6	12	12	1	0	5	31	3	24	144
Cultivation & Agricultural Laborer	87	30	55	2	50	9	2	5	19	27	14	165	465
Cultivation & Business	23	17	10	1	10	5	2	1	3	6	0	63	141
Cultivation & Service	5	1	0	0	4	1	0	0	0	2	0	0	13
Agricultural Labor & Petty Trading	3	2	0	0	1	3	0	0	0	1	0	2	12
Cultivation, Agricultural Laborer & Business	0	0	0	0	1	0	0	0	0	0	0	0	1
Cultivation & Other	28	11	0	0	0	0	0	0	0	0	0	0	39
Agricultural Laborer & Service	0	2	0	0	0	0	0	0	0	0	0	11	13

Source: Field survey conducted in 2007–2008.

* Only local people.

Notes

Chapter 1. Introducing Chars

1. In places, we have used chars and charlands synonymously because chars are often called in Bengali "charbhumi" ("bhumi" in Bangla means "land"). Such use of terms does not imply the predominance of land over water.

2. Some even suggest that we are living in a "postnatural" condition where the human-fabricated phenomena pervade all parts of the biosphere and where the "environmental threats" are more often than not human-induced.

3. Classical geomorphologists' views privileged land, while acknowledging the inherent definitional and classificatory difficulties of *terra firma*, or "dry land," which excludes swamps, estuaries, tidal areas, lakes, ponds, and streams. William M. Davis (1900: 10–11), the geomorphologist who described fluvial landscape evolution as "cycles" of youth, maturity, and old age, comments that "[l]and is surprisingly difficult to define"; land is immobile, finite, and reproducible, and can be defined as a part of the earth's surface that, together with everything annexed to it whether by nature or by the handiwork of humans, can be owned as property.

4. About the indeterminate and shifting boundaries of land and water in Kakadu National Park in the northern territory of Australia, Howitt (2001: 239–240) says: "The tide constantly redefines the position of the frontier; heavy sediment loads produce muddy estuaries with shifting muddy tidal meanders that are colonised by mangroves and flattened by cyclones, the wet season regularly inundates coastal plains so that the 'land' looks very much like a swamp whose continuities with estuarine environments are at least as notable as their continuities with terrestrial ones. Sea, sky and land mixes up as Country, saltwater, freshwater and the land entwine and interpenetrate in a complex and fecund embrace of coexistence, rather than confined in zones of exclusion and non-interference."

5. According to Coones (1983: 95), Anuchin opposed the prevailing "fissiparous tendencies" in geography which separated the study of society from that of nature and

promoted the division of the subject into specializations, systematic branches (or "adjectival geographies"), and spatial abstractions. Indeed, Anuchin argued powerfully in favor of a unified geography, concrete complexity, and the indivisibility of the "seamless" geographical environment. Rejecting his vision of a unity in geography on the grounds that nature and society operate according to different sets of laws, the opponents of Anuchin maintained that a mixture of the two spheres was contrary to Marxist theory (Matley 1966).

6. One must not forget the deterministic views of Griffith Taylor, who wrote his geographical works around the same time.

7. Interesting descriptions of these lands and waters can be found from colonial documents. For example, O'Malley's (1911) *Bengal District Gazetteers: Purnea* notes that in the 1877 flood of the Kosi, the fluvial material brought down by the river was so immense that the chimneys of a nearby indigo factory were covered by silt.

8. Sir Francis Hamilton Buchanan's 1828 account of Purnea district describes only those lands that are overgrown with a coarse prairie-type grass as chars. The stronger, reed-like grass is described by him as "*janggala*."

9. As opposed to *pucca*, or more permanent lands.

10. W. W. Hunter noted it as a vast alluvial plain, where the process of land formation was ongoing, and presented it as "a sort of drowned land, covered with jungle, smitten by malaria, and infested by wild beasts" (1875: 285–346). Hunter also portrayed the Sundarbans as an area "intersected by a thousand river channels and maritime backwaters, but gradually dotted, as the traveller recedes from the seaboard, with clearings and patches of rice land" (p. 287).

11. The term derives from Persian *zamin* (land) and *dar* (holder); technically, a zamindar is a local landlord, but in Company-ruled Bengal, the zamindars performed a dual role. Simultaneously, they were hereditary rulers, or rajas, of a territory in which they generally enjoyed broad autonomy and they were also servants of the state, pledged to keep order and promote the welfare of the subjects, and removable if they failed to pay the revenue demanded by the state (McLane 1993: 8). The system of landlordism that came into existence in rural Bengal is described in detail in chapter 3.

12. Whitehead (2010: 85) says: "The category of wasteland became the hidden opposition to the category of value in Locke's *Second Treatise*, in the sense that it is land that lacked in value because it had not (yet) been enclosed, privatized, and commodified. Wasteland and value-producing land became a foundational binary for multiple, ramifying oppositions that Locke constructed between the state of nature and a state of culture, savagery and civilization."

13. Under the Convention on Wetlands (see http://www.ramsar.org) "wetlands" are defined by articles 1.1 and 2.1. The first states that: "*For the purpose of this Convention wetlands are areas of marsh, fen, peat land or water, whether natural or artificial, permanent or temporary, with water that is static or flowing, fresh, brackish or salt, including areas of marine water the depth of which at low tide does not exceed six metres.*" Article 2.1 provides that wetlands: "*[M]ay incorporate riparian and coastal zones adjacent to the wetlands, and islands or bodies of marine water deeper than six metres at low tide lying within the wetlands.*"

14. The rational or purposive manipulation of the social and natural environments constitutes their approach to nature; this behavior is behind the current understanding of adaptive human behavior as multidimensional (see Bennet 1976, for example).

15. This point of Beck's thesis, that reflexive modernization does not mark a complete break from tradition, has been critiqued by Elliot (2002: 306–308), who highlights the multiplicity of world traditions, communities, and cultures as impacting upon current social practices and life-strategies.

16. "Orang" means "man" standing for a person or individual, "laut" is the sea.

17. The livelihoods of people on chars provide the embodiment of Pierre Bourdieu's conceptualization of *habitus*, a sense of place or a feel of the land, or the importance of experience in developing a practical sense. As Hillier and Rooksby (2005: 21) define: "Habitus is thus a sense of one's (and others') place and role in the world of one's lived environment." As we show in this book, habitus is an embodied, as well as a cognitive, sense of place. Although it is a product of history, habitus is also changeable, but the past does not speak to the present in the habitus by means of tradition, customs, or ceremonials. We argue that in the volatile place of chars, daily adjustment to nature to secure a livelihood gives rise to the sense of place.

18. The "livelihoods" perspective to studying the poor was popularized by Chambers and Conway in 1992 and has been central to development planning since then. Scoones (2009) believes that the idea has existed before and been enriched by a number of theoretical perspectives.

19. Saussier, a French photographer, used the phrase in 1998.

20. See www.eurasianet.org/departments/rights/articles/eav100101.shtml# (accessed on July 20, 2010).

21. Sarker et al. (2003: 61) note that in Bangladesh alone approximately six hundred thousand people live on chars. According to a more recent United Nations Development Programme (UNDP) report, there are three million char dwellers in Bangladesh. In India, no such major study has been undertaken yet to give a reliable estimate of the numbers involved. However, the figure would be much higher than that of Bangladesh, especially if those people living within the embankments along the rivers are taken into account. However, one must remember that this is a "floating" population, and, hence, these numbers are no more than (informed) guesstimates.

22. Khas lands are new lands coming under government control. A piece of land has to be in existence for at least twenty years on a continuous basis before it can be legally designated as "land." Thus, many charlands are nonlands, as the Bangladeshi residents on Damodar chars are nonpeople.

23. *Patta* is the legal right to land recorded in a document provided by the land revenue department. It is most important for a squatter to have a patta in order to establish ownership rights to the land. Obtaining the patta can be a bitterly prolonged affair of several years.

24. The migration began in 1947 with the Partition of British India into India and Pakistan. Bengal was partitioned into East Pakistan (now Bangladesh) and West Bengal. In the wake of the Partition, millions of people moved across the new borders between the two states that were carved out to accommodate the two main religious groups, Hindus and Muslims.

25. Although the hurried partition of land and territories by the Radcliffe Commission created these enclaves, today they pose challenges to binary constructions

of citizenship. Even though over six decades have passed since the Partition, people living in these enclaves (and exclaves) have remained stateless, completely beyond government assistance, and without any care. Chaki (2011) draws attention to the complete lack of human rights in the ninety-seven "Indian" enclaves located well within what is today Bangladeshi territory.

26. The research and all related activities were enabled by personal research funds of Lahiri-Dutt. We thank the Australian National University, particularly the Resource Management in Asia Pacific Program and its convenor, Dr. Colin Filer, for providing the funding.

Chapter 2. *Char Jage*

1. In Bengal, chars are seen as rising from the water, "jage" literally means "rising."

2. Chowdhury (2001: 4) defines charlands as "sandbars that emerge as islands within the river channel or as attached land to the riverbanks as a result of the dynamics of erosion and accretion in the rivers."

3. See, for example, the work by Chalov (2001) that explains the conditions of formation, morphology, and deformation of such channels in lowland rivers.

4. Gupta (2011) quotes Alexander von Humboldt, the great traveler-geographer and polymath: "The tropics are my element, and I have never been so constantly healthy as in the last two years [of living in the tropics]." Yet, not unlike scholars of his time, Humboldt viewed the tropics through a lens shaped by training in the temperate lands, and neglected to deeply investigate the different fluvial processes.

5. About tropical rivers, Gupta observes: "A river on a steeper gradient with high seasonal variability in flow and transporting coarse-grained sediments is likely to have a braided appearance. This river will consist of several interlocking channels separated by a number of bars. . . . A river where very large floods recur at an interval of several decades may have a wide channel with high steep banks and bars may form at the foot of such banks" (1994: 58).

6. He also wrote about the multiple roles played by rivers in India and equated those in the plains of Bengal to "arteries in a living body": as highways of the country, the rivers played an important role in "cheap transit" for the collection and distribution of agricultural produce. But then, he also warned that these rivers were not all benign benevolence embodied: "But the very potency of their energy sometimes causes terrible calamities. Scarcely a year passes without floods, which sweep off cattle and grain stores and the thatched cottages, with anxious families perched on the roofs" (Hunter 1882: 31).

7. The Bengal basin occupies an area of about ninety thousand square kilometers, extending southward well into the offshore regions of the Bay of Bengal. Geographically, the basin includes West Bengal and Bangladesh.

8. Majuli is on UNESCO's World Heritage list. See http://whc.unesco.org/en/tentativelists/1870 (accessed on July 20, 2010).

9. Erosion on the southern side of Majuli is due to the erosive actions of the Brahmaputra and on its northern side to the Subansiri river. Kotoky et al. think that the

erosion is mainly due to "extreme sediment charge and to the main river traversing through a series of deep and narrow throats, and the formation of sand bars in the midst of the river" (2003: 929). The heterogeneous nature of the bank material also contributes to the slumping of riverbanks through undercutting and the flow of highly saturated sediments during the dry season.

10. An example could be that of the Jamuna, as the main course of the Brahmaputra is known in Bangladesh. The Jamuna is a braided river with bank materials that are highly susceptible to erosion. Over a period of nearly thirty years, the bed of the river widened by eroding a significant amount of floodplains, but the water area within the braided belt of the river had not changed, indicating that the area of sand and vegetated land within this belt had increased at a rate corresponding to the rate of erosion. This accreted land consists of coarser material than that of the floodplain, implying that within this period a huge amount of coarser materials was deposited and finer materials were washed away from the bed of the Jamuna (EGIS 2000: 21–22). Goswami (1985), in his study of the fluvial dynamics of the Brahmaputra river in Assam, also noticed that in the 1950s and the early 1960s, the Brahmaputra aggraded rapidly following the dumping of huge amounts of sediments into the river system that resulted from the earthquake of 1950. Subsequently, this enormous amount of sediments traveled downstream to reach Bangladesh in the late 1960s or the early 1970s. This additional supply of sediments, which was beyond the transporting capacity of the river, resulted in a deposition of sediments in the riverbed and an erosion of the finer sediments from the riverbank that maintained its flow area, thereby causing a widening of the river.

11. EGIS (2000: 1) notes that charland environment is "fickle" and not at all "constant," and observes that although the chars offer significant amounts of land for settlement and cultivation, living and working conditions there are very harsh. According to the report, these lands are prone to acute flooding, erosion hazards, fierce storms, and sand carpeting, which suddenly renders cultivable lands nonarable and may ruin standing crops.

12. In this book, we have used the terms synonymously, but have preferred the latter as the first term is more commonly used only among the Bangladeshi migrants.

13. For example, Urdu flood vocabulary contains over one hundred words, each with a definite meaning, each describing a specific *kind* of flood (Barrows 1948: 626).

14. Even for a country such as Bangladesh, into which international donors pour billions every year, the chars livelihoods program is a huge, high-profile initiative (£50 million over seven years). An article by the consultants Brocklesby and Hobley (2003) describes the design process of this program.

15. The term "khas land" is used in Bangla to mean unoccupied land that is legally owned by the government and managed by the Ministry of Land. Mitra's treatise on *The Land-Law of Bengal* defined it thus: "A Khas Mahal is an estate in the private possession of the Government as proprietor. Waste lands not included within the area of any permanently settled estate, islands thrown up in large navigable rivers, resumed revenue-free lands, and settled estates which have lapsed to Government are included within this definition" (1898: 32). Although the legal framework that designates land as khas has changed over time, the main sources of khas are: land already possessed by the

government, accredited lands from the sea or rivers, land vested in the government as ceiling surplus, land purchased by the government in auction sales, miscellaneous sources such as surrendered land, and abandoned or confiscated land (Momen 1996: 100). We will come across this term again in the next chapter.

16. Burdwan is spelled in different ways. Traditionally, the Sanskritized version was Vardhamana, which is noted in some Jain and Buddhist literature. Currently, it is spelled Barddhaman. The old spelling has been retained here to avoid confusion.

17. In a personal communication, Dinesh K. Mishra pointed out that in *Sapta Jangal Bibaran, Digvijay Prakash* (from the sixteenth century), the Damodar gets a mention as "*Vishnupadambujatah Damodar jaladwahi*" (Give me the water of the river Damodar that rises from the feet of Vishnu).

18. Professor Mahua Sarkar of the History department of Javadpur University in Kolkata speaks of the competing histories that clamor. She mentions a Jhumur (Bengali folk) song that celebrates its cool waters and gentle flow: "*Jhiri jhiri nadia, patal shital pania*" (The river flows swiftly, its deep water is cool). In a Tusu (also Bengali folk) song, the river is imagined as the matrimonial home, warning girls of playing in that water: "*Damodare jale khelo, Jale tomar ki ache, Apan mone bhebe dekho, Jale sasurghar ache*" (Don't play in Damodar waters, it is as bad as the in-laws' house). Another, Bhadu (also Bengali folk) song praises its width and dense forests on its banks: "*Ipare opare lodi, Tar pare mongolphul, Damodarer jale Bhadu, Khunje paina tab phul*" (The river is so wide, the flowers are on its bank. When we worship Bhadu with Damodar waters, we cannot find the flowers).

19. Meghnad Saha, the famous Bengali scientist and one of the key architects of the river control measures considered this "maldistribution" the "source of trouble": "the rainfall coming in abrupt surges and lasting only for a short period in the year during the monsoon months" (Saha and Ray 1942).

20. Throughout this book, the term "mainland" has been used to imply the land areas that are *not within* the two embankments of the river, but lying across the banks and outside of the river's boundaries. How the char people see these lands is described in chapter 4. However, by using the term "mainland" in opposition to "charlands," a dichotomy or subscription to yet another binary opposition is not implied. In fact, as shown in this book, there are intimate links and reciprocities between the charlands and the lands and peoples living beyond them.

21. Before 1793, the amount of revenue was decided every ten years (the Decennial Settlement) depending on whether pieces of land were productive or not. If the farmers could not produce because their lands were inundated or suffering from droughts, they were allowed concessions and revenue holidays. Hill interprets the introduction of the Permanent Settlement as a "sternly Eurocentric fashion . . . to limit the variables involved in revenue collection" (1997: 31).

22. Buchanan was one of the earliest and strongest proponents of commercializing the diara lands of the Kosi. He claimed that "the zamindars endeavoured to represent waste lands as less important than they in reality are: for there is reason to suspect that they consider their claim to the property of these lands very doubtful" (1828: 3).

Chapter 3. Controlling the River to Free Up Land

1. Bhattacharyya (1998) notes that over 8,000 cubic meters of peak flow of water per second (m^3/s) could give rise to "abnormal" level floods, whereas a "normal" flood resulted with about 5,500 to 8,000 m^3/s peak flow. "Extremely abnormal" floods were the ones with over 12,000 m^3/s peak flow, which occurred at least four times during the twentieth century—in 1913, 1935, 1941, and 1978.

2. In Ain-i-Akbari (AD 1590), Burdwan is mentioned as a *mahal* or *pargana* of Sarkar Sarifabad. The Nawab of Bengal, Murshid Kuli Khan, in 1722 revised the settlement and mentioned Burdwan as a *chakla*, a much bigger entity containing sixty-one parganas. On September 27, 1760, Burdwan (which then contained an area of over five thousand square miles, and was described as the most productive district within the whole province or Subah of Bengal) was ceded to the East India Company by Nawab Mir Muhammad Kasim Khan, the Governor of Bengal (Chaudhuri et al. 1994: 379).

3. As per Nalini Mohan Pal's 1929 treatise, the diwani meant that the Company had only zamindari rights over the territory. Burdwan, Midnapore, and Chittagong were "ceded" in 1760, which meant that the Company had "absolute rights" to the revenue arising from the territory (p. 2).

4. Other scholars support the view, noting that the ancient notion in India as to the origin of property in land is still prevalent where Mughal or British influence has not been much felt. Mitra (1898: 2) quotes Manu, the ancient sage who established basic rules of life and living in ancient India: "A field . . . is his who clears it of jungle, game is his who first pierced it." Nationalist scholars of Indian history, such as Mookerjee (1919), have also shown that proprietary right of land had always belonged to the cultivator in pre-British times, and that the king was only entitled to a share of its produce and was never regarded as the proprietor of the land. The proprietary rights carried with them the right of possession, but the cultivators began to lose the right to occupy the land that they had enjoyed since ancient times (see also Chaudhuri 1927).

5. Pal wrote that the changes occurred during the Mughal rule: "During Mohammedan misrule, zemindars, who were merely revenue farmers, had in many places usurped the rights of the peasants. But the property in land belonged, of right, to the peasants, and it was good policy to regard it as such" (1929: 18). And indeed, Banerjee's view reiterates this: "Like *abwabs*, illegal perquisites were a characteristic feature of the Mughal revenue system" (1980: 12).

6. Hill quotes the Act: "The Governor General in Council accordingly declares to the zamindars . . . and other actual proprietors of the land, with or on behalf of whom a settlement has been concluded under the regulations above-mentioned, that at the expiration of the terms of the settlement, no alteration will be made in the assessment which they have respectively engaged to pay, but they and their heirs and lawful successors, will be allowed to hold their estates at such assessments forever" (1997: 30).

7. Although the "Bengal System," associated with Cornwallis's enormous personal credibility, became the reigning model of Company governance in India, elsewhere in India, alternative land revenue models such as the Raiyatwari system emerged under different administrators, such as Thomas Munro (see Swamy 2011).

8. The legal institutional entity within which the economic phenomenon of subinfeudation developed was the *taluk* (or *talook*), an Arabic word, meaning "something hanging or dependent." *Taluks*, or "tenures," in the sense of intermediate interests between the zamindar and the ryots, or *raiyats*, were well known during the Mughal rule in Bengal. One class of talukdars sprung from the ancient rajas who were allowed to retain their possessions, against payment of revenue demanded by the state. Such talukdars originally differed little, if at all, from the zamindars, and some of them, in the course of time, gradually grew up to be zamindars themselves. The difference between them is the degree of proximity to the state; the talukdar did not represent the state to the same extent that zamindars did.

9. A *gantie*, or *ganthe*, was a hereditary tenure at a fixed rent.

10. *Howala*, or *howla*, is the local name in eastern Bengal for a small taluk. There could be an *ousat-howla*, which was a general name for tenures intermediately between those of the zamindar and the ryot. There could also be *nim-howla*s, which meant a half-howla and *by-howla*, or subdivisions of a nim-howla (Bhattacharyya 1985: 14).

11. The term "cadastral" is derived from the French word *cadastre*, which means the "registration of landed property." Cadastral Maps are meant to register the ownership of landed property by demarcating the boundaries of fields and the like for the realization of revenue from the land. Once done, the ownership of property can only be mutated in each new buyer's name. The Revenue Survey identifies the nature of the land against each plot of the Cadastral Maps (but does not prepare maps). In Burdwan region, the second large-scale settlement operation took place in 1953, primarily aimed at the abolition of all intermediary rights (on payment of compensation) and to effect equitable distribution of lands by imposing ceilings on holdings retained by an individual intermediary/ryot.

12. Willcocks noted: "These breaches were considered by the authorities as breaches made by the uncontrolled floods of the rivers, and the Government had set itself to put an end to such discreditable [acts from] occurring. It never seems to have struck anybody that the breaches were made secretly by the peasantry for irrigation. And yet it ought to have been evident that 40 or 50 breaches in a heavily embanked river of inconsiderable length in a single year could not have been made by the river itself; for one or two breaches eased the situation" (1930: 22–23).

13. Or on June 5, 1789, to Lawrence Mercier, Collector of Burdwan: "[It has been] represented to me that the neglect of the repairs of the embankments at Callagautchy in your district exposes some villages in Cossyoora to be entirely inundated" (Mitra 1955: 74).

14. See "Banglapedia: National Encyclopedia of Bangladesh." Available online at http://www.banglapedia.org/httpdocs/HT/A_0209.HTM (accessed on July 25, 2010).

15. See http://www.archive.org/stream/imperialgazettee14hunt/imperialgazettee14hunt_djvu.txt (accessed on July 13, 2011).

16. After the abolition of zamindari in 1956, the right of ownership of chars in the case of these smaller rivers was also vested in the state.

17. Such a change is not unusual and has happened elsewhere in India. A historical example has been provided by Talwar-Oldenburg, who has shown how changes in the

land revenue system in rural Punjab during the colonial period, which purported to modernize the world of peasants, severely enhanced the masculinity of the farming communities, who had used land and water resources for generations. As land became owned by men, such ownership of land became equated with social prestige, and the multitude of tasks that rural women performed on the land lost their importance to society (2010: 97–98). This created a fierce desire for sons and reduced the value of girls in Punjab. Today's rural Punjab, while known for its agro-based prosperity, continues to bear this patriarchal burden in its low sex ratio and disposability of women.

18. As early as 1925, Dr. C. A. Bentley advocated the reintroduction of floodwaters into the Bhagirathi-Damodar *doab* as well as into the trans-Damodar tract. In 1931, Mr. C. Adams Williams stated that the silt-laden waters should be used to increase the fertility of the soil and decrease the ravages caused by malaria.

19. This measure was undertaken to protect the newly constructed railway line and the Grand Trunk Road lying on the left bank, but resulted in disconnecting several left-bank distributaries such as the Khari, Banka, and the Behula, and caused a disintegration of the drainage system. The flood season of 1859 saw the Damodar, unrestrained by embankments, breaching at Begua hana on the right.

20. A 1863 report by Colonel J. F. Stoddart, the superintending engineer of South-Western Circle, noted the distributaries of the Damodar as "a succession of stagnant and offensive pools, much choked with rank and decomposing vegetation and other organic matter, and highly insalubrious." He also noted that this was partially caused by the cutting-off of the Damodar floodwater distribution channels and by the zamindars neglecting to keep them clear of silt and obstruction (quoted in Inglis 2002: 155–156).

21. Henry C. Hart gives an unparalleled description of the flood: "On the morning of 14 July 1943, rain began to fall steadily at Asansol. On the next day, a real cloudburst began; in 24 hours ending on the 16th, the Damodar River, a flashy monsoon stream, rose quickly. By midnight on the 16th, it was carrying 350,000 cusecs of water past Burdwan, 70 miles below. This was not an exceptionally high flood; the most moderate, in fact in the last three years. But this time, the Damodar found a weak spot in the century-old embankment defending its northern bank" (1956: 59).

22. See http://www.dvcindia.org/index.htm (accessed on 29 November 2009).

23. On the effectiveness of this manual in coping with the 1978 floods, Pathak notes: "The vagaries of monsoonal rainfall . . . belied the DVC water release manual because of heavy downpour of 72cm. during September 26–28 in 1978. The DVC reservoirs received an all time record inflow of 851,000 cu. ft. According to the manual, the DVC was to release 200,000 cu.ft/sec. whereas it released only 160,000 considering the heavy rainfall; but at Durgapur barrage point it was 380,000 cu.ft/sec. threatening the barrage itself. Besides, other rivers in the lower Bengal—like Silavati, Darkeswar, Kansavati, Ajoy and Moyurakshi—were swollen and added to the Damodar flood" (1981: 629).

Chapter 4. *Bhitar o Bahir Katha*

1. For example, when an agricultural scientist thinks about soil fertility or an economist plans for rural development, she or he would think of *this* land.

2. For example, Panchanan Tarkaratna, an ancient historian, while noting the Ugrakhatriya as a powerful, generous, and hospitable caste, suggested that the community originated from the cohabitation of Kshatriya men and Shudra (menial laborer or lowest-caste) women. "Aguri" is the term used in popular parlance. Some Aguris customarily wore the sacred thread and saw themselves as "twice-born."

3. Bengal has been conventionally divided into a number of ecological units: Radh comprises the western part of the Ganga and is equivalent to the Chota Nagpur Plateau fringe. Among other such units, Barind comprises the uplands located in the north and Bagri comprises the eastern part of the Ganga.

4. Although Bose observed that "[b]etween 1891 and 1931, the cultivated area contracted by something like 50% in Burdwan, 60% in Hooghly, 30% in Jessore and 20% in Nadia and Murshidabad" (1986: 45).

5. There is no "official record" to support this, but much anecdotal evidence, particularly from older residents of Burdwan and local historical books, points to this fact. For example, Shakti Hazra, an elderly member of the CPI, remembers that large ships and barges carried a river-borne trade of rice, coal, and other produce until the late 1940s.

6. C. A. Bentley, the colonial director of public health in Bengal, in his treatise written in 1925 considered malaria as the result of seven decades of mismanagement of the delta. Bandopadhyaya (2009: iii) reiterates Bentley's view that the soaring mosquito population resulted in the decline of agricultural fertility and deterioration of public health. Klingensmith supports Bentley's cause-effect relationship explanation (between mosquitoes caused by a choked drainage system and malaria) and writes: "Out of a provincial population of around 45 million people in 1911, Bentley estimated that 30 million in Bengal were afflicted by malaria, more than 10 million severely so" (2007: 34).

7. This operation was undertaken by the newly elected West Bengal government, which was launched in October 1978 to register sharecroppers, or tenants on farming land, who had sometimes been farming these lands for generations, but had no legal recognition or rights over these lands. The sharecroppers provided labor; other cost-sharing arrangements were intricately detailed and for only part of the harvest.

8. Very little is written about the cooperative in Shodya village in Burdwan, but in his memoir written in Bangla, Syed Shahedullah (1991), a veteran of the Communist movement, touched upon the expansion of this ideology-based rural change in Burdwan in the 1950s and the 1960s.

9. Other demands were: no eviction; two-thirds share; right to stock harvested crop in the bargadar's farmyard; and reduction in the exorbitant interest rates on advances and the elimination of all illegal exactions (abwabs).

10. The compound rate of growth of the real daily wage of male agricultural laborers between 1979–1980 and 1992–1993 among all the states of India was highest in West Bengal at 280 percent (Rawal and Swaminathan 1998).

11. See Ruud 1999 and 2003 for more on how the supporters of the CPI(M) rose in social status and accumulated wealth as they gained political power.

Chapter 5. Silent Footfalls

1. Prior to 1971, Bangladesh was known as East Pakistan.

2. The most famous depiction of the decline in livelihoods of a fishing community with char formation and shifting river courses is in the novel *Titas Ekti Nadir Naam* by Adwaita Mallabarman (1956). Another well-known novel, *Kalindi*, by Tarashankar Bandyopadhyay, starts with the description of a newly rising char and the conflicts over its ownership.

3. See *Dainik Damodar*, September 10, 1950, vol. 2, no. 2.

4. See *Dainik Damodar*, May 12, 1950, vol. 2, no. 70.

5. See *Dainik Damodar*, August 4, 1950, vol. 3, no. 94.

6. We must mention that this rule operates informally and is not set in concrete as a law. However, it is this informal rule that defines char dwellers' access to and rights over the lands.

7. Locals from the mainland still say about a Mahadeb teacher that he was a "sardar of dacoits," that hundreds of people ran to help him at his call.

8. On migration from Bihar see the Government of India National Informatics Centre (NIC) website, http://mospi.nic.in/ (accessed on March 25, 2004).

9. See http://www.bharattimes.com.

10. Siddiqui (2003) observes that twenty-five million people (about 20 percent of the total population) live in extreme poverty, with the incidence of poverty being greatest among women. In absolute terms, population is burdensome for Bangladesh, a small deltaic country of about 150,000 square kilometers, with the eighth largest population in the world.

11. Samaddar elaborates (1999: 156–157) that "successive Flood Action Programmes (FAP) have affected the wetlands, fisheries and charlands, leading to further erosion, salinity, and the decline of the employment potential for women in particular. Floods were identified as the 'problem' and the control of floods as the corresponding 'solution' by consultants appointed by the donor agencies and the rulers."

12. Alam says: "In the face of unprecedented environmental crises and consequent socio-economic pressure faced by the people and inadequate measures taken by the state to address the same, it can be said that the flow of population from Bangladesh to India will continue unabated, perhaps at an even greater pace" (2003: 7).

13. Others (for example, Barkat and Zaman 2000; Malik 2000; Samad 1998) have documented the forcible eviction from landed property of the Bangladeshi Hindus.

14. Rahman and van Schendel have drawn attention to the reverse flow as well. They say: "In the literature, the dominant image of the refugee is that of the Bengali Hindu fleeing from east Pakistan to Calcutta in West Bengal. We need to broaden this image to include many other groups, particularly Muslims fleeing from Assam, Tripura, West Bengal, Bihar and Uttar Pradesh and finding a new home in East Pakistan" (2003: 559).

15. Rather than, as in the title of Salman Rushdie's celebrated book, "Midnight's Children."

16. Tin Bigha is an Indian parcel of land in north Bengal that was left outside India's borders and can only be reached by crossing Bangladeshi terrain.

17. In the mangrove end of the Bengal delta, riverine silt builds up islands continuously.

18. Since none of the countries involved are signatories to the 1951 UN Convention, India can only have the Bangladeshi Hindus as "undeclared refugees" or infiltrators. Consequently, Hindus (as well as Muslims) who cross the border with the hope of settling in India are invariably labeled as illegal immigrants and have received poor treatment historically.

19. The scale of illegal migration is apparent from the fact that some 2.1 million illegal entrants to Malaysia were apprehended between 1992 and 2000 (Hugo 2002).

20. See http://www.southasiaanalysis.org/%5Cpapers7%5Cpaper632.html (accessed on November 29, 2010).

21. Mallick (1999) gave some concrete figures; he writes that out of the 14,388 families who deserted (for West Bengal), 10,260 families returned to their previous places and the remaining 4,128 families perished in transit, died of starvation or exhaustion, or were killed in Kashipur, Kumirmari, and Marichjhapi by police gunfire.

22. These migrants' journey involved several changes of destination before settling on chars—their migration occurred in a step-by-step fashion.

23. This is close to the Indian threshold urban density of four hundred persons per square kilometer.

24. Joint families are traditional in many rural areas of India. They may comprise ten to twenty people living in one household—commonly the families of two or three brothers, together with their parents.

25. The Biharis are well known for choosing to migrate to other parts of India from their native north Bihar to escape severe poverty, which is exacerbated by natural factors such as floods, waterlogging, and shifting river courses.

26. The title of this section comes from a statement made by Morokvasic (1984: 886).

Chapter 6. Living with Risk

1. These are catchwords of the day, often seen from a positivist perspective, dealing with the issues of resilience and sustainable development, aiming to build "adaptive capacity" among human communities or even ecological systems or a "resilience framework" linking social and ecological systems.

2. For example, the vulnerability and adaptation guidelines formulated by the Intergovernmental Panel on Climate Change (IPCC), the United Nations Environment Programme (UNEP), and the United States Country Study Program (USCSP) for fulfilling the United Nations Framework Convention on Climate Change's (UNFCCC) core focus have highlighted the need to know the autonomous adaptation mechanisms in the various sectors of a society such as different classes or social groups. Another study by the USCSP, in collaboration with the Government of Bangladesh, has located vulnerability and adaptation of humans to environmental changes in various sectors (Smith et al. 1996).

Chapter 7. Livelihoods Defined by Water

1. Ginguld et al. (1997: 577) see livelihood as a set of strategies undertaken by a particular household in order to secure its economic well-being and especially its long-term survival. This idea is drawn from a tradition set by Pearson (1977) where he analyzes the emergence of economic transactions and the origin and development of trade, money, and market as part of human livelihood. Some recent studies such as that by Valdivia and Gilles (2001: 7) also view livelihood strategies as a portfolio of activities and the social relations by which families secure or improve their condition or cope with crises. According to Frankenberger (1996), livelihoods consist of on-farm and off-farm activities, which together provide a variety of procurement strategies for food and cash.

Chapter 8. Living on Chars, Drifting with Rivers

1. Aldo Leopold (1966) has described the functioning of an ecosystem as a "round river" to emphasize the cycling of nutrients and energy.

Glossary

Aal	Raised demarcation bounding farm plots
Abwab	Additional cess ("good luck") amount demanded by Mughal revenue collectors on top of assessed revenues A kind of bribe
Aman	Late-growing kharif paddy
Babu	Gentlefolk
Bada	Another word for chars/river islands
Baet	Mound-like land, rising between two branches of (usually) the Indus river in Pakistan
Bagri	Moribund part of the Bengal delta
Banberal	Feral or wild cat
Bandaki lease	Lease of mortgage
Bandher bhitarer jami	Mainland, land across the embankments ("bhitar" literally means "inside")
Bangal	A derogatory term for people from the part of Bengal that is now Bangladesh
Baor	Discarded river channel, often shaped like an oxbow, created by a meandering river
Bargadar	Registered sharecropper
Bastuhara	Someone who has lost his or her home
Bastutyagi	Someone who has left his or her home
Baze zameen	Wasteland
Beel	Water body or lake-like depression
Bena	Locally grown tall grass
Bhadralok	"Genteel" people; educated middle-class Bengalis, usually men

Bhagchashi	Sharecropper
Bhanga	To break something
Bhaoli jami	Land for which rent is paid in kind, usually a share of the produce
Bhil	Old shallow and choked-up river course
Bhitabari	Residential, often ancestral home
Bhiti jami	Land, generally raised; site suitable for residence
Bhurbhuri bhanga	String of bubbles created by bank erosion
Bidi	Indigenous cigarette
Bigha	A Bengali system of land measurement; 1 bigha equals 0.5 hectare, or one-third of an acre
Boka bhanrh	An earthen piggy bank
Borodhan	Summer paddy crop
Bund / Bandh	Embankment
By-howla	Subdivision of a *nim-howla*
Chakla	Larger administrative unit in Mughal period
Chalaghar	Makeshift hut, usually temporary
Chap	Large chunk of soil
Chapa bhanga	Breaking of the river bank into chunks
Chapatti	Handmade bread made of coarse flour
Charbhumi	Charland
Char Mana	Island char or bar, unattached to the riverbank
Chechra bhanga	Washing away of large amounts of loose sand
Chhat Puja	Festival of sun worshipping, popular in Bihar
Chira	Flattened rice
Chorua	Char dweller; term is more widely used in West Bengal, India
Choura	Char dweller; term is more widely used in Bangladesh
Dadan	Traditional system of advancing loans against the harvest
Dah and *modar*	Sacred waters
Dakshin	South (direction)
Dal	Lentil soup
Damuda	Aboriginal name of Damodar, different spelling of the river's name
Dam-udar	The river with a fiery belly
Danga jami	Higher and drier land
Dar-patni	Subtenure or perpetual lease
Dar-patnidar	The holder of subtenure or perpetual lease
Dash dalil	Literally, "deed of ten"; informal land transaction record
Dewani	Imperial grant of the revenue authority. Also spelled as *diwani*.
Dhnayakarari	Peasant working on a farm on "paddy contract"

Diara	River island in north Bihar, both Ganga and Kosi floodplains
Gantie	Hereditary tenure at a fixed rent
Ghurni	Eddies, or circular currents
Goala	Milkman; can also imply the cattle-herder caste
Goalghar	Cowshed
Haat	Periodic rural market
Hanria bhanga	Breakage of a hanging piece of riverbank
Haor	Wide, saucer-shaped interfluvial water body in Sylhet
Harka ban	Flash flood
Howala	A small taluk
Izaradar	Leaseholder
Jage	Rises
Jalmahal/Jalkar	Privately owned part of the river
Jami-dakhal	Occupation of others' land by force
Jotedar	Owner of a large farm; rich farmer
Janggal	Jungle, forest
Kachha/kuchha	Fragile or wet land in the Indus valley in Pakistan, the equivalent of chars
Kana nadi	Dead river; literally, a river that is "blind in one eye"
Kanwa/Hana	Cut in the embankment or the canal bank, escape route for a spill channel
Karbar	Business, trade
Katha	Local measure of land, one-twentieth of a bigha
Khajna	Rent
Khalsa	Subordinate of a landlord/zamindar
Khal	Natural or artificial water channel
Kharif	Main (monsoon) paddy
Khas	Unoccupied land vested to the government. These are lands from which revenues or rents are collected directly by the government or zamindars (without an intermediary).
Khas mahal	Land that is in the private possession of the state
Khatia	Basic bed frame usually made of coconut string
Kirtan	Bengali folk devotional songs
Kist/Kisti	Installment
Krishak Sabha	The political platform for farmers, initiated by undivided Communist Party in West Bengal (also, *Kishan Sabha*)
Lakh	Hundred thousand
Lathiyal	"Stick-wielder"; also, as a group, a local force or army maintained by the landlord
Lethel	Stick-wielding local strongman, or people skilled in pole fight

Mahajan	Moneylender
Mahal/Pargana	Mughal administrative unit
Maharaja	A superior king
Majhhi-malla lok	Boatmen
Mana	"Attached" chars, physically contiguous to the river-bank, a term that is more widely used in West Bengal
Mantra	Ritualistic lines, usually prayer
Mastermasai	Affectionate or informal respectful name for a teacher
Matbar	Leader
Mesta	A fiber crop like jute, red in color, which grows without much water and nourishment
Mohkuma	A subdivision of the district
Morol	Leader, usually of a group or a village
Mouza	Lowest level of rural unit for revenue collection
Muchlekha	A written bond
Mutseddies	Underlings of the landlord/zamindar
Nakdi/Nekdi	Land on which rent is paid in cash at a certain rate per bigha
Namashudra	The lowest caste group in Hindu caste hierarchy
Nawab	Muslim equivalent of king
Nikashi	Drainage outlet or spill area
Nim-howla	A half-*howla*
Nimnobarno	Lower-caste communities
Nishi bhanga	Riverbank erosion during the night
Ousat-howla	The general name for intermediate tenures between the zamindar and ryot
Orang-laut	People of the sea or sea gypsies
Panchayat	Elected village-level council, the lowest in three-tier rural administration
Panchayati raj	The system of elected village-level councils
Parcha	Revenue record
Parichalan	Management
Patni	Tenure or perpetual lease
Patnidar	The holder of tenure or perpetual lease
Patta	Legal document of landownership
Pradhan	Head, usually elected, of a village
Praja	Subjects of a king
Probol bhanga	A devastating breakage of the riverbank
Pucca	Concrete (regarding constructions), more permanent (regarding lands)
Puja	Worshipping (usually of gods and goddesses in Hindu religion)
Pulbandi	Original, pre-British, low embankment
Rabi	Winter crop

Radh	Western bank of the Hooghly river in West Bengal
Raja	King
Ryot	Peasant, farmer
Sali jami	Land suitable for rice farming, submerged during the rains
Sardar	Leader
Se-patnidar	The holder of subtenure or perpetual lease
Sharonarthi	Refugee
Shimul	Cotton fiber tree
Sipoy	Sentry
Subah	Large, regional administrative unit
Suna jami	Land suitable for rice farming, but which is not submerged
Taluk	A piece of subtenured land
Talukdar	The holder of a piece of subtenured land
Tanbu	Tent, usually made of plastic sheets, bamboo, and tin
Thika	Contract
Thika contract	A special type of contract of land for a specific crop against a fixed rent amount
Ugrakhatriya	One of the caste groups of Burdwan, also called the "Aguris"
Uthbandi/Ootbundee	Land that is actually cultivated by the peasant, with rent paid according to the amount put under crops
Zamindar	Local landlord
Zamindari	System or tenure of land in which land is owned by someone other than the peasant

References

Abrar, C. R., and S. Nurullah Azad. 2003. *Coping with Displacement: Riverbank Erosion in Northwest Bangladesh*. Dhaka: Rangpur Dinajpur Rural Service and North Bengal Institute.

Achariya, J. M., M. Gurung, and R. Samaddar. 2003. "No-where People on the Indo-Bangladesh Border," Working Paper No. 14. Kathmandu: South Asia Forum for Human Rights.

Adger, W. N. 2006. "Vulnerability," *Global Environmental Change*, 16: 268–281.

Agergard, J., N. Fold, and K. V. Gough (eds.). 2010. *Rural-urban Dynamics: Livelihoods, Mobility and Markets in African and Asian Frontiers*. London and New York: Routledge.

Agrawal, A., and K. Sivaramakrishnan. 2001. *Social Nature: Resources, Representations and Rule in India*. New Delhi: Oxford University Press.

Agrawal, B. 1994. "Gender and Command over Property: A Critical Gap in Economic Analysis and Policy in South Asia," *World Development*, 22(10): 1455–1478.

Ahmad, I. 1997. "Indo-Bangladesh Relations: Trapped on the Nationalist Discourse," in B. De and R. Samaddar (eds.), *State, Development and Political Culture: Bangladesh and India*. New Delhi: Har-Anand Publishers, pp. 55–75.

Ahmed, S., C. Castaneda, A. M. Fortier, and M. Sheller. 2003. *Uprootings/Regroundings: Questions of Home and Migration*. Oxford: Berg.

Aich, B. N. 1998. "Five Decades of DVC," *Science and Culture*, 64(5/6): 77–86.

Akbar, M. J. 2003. "Migration and Poverty Go Hand-in-Hand in Bihar," *Gulf News*, November 24.

Alam, S. 2003. "Environmentally Induced Migration from Bangladesh to India," *Strategic Analysis: A Monthly Journal of the IDSA*, 27(3): 422–438.

Alim, A. 2009. "Land Management in Bangladesh with Reference to Khas Land: Need for Reform," *Drake Journal of Agricultural Law*, 14: 245–265.

Alkire, S. 2002. "Conceptual Framework for Human Security," in *Working Definition and Executive Summary: Report of the Commission on Human Security*. New York: CHS Secretariat.

Altman, J. 2009a. "The Hybrid Economy as Political Project: Reflections from the Indigenous Estate," Keynote address to the "Indigenous Participation in Australian Economies" conference, November 9, Canberra. Available online at http://www.nma.gov.au/audio/detail/the-hybrid-economy-as-political-project (accessed on August 20, 2011).

———. 2009b. "The Hybrid Economy and Anthropological Engagements with Policy Discourses: A Brief Reflection," *Australian Journal of Anthropology*, 20(3): 318–29. Available online at http://search.informit.com.au/fullText;dn=2010015007;res=APAFT (accessed on August 20, 2011).

Anderson, M. B., and P. J. Woodrow. 1989. *Rising from the Ashes: Development Strategies in Times of Disaster*. Boulder, CO: Westview.

Anuchin, V. A. 1977 [1957]. *Theoretical Problems of Geography*. Columbus: Ohio State University Press.

Araújo, M. B. 2002. "Biological Hotspots and Zones of Ecological Transition," *Conservation Biology*, 16(6): 1662–1663.

Araújo, M. B., and P. H. Williams. 2001. "The Bias of Complementary Hotspots towards Marginal Populations," *Conservation Biology*, 15: 1710–1720.

Aschawer, D. A. 1989. "Is Public Expenditure Productive?" *Journal of Monetary Economics*, 23(2): 177–200.

Ascoli, F. D. 1921. *A Revenue History of the Sundarbans from 1870 to 1920*. Calcutta: Bengal Secretariat Book Depot.

Ashley, S., K. Kar, A. Hossain, and S. Nandi, 2000. "Bangladesh: The Chars Livelihood Assistance Scoping Study," Draft paper. London: DFID.

———. 2003. *The Chars Livelihood Assistance Scoping Study*. Dhaka: DFID (Documents of Chars Livelihoods Assistance Project).

Asian Development Bank. 2001. *Country Assistance Plans: Bangladesh*. Manila: Asian Development Bank.

Asian Development Research Institute [ADRI]. 2004. "Socio-economic Status of Muslims in Bihar," Study sponsored by Bihar State Minorities Commission, Asian Development Research Institute, Patna.

Baden-Powell, B. H. 1892. *The Land Revenue Systems of British India: Being a Manual of the Land Tenures and of the Systems of Land Revenue Administration Prevalent in Several Provinces*, vol. 1. Oxford: Oxford University Press.

Bagchi, J., and S. Dasgupta (eds.). 2003. *The Trauma and the Triumph: Gender and Partition in Eastern India*. Kolkata: Stree.

Bagchi, K. G. 1944. *The Ganges Delta*. Calcutta: Calcutta University Press.

———. 1977. "The Damodar Valley Development and Its Impact on the Region," in A. G. Noble and A. Rudra (eds.), *Indian Urbanization and Planning: Vehicles of Modernization*. New Delhi: Tata McGraw-Hill, pp. 232–241.

Bakker, K. J. 2003. *An Uncooperative Commodity: Privatizing Water in England and Wales*. Oxford: Oxford University Press.

———. 2006. "Material Worlds? Resource Geographies and the 'Matter of Nature,'" *Progress in Human Geography*, 30(1): 5–27.

Bandhu, S. 2008. *Ugrakhatriya Parichiti O Gangaridi Prasango* [in Bengali]. Burdwan: Binoy Prakashani.

Bandopadhyaya, A. 2009. "The Changing Face of Bengal: Re-viewed after Seventy Years," in *Changing Face of Bengal: A Study in Riverine Economy*, revised ed. Calcutta: Calcutta University Press, pp. i–x. Originally published by Radhakamal Mukherjee in 1938.

Bandyopadhyay, D. 2001. "Tebhaga Movement in Bengal: A Retrospect," *Economic and Political Weekly*, 36(41): 3901–3907.

Bandyopadhyay, K., S. Ghosh, and N. Dutta. 2009. "Eroded Lives: Riverbank Erosion and Displacement of Women in West Bengal," in S. Roohi and R. Samaddar (eds.), *State of Justice in India: Issues of Social Justice, Key Texts on Social Justice in India*. New Delhi: Sage Publications, pp. 108–133.

Bandyopadhyay, N. 1995. "Agrarian Reforms in West Bengal: An Enquiry into Its Impact and Some Problems," Paper presented at the workshop on "Agrarian Growth and Agrarian Structure," Centre for Urban Studies, Calcutta University, July 18–19.

Bandyopadhyay, T. 1940. *Kalindi*. Kolkata: Mitra and Ghosh.

Banerjee, A. C. 1980. *The Agrarian Systems of Bengal*, vol. 1, *1582–1793*, Calcutta: K. P. Bagchi.

Banerjee, B. K. 1991. "Unified Development of the Damodar Valley and Its Impact on Environment," Workshop on Environmental Impact Assessment for Water Resource Projects. Calcutta: Institute of Engineers.

Banerjee, P. 2010. *Borders, Histories, Existences: Gender and Beyond*. New Delhi: Sage Publications.

Banerjee, P., and A. Basu Ray Chaudhury. 2011. *Women in Indian Borderlands*. Kolkata and New Delhi: Calcutta Research Group and Sage Publications.

Banerjee, P., S. Basu Ray Chaudhury, and S. Das (eds.). 2005. *Internal Displacement in South Asia*. New Delhi, Thousand Oaks, and London: Sage Publications.

Banerji, A. K. 1972. *West Bengal District Gazetteers: Howrah*. Calcutta: Government of West Bengal.

Baqee, A. 1998. *Peopling in the Land of Allah Jaane: Power, Peopling and Environment: The Case of Charlands of Bangladesh*. Dhaka: University Press Limited.

Barkat, A. 2004. *Poverty and Access to Land in South Asia: Bangladesh Country Study*. Kent: National Resources Institute.

Barkat, A., and S. uz Zaman. 2000. "Forced Outmigration of Hindu Minority: Human Deprivation due to Vested Property Act," in R. Abrar and Abdul Barkat (eds.), *Political Economy of the Vested Property Act in Rural Bangladesh*. Dhaka: Association for Land Reform and Development, pp. 21–30.

Barman, S. 1982. "Spatio-Temporal Aspects of Agriculture in Burdwan District," PhD thesis. Burdwan: The University of Burdwan.

Barnes, T. J. 2008. "History and Philosophy of Geography: Life and Death, 2005–2007," *Progress in Human Geography*, 32(5): 650–658.

Barnett, J. 2000. *The Meaning of Environmental Security*. London: Zed Books.

Barrows, H. K. 1948. *Floods: Their Hydrology and Control*. New York: McGraw-Hill.

Basu Ray Chaudhury, A. 2000. "Life after Partition: A Study on the Reconstruction of Lives in West Bengal." Available online at http://www.google.co.in/search?client=firefox-a&rls=org.mozilla%3Aen-US%3Aofficial&channel=s&hl=en&source=hp&q=Anasua%2BBasu%2BRaychaudhury%2B2000%2BRefugees%2BWest+Bengal&meta=&btnG=Google+Search (accessed on August 20, 2011).

Basu, S. 1982. "DVC: A Boon or a Calamity?" in *Geographical Mosaic*. Calcutta: Geographical Society of India, pp. 582–592.

Basu, S. K., and S. B. Mukherjee. 1963. *Evaluation of Damodar Canals (1959–'60): A Study of the Benefits of Irrigation in the Damodar Region*. New York: Asia Publishing House.

Battistella, G., and M. B. A. Maruja (eds.). 2003. "Southeast Asia and the Specter of Unauthorized Migration," in *Unauthorized Migration in Southeast Asia*. Quezon City: Scalabrini Migration Center, pp. 1–35.

Beck, T., and M. Ghosh. 2000. "Common Property Resources and the Poor: Findings from West Bengal," *Economic and Political Weekly*, 35(3): 147–153.

Beck, U. 1991. *Ecological Enlightenment: Essays on the Politics of the Risk Society*. Amherst, NY: Prometheus Books.

———. 1996. "World Risk Society as Cosmopolitan Society: Ecological Questions in a Framework of Manufactured Uncertainties," *Theory, Culture and Society*, 13(4): 1–32.

Bennet, J. 1976. *The Ecological Transition: Cultural Anthropology and Human Adaptation*. New York: Pergamon Press.

Bentley, C. A. 1925. "Malaria and Agriculture in Bengal," in W. L. Voorduin, *Preliminary Memorandum on the Unified Development of the Damodar River*. Kolkata: Central Technical Power Board, pp. 29–45.

Berkes, F., and C. Folke (eds.). 1998. "Linking Social and Ecological Systems for Resilience and Sustainability," in *Linking Social and Ecological Systems*. Cambridge: Cambridge University Press, pp. 1–25.

Bernier, F. 1891 [1815]. *Travels in the Moghul Empire, AD 1656–1668*, trans. Archibald Constable. Edinburgh: Humphrey Milford.

Best, J. L., P. J. Ashworth, C. S. Bristow, and J. E. Roden. 2003. "Three-dimensional Sedimentary Structure of a Large, Mid-channel Sand Braid Bar, Jamuna River, Bangladesh," *Journal of Sedimentary Research*, 73: 516–530.

Best, J. L., P. J. Ashworth, M. H. Sarker, and J. E. Roden. 2007. "The Brahmaputra-Jamuna River, Bangladesh," in A. Gupta (ed.), *Large Rivers: Geomorphology and Management*. Chichester: John Wiley & Sons, pp. 395–432.

Bhabha, H. 1990. "The Third Space," Interview with Homi Bhabha in J. Rutherford (ed.), *Identity, Community, Culture, Difference*. London: Lawrence and Wishart, pp. 202–221.

———. 1994. *The Location of Culture*. London: Routledge.

Bhattacharya, D. 2007. *Paippalada-Samhita of the Atharvaveda*, vol. 2. Calcutta: The Asiatic Society.

Bhattacharyya, H. 1985. *Zamindars and Patnidars: Study of Subinfeudation under Permanent Settlement*. Burdwan: The University of Burdwan.

Bhattacharyya, K. 1998. "Applied Geomorphological Study in a Controlled Tropical River: The Case of the Damodar between Panchet Reservoir and Falta," PhD thesis. Burdwan: The University of Burdwan.

Bhaumik, S. K. 1993. *Tenancy Relations and Agrarian Development: A Study of West Bengal*. New Delhi: Sage Publications.

Biswas, A. 1982. "Why Dandakaranya a Failure, Why Mass Exodus, Where Solution?" *Oppressed Indian*, July, pp. 16–19.

Blaikie, P., T. Cannon, I. Davis, and B. Wisner. 1994. *At Risk: Natural Hazards, People's Vulnerability and Disasters*. London: Routledge.

Blok, A., and T. E. Jensen. 2011. *Bruno Latour: Hybrid Thoughts in a Hybrid World*. London and New York: Routledge.

Blumberg, R. L. 1995. "Introduction: Engendering Wealth and Well-being in an Area of Economic Transformation," in R. L. Blumberg, C. A. Rakowski, I. Tinker, and M. Monten (eds.), *EnGENDERing Wealth and Well-being: Empowerment for Global Change*. Boulder, CO: Westview, pp. 165–178.

Bogardi, J. J. 2004a. "Hazards, Risk and Vulnerability: A New Look on the Flood Plains," Proceedings of the international workshop on "Water Hazards and Risk Management," Tsukuba, January 20–22.

———. 2004b. "Water Hazards, Risks and Vulnerabilities in a Changing Environment," International conference on "Space and Water: Towards Sustainable Development and Human Security," Santiago, Chile, April 1–2.

Bohle, H. G. 2002. "Land Degradation and Human Security," International workshop on "Environment and Human Security," United Nations Research and Training Centre, Bonn, March 1–6.

Bond, G. C., and A. Gilliam. 1994. *Social Reconstruction of the Past: Representation as Power*. London: Routledge.

Bose, P. K. (ed.). 2000. *Refugees in West Bengal: Institutional Practices and Contested Identities*. Calcutta: Calcutta Research Group.

Bose, S. 1986. *Agrarian Bengal: Economy, Social Structure and Politics, 1919–1947*. Cambridge: Cambridge University Press.

Bose, S. C. 1948. *The Damodar Valley Project*. Calcutta: Government of West Bengal.

———. 1999. "Agricultural Growth and Agrarian Structure in Bengal: A Historical Overview," in B. Rogaly, B. Harriss-White, and S. Bose (eds.), *Sonar Bangla? Agricultural Growth and Agrarian Change in West Bengal and Bangladesh*. New Delhi: Sage Publications, pp. 41–59.

Bose, T. 2000. "Protection of Refugees in South Asia," Working Paper No. 6. Kathmandu: South Asia Forum for Human Rights.

Boyce, J. K. 1990. "Birth of a Megaproject: Political Economy of Flood Control in Bangladesh," *Environmental Management*, 14(4): 419–428.

Brammer, H. 1990. "Floods in Bangladesh II: Flood Mitigation and Environmental Aspects," *Geographical Journal*, 56(2): 158–165.

———. 2004. *Can Bangladesh Be Protected from Floods?* Dhaka: University Press Limited.

Brice, J. C. 1964. "Planform Properties of Meandering Rivers," in C. M. Elliot (ed.), *River Meandering*. New York: ASCE, pp. 1–15.

Bridge, J. S. 2003. *Rivers and Floodplains: Forms, Processes, and Sedimentary Record*. Oxford: Blackwell.

Brittain, Robert E. 1959. *Rivers and Man*. London: Longmans, Green.

Brocklesby, M. A., and M. Hobley. 2003. "The Practice of Design: Developing the *Chars* Livelihoods Programme in Bangladesh," *Journal of International Development*, 15(7): 893–909.

Brooks, N. 2003. *Vulnerability, Risk and Adaptation: A Conceptual Framework*, Working Paper No. 38. Norwich: Tyndall Centre for Climate Change Research, University of East Anglia.

Buchanan, F. H. 1798. *An Account of the Journey Undertaken by Order of the Board of Trade through the Province of Chittagong and Tiperah, in order to Look Out for the Places Most Proper for the Cultivation of Spices*. London: India Office Records.

———. 1828. *An Account of the District of Purnea in 1809–1810*. Patna: Bihar and Orissa Research Society.

Burrard, S. 1933. "Movements of the Ground Level in Bengal," *Royal Engineers Journal*, 47: 234–240.

Burton, I., and R. W. Kates. 1964. "The Perception of Natural Hazards in Resource Management," *Natural Resources Journal*, 3: 412–421.

Burton, I., R. W. Kates, and R. E. Snead. 1969. "The Human Ecology of Coastal Flood Hazard in Megalopolis," Research Paper No. 115. Chicago: Department of Geography, University of Chicago.

Buvinic, M., and G. Rao Gupta. 1997. "Female-headed Households and Female-maintained Families: Are They Worth Targeting to Reduce Poverty in Developing Countries?" *Economic Development and Cultural Change* 45(2): 259–280.

Campbell, Sir G. 1921. *Report on the Administration of Bengal: 1918–1919*. Calcutta: Graphic.

Canclini, N. G. 1995. *Hybrid Cultures: Strategies for Entering and Leaving Modernity*. Minneapolis: University of Minnesota Press.

Carpenter, S. R., and W. A. Brock. 2006. "Rising Variance: A Leading Indicator of Ecological Transition," *Ecology Letters*, 9: 311–318.

Chaki, D. 2011. *Bratyajaner Britanto: Prasango: Bharat-Bangladesh Chhitmahal*. Calcutta: Sopan.

Chakrabarti, P. 1990. *The Marginal Men: Refugees and the Left Political Syndrome in West Bengal*. Kalyani: Lumierre Books.

Chakraborty, D., G. Gupta, and S. Bandyopadhyay. 1997. "Migration from Bangladesh to India, 1971–1991: Its Magnitude and Causes," in B. De and R. Samaddar (eds.), *State, Development and Political Culture: Bangladesh and India*. New Delhi: Har-Anand Publishers, pp. 75–90.

Chalov, R. S. 2001. "Intricately Braided River Channels of Lowland Rivers: Formation Conditions, Morphology, and Deformation," *Water Resources*, 28(2): 145–150.

Chambers, R. 1989. "Vulnerability, Coping and Policy," *IDS Bulletin*, 20: 1–8.

Chambers, R., and G. Conway. 1992. "Sustainable Rural Livelihoods: Practical Concepts for the 21st Century," *Discussion Paper No. 296*. Brighton: Institute of Development Studies.

Chan, A. B. 1996. *Li Ka Shing: Hong Kong's Elusive Billionaire*. Toronto: Macmillan.

Chan, K. B. 1997. "A Family Affair: Migration, Diaspora and the Emergent Identity of the Chinese Cosmopolitan," *Diaspora*, 6: 195–213.

Chandrasekhar, C. P. 1993. "Agrarian Change and Occupational Diversification: Non-agricultural Employment and Rural Development in West Bengal," *Journal of Peasant Studies*, 20(2): 205–270.

Chapman, G., and K. Rudra. 1995. *Water and the Quest for Sustainable Development in the Ganges Valley*. London: Mansell.

———. 2007. "Water as Friend, Water as Foe: Lessons from Bengal's Millennium Flood," *Journal of South Asian Development*, 2(1): 19–49.

Chatterjee, N. 1995. "The East Bengal Refugees: A Lesson in Survival," in S. Chaudhuri (ed.), *Kolkata: The Living City*, vol., 2, *Present*. New Delhi, Kolkata, and Madras: Oxford University Press, pp. 70–77.

Chatterjee, S. P. 1947. *The Partition of Bengal*. Kolkata: Geographical Society of India.

Chatterjee, S. P. 1967. "Technical Advisory Committee Report on the Lower Damodar Valley Region," Joint Committee for a Diagnostic Survey of Damodar Valley Region, Government of India. Calcutta: Damodar Valley Corporation.

Chaudhuri, K. C. 1927. *The History and Economics of the Land System in Bengal*. Calcutta: Book Company.

Chaudhuri, S. B, B. De, S. Mukherjee, P. Ray, S. Sengupta, A. Sen, S. P. Mukherjee, N. Sen, K. S. Sengupta, R. N. Nag, S. Som, and T. Pal. 1994. *West Bengal District Gazetteers: Barddhaman*. Calcutta: Government of West Bengal.

Chorley, R. J., S. A. Schumm, and D. E. Sugden. 1984. *Geomorphology*. London: Methuen.

Chowdhury, M. 2001. "Women's Technological Innovations and Adaptations for Disaster Mitigation: A Case Study of Charlands in Bangladesh," Expert Group Meeting on "Environmental Management and the Mitigation of Natural Disasters: A Gender Perspective," Ankara, Turkey, November 6–9.

Cleary, D. 1993. "After the Frontier: Problems with Political Economy in the Modern Brazilian Amazon," *Journal of Latin American Studies*, 25(2): 331–249.

Cleaver, F. 1998. "Choice, Complexity, and Change: Gendered Livelihoods and the Management of Water," *Agriculture and Human Values*, 15: 293–299.

Code, L. 2006. *Ecological Thinking: The Politics of Epistemic Location*. Oxford: Oxford University Press.

Colebrooke, H. T. 1806. *Remarks on the Husbandry and Internal Commerce of Bengal*. London: Blacks and Parry.

Collins, D., J. Morduch, S. Rutherford, and O. Ruthven. 2009. *Portfolios of the Poor: How the World's Poor Live on $2 a Day*. Princeton and Oxford: Princeton University Press.

Coones, P. 1983. "A Russian Interpretation of Classical Geography," *Geographical Review*, 73(1): 95–109.

Cosgrove, D., and G. Petts. 1990. *Water, Engineering and Landscape: Water Control and Landscape Transformation in the Modern Period*. London and New York: Belhaven Press.

Costa, J. da Silva, R. W. Ellson, and R. C. Martin. 1987. "Public Capital, Regional Output, and Development: Some Empirical Evidence," *Journal of Regional Science*, 27: 419–437.

Costa, J. E. 1988. "Floods from Dam Failures," in V. R. Baker, R. C. Koehel, and P. C. Patrons (eds.), *Flood Geomorphology*. New York: John Wiley, pp. 439–464.

Cronon, W. 1992. "A Place for Stories: Nature, History, and Narrative," *Journal of American History*, 78: 1347–1376.

Cutter, S. L., B. J. Boruff, and W. L. Shirley. 2003. "Social Vulnerability to Environmental Hazards," *Social Science Quarterly*, 84(2): 242–261.

Daly, C. C., and V. Mahendra. 2001. "Human Rights and Trafficking: Supporting Women in Nepal," *Global AIDSlink*, 69(1): 1–2.

Damodar Valley Corporation [DVC]. 1948. *Why the Damodar Scheme Deserves Top Priority among India's Development Projects*. Calcutta: Damodar Valley Corporation.

Das, S. K. 2005. "India: Homelessness at Home," in P. Banerjee, S. Basu Ray Chaudhury, and S. K. Das (eds.), *Internal Displacement in South Asia*. New Delhi: Sage Publications, pp. 113–143.

Dasgupta, Abhijit. 2001. "The Politics of Agitation and Confession: Displaced Bengalis in West Bengal," in S. K. Ray (ed.), *Refugees and Human Rights: Social and Political Dynamics of Refugee Problem in Eastern and Northeastern India*. Rawat: Jaipur, pp. 92–100.

Dasgupta, Amal. 2010. *Phanerozoic Stratigraphy of India*. Kolkata: World Press.

Das Gupta, A. B. 1997. "Geology of Bengal Basin," *Quarterly Journal of Geological Survey of India*, 69(2): 161–176.

Das Gupta, A. B., and B. Mukherjee. 2006. *Geology of Northwest Bengal Basin*. Kolkata: Geological Society of India.

Datta, D., and I. Hossain. 2003. *Reaching the Extreme Poor: Learning from Concern's Community Development Programme in Bangladesh*. Dhaka: Concern.

Datta, P. 2004. "Push-pull Factors of Undocumented Migration from Bangladesh to West Bengal: A Perception Study," *Qualitative Report*, 9(2): 335–358.

Davis, W. M. 1900. "The Physical Geography of the Lands," *Popular Science Monthly*, 2: 157–170.

Deb Sarkar, M. 2009. *Geo-political Implications of Partition in West Bengal: Looking Back at Partition of Bengal*. Kolkata: K. P. Bagchi & Company.

Deb, U. K., G. D. Nageswara Rao, Y. M. Rao, and R. Slater. 2002. "Diversification and Livelihood Options: A Study of Two Villages in Andhra Pradesh, India, 1975–2001," Working Paper No. 178. London: Overseas Development Institute.

de Haan, A. 1999. "Livelihood and Poverty: The Role of Migration, A Critical Review of the Migration Literature," *Journal of Development Studies*, 36(2): 1–47.

———. 2000. "Migrants, Livelihoods, and Rights: The Relevance of Migration in Development Policies," Working Paper No. 4. London: Social Development Department, DFID.

———. 2002. "Migration and Livelihoods in Historical Perspective: A Case Study of Bihar, India," *Journal of Development Studies*, 38(5): 115–142.

de Haan, A., K. Brock, G. Carswell, N. Coulibaly, H. Seba, and K. Ali Toufique. 2000. "Migrants, Livelihoods: Case Studies in Bangladesh, Ethiopia and Mali," *Research Report No. 46*. Brighton: Institute of Development Studies.

Demeritt, D. 1994. "The Nature of Metaphors in Cultural Geography and Environmental History," *Progress in Human Geography*, 18(2): 163–185.

Department for International Development [DFID]. 2002. "Better Livelihoods for Poor People: The Role of Agriculture," Draft paper, March. London: DFID.

Deshingkar, P., and D. Start. 2003. "Seasonal Migration for Livelihoods in India: Coping, Accumulation and Exclusion," Working Paper No. 220. London: Overseas Development Institute.

D'Souza, R. 2003. "Canal Irrigation and the Conundrum of Flood Protection: The Failure of the Orissa Scheme of 1863 in Eastern India," *Conservation and Society*, 1(2): 317–332.

———. 2004. "Rigidity and the Affliction of Capitalist Property: Colonial Land Revenue and the Recasting of Nature," *Studies in History*, 20(2): 237–272.

———. 2007. *Drowned and the Dammed: Colonial Capitalism and Flood Control in Eastern India*. New Delhi: Oxford University Press.

———. 2009. "Rivers as Resource and Land to Own: The Great Hydraulic Transition in Eastern India," Paper presented at the conference "Asian Environments Shaping the World: Conceptions of Nature and Environmental Practices," National University of Singapore, Singapore, March 20–21, 2009.

Dutta, A. K. 2002. *Economy and Ecology in a Bengal District*. Calcutta: Formal KLM.

Duyne-Barenstein, J. 2008. "Endogamous Water Resources Management in North-east Bangladesh: Lessons from the Haor Basin," in Kuntala Lahiri-Dutt and Robert J. Wasson (eds.), *Water First: Issues and Challenges for Nations and Communities in South Asia*. New Delhi: Sage Publications, pp. 349–371.

East, G. 1938. *The Geography behind History*. London: T. Nelson.

Elahi, K. M., K. S. Ahmed, and M. Mufiazuddin. 1991. *Riverbank Erosion, Flood and Population Displacement in Bangladesh*. Riverbank Erosion Impact Study. Dhaka: Jahangirnagar University.

Elahi, K. M., and J. R. Rogge (eds.). 1990. "Riverbank Erosion, Flood and Population Displacement in Bangladesh," in *Riverbank Erosion Impact Study*. Dhaka: Jahangirnagar University.

Elliott, A. 2002. "Beck's Sociology of Risk: A Critical Assessment," *Sociology*, 36(2): 293–315.

Ellis, F. 1998. "Household Strategies and Rural Livelihood Diversification," *Journal of Development Studies*, 35(1): 1–38.

———. 1999. "Rural Livelihood Diversity in Developing Countries: Evidence and Policy Implications," in *Natural Resource Perspectives 40*. London: Overseas Development Institute.

———. 2000. *Rural Livelihoods and Diversity in Developing Countries*. Oxford: Oxford University Press.

Engle, P. 1995. "Father's Money, Mother's Money and Parental Commitment: Guatemala and Nicaragua," in R. L. Blumberg, C. A. Rakowski, I. Tinker, and M. Monten (eds.), *EnGENDERing Wealth and Well-being: Empowerment for Global Change*. San Francisco: Westview, pp. 235–265.

Environment and GIS Support Project for Water Sector Planning [EGIS]. 2000. *Riverine Chars in Bangladesh: Environmental Dynamics and Management Issues*. Environmental and Geographical Information Systems Support, Dhaka: University Press Limited.

Evans, C., and P. Bhattarai. 2003. *Trafficking in Nepal: Intervention Models—A Comparative Analysis of Anti-trafficking Intervention Approaches in Nepal*. Kathmandu: Asia Foundation/Population Council/Horizons.

Fairhead, J., and M. Leach. 1996. "Enriching the Landscape: Social History and the Management of Transition Ecology in the Forest Savanna Mosaic of the Republic of Guinea," *Journal of the International African Institute*, 66(1): 14–36.

Febvre, L. 1962 [1923]. Review of Vidal de la Blache's *Geography Textbook: A Geographical Introduction to History*. Reprinted in *Pour une Histoire à Part Entière*. Paris: S.E.V.P.E.N.

Field, C. D. 2010 [1883]. *Landholding and the Relation of Landlords and Tenants in Various Countries*, The Making of Modern Law, Collection of Legal Archives, MOML Legal Treatises, 1800–1926. Farmington Hills, MI: Gale.

Folbre, N. 1991. "Women on Their Own: Global Patterns of Female Headship," in R. S. Gallin and A. Fergusen (eds.), *The Woman and International Development Annual*, vol. 2. Boulder, CO: Westview, pp. 89–128.

Forbes, G. H. 1999 [1975]. *Positivism in Bengal: A Case Study in the Transmission and Assimilation of an Ideology*. Kolkata: Papyrus.

Fouron, G. E., and N. Glick Schiller. 2001. "All in the Family: Gender, Transnational Migration and the Nation-state," *Identities*, 44: 539–582.

Fox, C. S. 1930. *Annual Report*. Calcutta: River Research Institute.

Francis, E. 1998. "Gender and Rural Livelihoods in Kenya," *Journal of Development Studies*, 35(2): 72–95.

———. 2002. "Gender, Migration and Multiple Livelihoods: Cases from Eastern and Southern Africa," *Journal of Development Studies*, 38(5): 167–190.

Frankenberger, T. R. 1996. "Measuring Household Livelihood Security: An Approach for Reducing Absolute Poverty," Paper prepared for the "Applied Anthropology Meeting," Baltimore, March 27–30.

Franklin, P. 1986 [1861]. "The Ganges and the Hooghly: How to Connect These Rivers by Converting the Matabhanga into a Navigable Canal," in Sunil Sen Sharma (ed.), *Farakka—A Gordian Knot: Problems of Sharing Ganges Waters*. Calcutta: Calcutta University Press, pp. 20–30.

Gadgil, M., and R. Guha. 1992. *This Fissured Land: An Ecological History of India*. New Delhi: Oxford University Press.

Ganguly, D. S. 1982. "Damodar Valley Corporation and Regional Economy: An Appraisal," in *Geographical Mosaic*. Calcutta: Geographical Society of India, pp. 568–81.

Gaston, K. J., A. S. Rodrigues, B. J. van Rensburg, P. Koleff, and S. L. Chown. 2001. "Complementary Representation and Zones of Ecological Transition," *Ecology Letters*, 4: 4–9.

Gastrell, J. E. 1863. *Statistical and Geographical Report of the District of Bancoorah*. Calcutta: Bengal Secretariat Press.

Gazdar, H., and S. Sengupta. 1999. "Agricultural Growth and Recent Trends in Well-being in Rural West Bengal," in B. Rogaly, B. Harriss-White, and S. Bose (eds.), *Sonar Bangla? Agricultural Growth and Agrarian Change in West Bengal and Bangladesh*. New Delhi: Sage Publications, pp. 71–98.

Ghatak, M. 1995. "Reforms, Incentives and Growth in West Bengal Agriculture," Paper presented at the workshop on "Agricultural Growth and Agrarian Structure in Contemporary West Bengal and Bangladesh," Centre for Studies in Social Sciences, Calcutta, January 9–12.

Ghosal, U. N. 1930. *The Agrarian System in Ancient India*, Calcutta University Readership Lectures. Calcutta: University of Calcutta.

Ghosh, Aditya. 2004. "Shifting River Erases Villages and Identities," *Times of India*, Kolkata, November 24.

Ghosh, Amitav. 2004 *The Hungry Tide*. New Delhi: Ravi Dayal.

Ghosh, B. 1998. *Huddled Masses and Uncertain Shores: Insights into Irregular Migration*. The Hague: International Organisation for Migration and Martinus Nijhoff.

Ghosh, B., and P. De. 1998. "Role of Infrastructure in Regional Development," *Economic and Political Weekly*, 33(47): 3039–3048. .

Ghosh, M. 1998. "Agricultural Development, Agrarian Structure and Rural Poverty in West Bengal," *Economic and Political Weekly*, 33(47): 2987–2996.

Ghosh, M. G. 1995. "Common Property Resource Use by Poor in West Bengal," Paper presented at Fifth Common Property Conference, "Reinventing the Commons," Bodø, Norway, May 24–28.

Gibson-Graham, J. K. 2006. *A Post Capitalist Politics*. Minneapolis and London: University of Minnesota Press.

Ginguld, M., A. Perevolotsky, and E. D. Ungar. 1997. "Living on the Margins: Livelihood Strategies of Bedouin Herd-owners in the Northern Negev, Israel," *Human Ecology*, 25(4): 567–591.

Gleditsch, N. P. 2001. "Armed Conflict and the Environment," in P. F. Diehl and N. P. Gleditsch (eds.), *Environmental Conflict*. Boulder, CO: Westview, pp. 251–272.

Goodbred, S. L., Jr. 2003. "Response of the Ganges Dispersal System to Climate Change: A Source-to-sink View since the Last Interstade," *Sedimentary Geology*, 162: 83–104.

Goodbred, S. L., Jr., and S. A. Kuehl. 2000. "Enormous Ganges—Brahmaputra Sediment Discharge during Strengthened Early Holocene Monsoon," *Geology*, 28: 1083–1086.

Goswami, D. C. 1985. "Brahmaputra River, Assam, India: Basin Denudation and Channel Aggradation," *Water Resources Research*, 21(7): 959–978.

Government of India [GoI]. 2001. *Data Highlights, Migration Tables*. New Delhi: Census of India, GoI.

Gowda, M. N., and P. M. Savadatti. 2004. "CPRs and Rural Poor: Study in North Karnataka," *Economic and Political Weekly*, 39(33): 3752–3757.

Grove, R. 1995. *Green Imperialism: Colonial Expansion, Tropical Island Edens and the Origins of Environmentalism, 1600–1800*. Cambridge: Cambridge University Press.

Grove, R., and V. Damodaran. 2006. "Imperialism, Intellectual Networks, and Environmental Change: Origins and Evolution of Global Environmental History, 1676–2000," part 1, *Economic and Political Weekly*, 41(41), October 14: 4345–4356.

Grunwald, M. 2007. *The Swamp: The Everglades, Florida, and the Politics of Paradise*. New York: Simon & Schuster.

Guha, R., and J. Martinez-Alier. 1997. *Varieties of Environmentalism: Essays North and South*. New Delhi: Oxford University Press.

Guha, Ramachandra (ed.). 1994. *Social Ecology*. New Delhi: Oxford University Press.

Guha, Ranajit. 1963. *A Rule of Property for Bengal: An Essay on the Idea of Permanent Settlement*. Paris: Mouton & Co.

Gulati, L. 1993. *Women Migrant Workers in Asia: A Review*, UNDP/ILO Asian Regional Program on International Labor Migration. New Delhi: ILO.

———. 1997. "Asian Women in International Migration with Special Reference to Domestic Work and Entertainment," *Economic and Political Weekly*, 32: 3029–3035.

Gupta, A. 1994. "Fluvial Geomorphology in the Tropics with Special Reference to the Indian Rivers," in K. R. Dikshit, V. S. Kale, and M. N. Kaul (eds.), *India: Geomorphological Diversity*. Jaipur: Rawat Publications, pp. 57–66.

———. (ed.). 2007. *Large Rivers: Geomorphology and Management*. Chichester: John Wiley & Sons.

———. 2011. *Tropical Geomorphology*. Cambridge: Cambridge University Press.

Hampshire, K. 2002. "Fulani on the Move: Seasonal Migration in the Sahel as a Social Process," *Journal of Development Studies*, 38(5): 15–36.

Hapke, H. M., and D. Ayyankeril. 2004. "Gender, the Work-life Course, and Livelihood Strategies in a South Indian Fish Market," *Gender, Place and Culture*, 11(2): 229–256.

Harper, K. A., S. E. MacDonald, P. J. Burton, J. Chen, K. D. Brosofske, S. C. Saunders, E. S. Euskirchen, D. Roberts, M. S. Jaiteh, and P.-A. Esseen. 2005. "Edge Influence on Forest Structure and Composition in Fragmented Landscapes," *Conservation Biology*, 19: 1–15.

Harris, C. 2004. *Making Native Space: Colonialism, Resistance and Reserves in British Columbia*. Vancouver: University of British Columbia Press.

Harriss, J. 1992. "Does the 'Depressor' Still Work? Agrarian Structure and Development in India: A Review of Evidence and Argument," *Journal of Peasant Studies*, 19(2): 189–227.

———. 1993. "What Is Happening in Rural West Bengal? Agrarian Reform, Growth and Distribution," *Economic and Political Weekly*, 28(24): 1237–1247.

Hart, H. C. 1956. *New India's Rivers*. Bombay: Orient Longman.

Hayzer, N., and V. Wee. 1994. "Domestic Workers in Transient Overseas Employment: Who Benefits and Who Profits?" in N. Hayzer, G. Lycklama, and N. Weerakoon (eds.), *The Trade in Domestic Workers; Causes, Mechanisms and Consequences of International Migration*, vol. 1. London: Zed Books, pp. 1–25.

Hazarika, S. 2000. *Rites of Passage: Border Crossings, Imagined Homelands, India's East and Bangladesh*. New Delhi: Penguin.

Head, L. 2007. "Cultural Ecology: The Problematic Human and the Terms of Engagement," *Progress in Human Geography*, 31(6): 837–846.

———. 2010. "Cultural Ecology: Adaptation—Retrofitting a Concept?" *Progress in Human Geography*, 34(2): 234–242.

Head, L., and P. Muir. 2007. *Backyard: Nature and Culture in Suburban Australia*. Wollongong: University of Wollongong Press.

Henningham, S. 1990. *A Great Estate and its Landlords in Colonial India: Darbhanga, 1860–1942*. New Delhi: Oxford University Press.

Hewitt, K. 1997. *Regions of Risk: A Geographical Introduction to Disasters*. Essex, UK: Longman.

Hill, C. V. 1997. *River of Sorrow: Environment and Social Control in Riparian North India, 1770–1994*. Ann Arbor: Association for Asian Studies.

———. 2008. *South Asia: An Environmental History*. Santa Barbara: University of California Press.

Hillier, J., and E. Rooksby (eds.). 2005. *Habitus: A Sense of Place*. Ashgate: Aldershot.

Hofer, T., and B. Messerli. 1997. *Floods in Bangladesh: Process Understanding and Development Strategies*. Berne: Institute of Geography, Swiss Agency for Development and Cooperation, and the United Nations University.

Homer-Dixon, T. F. 1991. "On the Threshold: Environmental Changes as Causes of Acute Conflict," *International Security*, 16(2): 76–116.

———. 1994. "Environmental Scarcities and Violent Conflict: Evidence from Cases," *International Security*, 19(1): 5–40.

Hossain, I. M., I. A. Khan, and J. Selley. 2003. "Surviving on Their Feet: Charting the Mobile Livelihoods of the Poor in Rural Bangladesh," Paper presented at the conference "Staying Poor: Chronic Poverty and Development Policy," Manchester, April 7–9.

Howitt, R. 2001. "Frontiers, Borders, Edges: Liminal Challenges to the Hegemony of Exclusion," *Australian Geographical Studies*, 39(2): 233–245.

Hugo, G. 2002. "Introduction," in *Migration and the Labour Market in Asia: Recent Trends and Policies*. Paris: OECD, pp. 7–16.

Human Rights Features. 2001. "Attacks on Hindu Minorities in Bangladesh," *Human Rights Features*, 48: 1–4.

Hunter, W. W. 1875. *A Statistical Account of Bengal*, vol. 1, *District of 24 Parganas and Sundarbans*. London: Truebner.

———. 1876. *A Statistical Account of Bengal*, vol. 4, *Burdwan, Bankura and Birbhum*. London: Truebner.

———. 1882. *The Indian Empire: Its Peoples, History and Products*. London: Trubner.

———. 1887. *The Imperial Gazetteer of India*. London: Trubner.

Huxley, Aldous. 1929. "Wordsworth in the Tropics," in *Do What You Will*. London: Chatto and Windus, pp. 113–115.

Ifekwunigwe, Jayne O. 2004. *"Mixed Race" Studies: A Reader*. London and New York: Routledge.

Ikeme, J. 2003. "Equity, Environmental Justice and Sustainability: Incomplete Approaches in Climatic Change Politics," *Global Environmental Change*, 13: 195–206.

India News. 2004. "Bihari Migration," *India News*, Patna, October 27.

Inglis, D., and J. Bone. 2006. "Boundary Maintenance, Border Crossing and the Nature/Culture Divide," *European Journal of Social Theory*, 9(2): 272–287.

Inglis, W. A. 1909. *The Canals and Flood Banks of Bengal*. Calcutta: Bengal Secretariat Press.

———. 2002. *Rivers of Bengal*. Kolkata: West Bengal District Gazetteers, Government of West Bengal. Reprint edition.

Intergovernmental Panel on Climate Change [IPCC]. 2001. *Climate Change 2001: Impacts, Adaptation, and Vulnerability*. IPCC Third Assessment Report. Geneva: United Nations, IPCC. Available at http://www.ipcc.ch/ipccreports/tar/index.htm.

International Strategy for Disaster Reduction [ISDR]. 2004. "Water and Disaster: Be Informed and Be Prepared," Publication No. 971. Geneva: United Nations, World Meteorological Organization.

Iqbal, I. 2010. *The Bengal Delta: Ecology, State and Social Change*, Cambridge Imperial and Post Colonial Series. Basingstoke: Palgrave Macmillan.

Jackson, R. G., II. 1975. "Hierarchical Attributes and a Unifying Model of Bed Forms Composed of Cohesionless Material and Produced by Shearing Flow," *Geological Society of America Bulletin*, 86: 1523–1533.

Jacques, K. 2001. *Bangladesh, India and Pakistan: International Relations and Regional Tensions in South Asia*. New Delhi: Macmillan.

Jahan, R. 1995. *The Elusive Agenda: Mainstreaming Women in Development*. London: Zed Books.

Jalais, A. 2005. "Dwelling on Morichjhanpi: When Tigers Became 'Citizens,' Refugees 'Tiger-food,'" *Economic and Political Weekly*, 40(17), April 23: 1757–1762.

———. 2010. *Forest of Tigers: People, Politics and Environments in the Sundarbans*, London: Routledge.

Jones, R. 2009. "Categories, Borders and Boundaries," *Progress in Human Geography*, 33(2): 174–189.

Joshi, S. 2004. "Female Household-headship in Rural Bangladesh: Incidence, Determinants and Impact on Children's Schooling," Discussion Paper No. 894. New Haven: Economic Growth Centre, Yale University.

Kabeer, N. 1991. *Gender, Production and Well Being: Rethinking the Household Economy*. Brighton: Institute of Development Studies.

Kabeer, N., and R. Subrahmanian. 1996. *Institutions, Relations and Outcomes: Framework and Tools for Gender-Aware Planning*. Brighton: Institute of Development Studies.

Kaplan, R. 1998. "The Coming Anarchy," in Ó. T. Garõid, S. Dalby, and P. Routledge (eds.), *The Geopolitics Reader*. Abingdon: Routledge, pp. 185–95.

Kar, S. 1998. "Rural Uplift: Case for State Help," *The Statesman*, December 8.

Karan, A. 2003. "Changing Patterns of Migration from Rural Bihar," in G. Iyer (ed.), *Migrant Labour and Human Rights in India*. New Delhi: Kanishka Publishers, pp. 102–139.

Karnath, G. K., and V. Ramaswamy. 2004. "From Market to Market: Changing Faces of Rural Livelihood Systems," in R. Baumgartner and R. Hogger (eds.), *In Search of Sustainable Livelihoods Systems: Managing Resources and Change*. New Delhi: Sage Publications, pp. 57–75.

Karvonen, A., and K. Yocom. 2011. "The Civics of Urban Nature: Enacting Hybrid Landscapes," *Environment and Planning A*, 43: 1305–1322.

Kates, R. W. 1962. "Hazard and Choice Perception in Flood Plain Management," Research Paper No. 78. Chicago: Department of Geography, University of Chicago.

Kelly, P. M., and W. N. Adger. 2000. "Theory and Practice in Assessing Vulnerability to Climate Change and Facilitating Adaptation," *Climatic Change*, 47: 325–352.

Kirk, W. 1950. "The Damodar Valley: 'Valles Optima,'" *Geographical Review*, 40(3): 415–443.

Klingensmith, D. 2007. *One Valley and a Thousand Dams: Nationalism, and Development*. Oxford: Oxford University Press.

Kotoky, P., D. Bezbaruah, J. Baruah, and J. N. Sarma. 2003. "Erosion Activity on Majuli: The Largest River Island of the World," *Current Science*, 84(7): 929–932.

Kudaisya, G. 1998. "Divided Landscapes, Fragmented Identities: East Bengal Refugees and Their Rehabilitation in India, 1947–1979," in D. A. Low and H. Brasted (eds.), *Freedom, Communities, Trauma: Northern India and Independence*. New Delhi: Sage Publications, pp. 105–131.

Kumar, A. 1994. "Rural Development in India: Back and Beyond," in A. Kumar (ed.), *New Approach in Rural Development*. New Delhi: Anmol, pp. 1–25.

Kumar, D., V. Damodaran, and R. D'Souza (eds.). 2011. "Introduction," in *The British Empire and the Natural World: Environmental Encounters in South Asia*. New Delhi: Oxford University Press, pp. 1–16.

Lahiri-Dutt, K. 1985. "Urbanisation in the Lower Damodar Valley: A Study in Urban Geography," PhD thesis. Burdwan: The University of Burdwan.

———. 1994. "Shifting of the Urban Nucleus: A Study of Kanchannagar and Burdwan Town," *Landscape Systems*, 5(3): 1–20.

———. 2000. "Imagining Rivers," *Economic and Political Weekly*, 35(27): 2395–2400.

———. 2003. "People, Power and Rivers: Experiences from the Damodar River, India," *Water Nepal, Journal of Water Resources Development*, Special issue on Water, Human Rights, and Governance, 9/10(1/2): 251–267.

———. 2006. "Nadi O Nari: Social Construction of Rivers as Women in Rural Bengal," in K. Lahiri-Dutt (ed.), *Fluid Bonds: Views on Gender and Water*. Calcutta: Stree, pp. 387–408.

———. 2008. "Negotiating Water Management in the Damodar Valley: Kalikata Hearing and the DVC," in K. Lahiri-Dutt and R. Wasson (eds.), *Water First: Issues and Challenges for Nations and Communities in South Asia*. New Delhi: Sage Publications, pp. 316–348.

———. 2012. "Large Dams and Changes in an Agrarian Society: Gendering the Impacts of Damodar Valley Corporation in Eastern India," in *Water Alternatives*, 5(2), June 2012: 529–542.

Lahiri-Dutt, K., and G. Samanta. 2002. "State Initiatives for the Empowerment of Women of Rural Communities," *Community Development Journal*, 37(2): 135–156.

———. 2004. "Fleeting Land, Fleeting People: Bangladeshi Women in a *Char*land Environment in Lower Bengal, India," *Asia Pacific Migration Journal*, 13(4): 475–495.

Land Revenue Records. 1851. "Embankments in Bengal: Note on Their Origin, Development and Utility (1772–1850)," in *Index to Land Revenue Records, 1838–1859*. New Delhi: National Archives of India.

Law, J. 2004. *After Method: Mess in Social Science Research*. London and New York: Routledge.

———. 2007. "Making a Mess with Method," in W. Outhwaite and S. P. Turner (eds.), *The Sage Handbook of Social Science Methodology*. Thousand Oaks: Sage Publications, pp. 595–606.

Leach, M., and J. Fairhead. 2000. "Fashioned Forest Pasts, Occluded Histories? International Environmental Analysis in West African Locales," *Development and Change*, 31: 35–59.

Leaf, M. 1997. "Local Control versus Technocracy: The Bangladesh Flood Response Study," *Journal of International Affairs*, 51(1): 179–200.

Lehner, G., F. John, and E. Kube. 1955. *The Dynamics of Personal Adjustment*. New York: Prentice-Hall.

Leopold, A. 1966. "The Round River," in *A Sand Country Almanac*. New York: Oxford University Press, pp. 1–25.

Leuchtag, A. 2003. "Human Rights, Sex Trafficking and Prostitution," *Humanist*, 63(1): 10–15.

Levy, M. 1995. "Is the Environment a National Security Issue?" *International Security*, 20(2): 35–62.

Lieten, G. K. 1994. "Rural Development in West Bengal: Views from Below," *Journal of Contemporary Asia*, 24(4): 515–530.

———. 1996. "Land Reforms at Centre Stage: The Evidence on West Bengal," *Development and Change*, 27: 111–130.

Limb, M., and C. Dwyer. 2001. *Qualitative Methodologies for Geographers*. London: Arnold.

Linklater, A. 1996. "The Achievement of Critical Theory," in S. Smith, K. Booth, and M. Zalewski (eds.), *International Theory: Positivism and Beyond*. Cambridge: Cambridge University Press, pp. 193–209.

Linton, J. 2010. *What Is Water? The History of a Modern Abstraction*. Vancouver: University of British Columbia Press.

Lowenthal, D. (ed.). 1967. "Environmental Perception and Behavior," Research Paper No. 109. Chicago: Department of Geography, University of Chicago.

Lucas, R. 1988. "On the Mechanics of Economic Development," *Journal of Monetary Economics*, 22: 3–42

Maity, P. K. 1989. *Human Fertility Cults and Rituals of Bengal: A Comparative Study*. New Delhi: Abhinav Publishers.

Makita, R. 2003. "Participation of the Landless Poor in the Rural Economy through the Non-farm Sector: A Case Study in Bangladesh," Final draft of research proposal for PhD thesis. Canberra: Australian National University.

Malik, S. 2000. "Refugees and Migrants of Bangladesh: Looking through a Historical Prism," in R. Abrar Chowdhury (ed.), *On the Margin: Refugees, Migrants and Minorities*. Dhaka: RMMRU, pp. 11–40.

Mallabarman, A. 1956. *Teetas Ekti Nadir Naam*. Calcutta: Punthighar.

Mallick, R. 1999. "Refugee Resettlement in Forest Reserves: West Bengal Policy Reversal and the Marichjhapi Massacre," *Journal of Asian Studies*, 58(1): 104–125.

Mantu, R. H. 1998. *Char Anchaler Jibanjatra O Manabadhikar* [in Bengali]. Dhaka: Massline Media Centre.

Masika, R., and S. Joekes. 1996. "Employment and Sustainable Livelihoods: A Gender Perspective," Bridge Report 37. Brighton: Institute of Development Studies.

Matley, I. M. 1966. "The Marxist Approach to the Geographical Environment," *Annals of the Association of American Geographers*, 56: 97–111.

Mazumdar, R. C. 2004. *History of Ancient Bengal*, vol. 1, *Ancient Period*. New Delhi: B. R. Publishing. Reprint edition.

McCarthy, J. J., O. F. Canziani, N. A. Leary, D. J. Dokken, and K. S. White (eds.). 2001. *Climate Change 2001: Impacts, Adaptation and Vulnerability*. Cambridge: Cambridge University Press.

McCay, B. 2000. "Edges, Fields and Regions," Presidential Address, Part 2, International Association for the Study of Common Property Conference, September, Bloomington, *Common Property Digest*, 54: 6–8.

McDowell, C., and A. de Haan. 1997. "Migration and Sustainable Livelihoods: A Critical Review of the Literature," Working Paper No. 65. Brighton: Institute of Development Studies, University of Sussex.

McKay, E. 2000. "Measurement of Cognitive Performance in Computer Programming Concept Acquisition: Interactive Effects of Visual Metaphors and the Cognitive Style Construct," *Journal of Applied Measurement*, 1(3): 257–286.

McLane, J. R. 1985. "Bengali Bandits, Police and Landlords: After the Permanent Settlement," in A. A. Yang (ed.), *Crime and Criminality in British India*, Monograph no. 42. Tucson: Association of Asian Studies and University of Arizona Press, pp. 26–48.

———. 1993. *Land and Local Kingship in Eighteenth Century Bengal*. Cambridge: Cambridge University Press.

Meade, R. H., 2007. "Transcontinental Moving and Storage—the Orinoco and Amazon Rivers Transfer the Andes to the Atlantic," in A. Gupta (ed.), *Large Rivers: Geomorphology and Management*. Chichester: John Wiley & Sons, pp. 45–63.

Michels, K., H. R. Kudrass, C. Hubscher, A. Suckow, and M. Wiedicke. 1998. "The Submarine Delta of the Ganges—Brahmaputra: Cyclone-dominated Sedimentation Patterns," *Marine Geology*, 149(1–4): 133–154.

Mikesell, M. 1960. "Comparative Studies in Frontier History," *Annals of the Association of American Geographers*, 50(1): 62–74.

Mishra, D. K. 1997. "The Bihar Flood Story," *Economic and Political Weekly*, 32(35): 2206–2217.

———. 1999. "The Embankment Trap," *Seminar*, No. 478, June, pp. 46–51.

———. 2003. "Life within the Kosi Embankments," *Water Nepal*, 10(1): 277–301.

Mitchell, J. K. 1974. "Community Response to Coastal Erosion: Individual and Collective Adjustments to Hazard on the Atlantic Shore," Research Paper 156. Chicago: Department of Geography, University of Chicago.

Mitra, A. 1955. *District Records: Burdwan*. Calcutta: Government of West Bengal.

Mitra, S. C. 1898. *The Land-law of Bengal*, Tagore Law Lectures, 1895. Calcutta: Thacker, Spink.

Mohanty, B. 2000. "Women and Seasonal Migration (Review)," *Indian Journal of Gender Studies*, 7(2): 336–339.

Mohsin, A. 1997. "Democracy and the Marginalization of the Minorities: The Bangladesh Case," *Journal of Social Studies*, 78: 92–93.

Momen M. A. 1996. "Land Reform and Landlessness in Bangladesh," PhD thesis. England: University of East London.

Moodie, A. E. 1947. *Geography behind Politics*. London: Hutchinson University Library.

Mookerjee, R. 1919. *Occupancy Right: Its History and Incidents Together with an Introduction Dealing with Land Tenure in Ancient India*. Calcutta: University of Calcutta.

Morgan, J. P., and W. G. McIntire. 1959. "Quaternary Geology of the Bengal Basin, East Pakistan and India," *Geological Society of America Bulletin*, 70: 319–342.

Morisawa, M. 1985. *Rivers: Form and Process*. London: Longman.

Morokvasic, M. 1984. "Birds of Passage Are Also Women," *International Migration Review*, 18(4): 886–907.

Mukherjee, R. 1938. *The Changing Face of Bengal: A Study in Riverine Economy*. Calcutta: University of Calcutta.

Nandy, Ashis. 2001 "Dams and Dissent: India's First Modern Environmental Activist and His Critique of the DVC Project," in *Futures*, Special issue on Water Futures in South Asia, 33(8/9): 709–732.

Neale, W. C. 1962. *Economic Change in Rural India: Land Tenure and Reform in UP, 1800–1955*. New Haven and London: Yale University Press.

Nehru, J. 1936. *An Autobiography: With Musings on Recent Events in India*. London: John Lane.

Newman, D. 2003. "Boundaries," in J. Agnew, K. Mitchell, and G. Toal (eds.), *The Companion to Political Geography*. Malden, MA: Blackwell, pp. 122–136.

O'Brien, K., S. Eriksen, and A. S. Lynn Nygaard. 2004. "What's in a Word? Conflicting Interpretations of Vulnerability in Climate Change Research," Working Paper No.

2004: 04. Norway: Centre for International Climate and Environmental Research, Blinden.

Odum, E. P. 1971. *Fundamentals of Ecology*, 3rd ed. Philadelphia: W. B. Saunders.

Oldham, T. 1870. *Proceedings of the Asiatic Society of Bengal*. Calcutta: Asiatic Society.

O'Malley, L. S. S. 1911. *Bengal District Gazetteers: Purnea*. Calcutta: Bengal Secretariat Press.

O'Malley, L. S. S., and M. Chakravarty. 1909. *Bengal District Gazetteers: Howrah*. Kolkata: Bengal Secretariat Book Depot.

Pal, B. K. 2010. *Barishal Theke Dandakaranya: Purbabanger Krishijibi Udbastur Punorbason Itihas*. Kolklata: Granthamitra.

Pal, N. M. 1929. *Some Social and Economic Aspects of the Land Systems of Bengal*. Calcutta: Book Company.

Panandikar, S. G. 1926. *Wealth and Welfare of the Bengal Delta*. Calcutta: Calcutta University.

Parker, P. A. M. 1949. *The Control of Water: As Applied to Irrigation, Power and Town Water Supply Purposes*. London: Routledge & Kegan Paul.

Paterson, J. C. K. 1910. *Bengal District Gazetteers: Burdwan*. Kolkata: Bengal Secretariat Book Depot.

Pathak, C. R. 1981. "Development in the Damodar Valley Region, India," *Habitat International*, 5(5/6): 617–635.

Pathania, J. 2003. "Illegal Migration of Bangladeshis in India," Paper No. 632. South Asia Analysis Group. Available online at http://www.southasiaanalysis.org/%5Cpapers7%5Cpaper632.html (accessed on November 30, 2010).

Pearson, H. W. (ed.). 1977. *The Livelihood of Man: Karl Polanyi*. New York: Academic Press.

Philips, A. 1876. *The Law Relating to Land Tenure of Lower Bengal*, Tagore Law Lectures, 1874–1875. Calcutta: Thacker, Spink.

Pielke, R. A. J. 1998. "Rethinking the Role of Adaptation in Climate Policy," *Global Environmental Change*, 8: 159–179.

Porter, M. E. 1990. *The Competitive Advantage of Nations*. London: Macmillan.

Postel, S., and B. Richter. 2003. *Rivers for Life: Managing Waters for People and Nature*. Washington, DC: Island Press.

Potter, P. E. 1978. "Significance and Origin of Big Rivers," *Journal of Geology*, 86: 13–33.

Prescott, J. R. V. 1987. *Political Frontiers and Boundaries*. London: Allen and Unwin.

Quayle, M., and T. D. van der Lieck. 1997. "Growing Community: A Case for Hybrid Landscapes," *Landscape and Urban Planning*, 39: 99–107.

Quisumbing, A. R., L. Haddad, and C. Pena. 1995. "Gender and Poverty: New Evidence from 10 Developing Countries," Discussion Paper No. 9. Washington, DC: International Food Policy Research Institute Food Consumption and Nutrition Division.

———. 2001. "Are Women Overrepresented among the Poor? An Analysis of Poverty in Ten Developing Countries," *Journal of Development Economics*, 66(1): 225–269.

Qvistrom, M. 2007. "Landscapes Out of Order: Studying the Inner Urban Fringe beyond the Rural-urban Divide," *Geografiska Annaler*, Series B, *Human Geography*, 89(3): 269–82.

Rahman, Md. M., and W. van Schendel. 2003. "'I Am Not a Refugee': Rethinking Partition Migration," *Modern Asian Studies*, 37(3): 551–584.

Ramachandran, S. 2003. "Operation Pushback: Sangh Parivar, State, Alums and Surreptitious Bangladeshis in New Delhi," *Economic and Political Weekly*, 38(7), February 15: 75–78.

———. 2005. "Indifference, Impotence and Intolerance: Transnational Bangladeshis in India," Global Migration Perspectives, No. 42. Geneva: Global Commission on International Migration.

Rao, C. H. H. 1994. *Agricultural Growth, Rural Poverty and Environmental Degradation in India*. New Delhi: Oxford University Press.

Ratzel, F. 1882. *Anthropogeography, or Outline of the Influences of Geographical Environment upon History*. Stuttgart: J. Engelhorn.

Rawal, V. 2001a. "Agrarian Reform and Land Markets: A Study of Land Transactions in Two Villages of West Bengal, 1977–1995," *Economic Development and Cultural Change*, 49(3): 611–629.

———. 2001b. "Expansion of Irrigation in West Bengal: Mid-1970s to Mid-1990s," *Economic and Political Weekly*, 36(42): 4017–4024.

Rawal, V., and M. Swaminathan. 1998. "Changing Trajectories: Agricultural Growth in West Bengal," *Economic and Political Weekly*, 33(40): 2595–2602.

Ray, M. 2009. "Illegal Migration and Undeclared Refugees—Idea of West Bengal at Stake," Paper presented at the "National Seminar on Migration and Its Impact on Indian State and Democracy," Department of Politics and Public Administration, University of Pune, Pune, March 13.

Rensburg, B. J. V., P. Koleff, K. Gaston, and S. L. Chown. 2004. "Spatial Congruence of Ecological Transition at the Regional Scale in South Africa," *Journal of Biogeography*, 31: 843–854.

Rigg, J. 2007. *An Everyday Geography of the Global South*. London and New York: Routledge.

Robinson, V. 2003. "An Evidence Base for Future Policy: Reviewing UK Resettlement Policy," in V. Gelsthorpe and L. Herlitz (eds.), *Listening to the Evidence: The Future of UK Resettlement*. London: Home Office RDS Conference Proceedings, pp. 111–138.

Roche, M. 2005. "Rural Geography: A Borderland Revisited," *Progress in Human Geography*, 29(3): 299–303.

Rogers, B. 1995. "Alternative Headships of Female Headship in the Dominican Republic," *World Development*, 23(12): 2033–2039.

Rosenhouse, S. 1989. "Identifying the Poor: Is 'Headship' a Useful Concept?" Working Paper No. 58. Washington, DC: World Bank Living Standard Measurement Study.

Roy, D. 1988. *Teestaparer Britanta* [The story from across the Teesta river banks; in Bengali]. Calcutta: Dey's Publishing.

Roy, Tathagata. 2001. *My People Uprooted*. Kolkata: Ratna Prakashan.

Roy, Tirthankar. 2010. "Rethinking the Origins of British India: State Formation and Military-Fiscal Undertakings in an Eighteenth Century World Region," Working Paper No. 142/10. London: London School of Economics.

Rudra, K. 1996. "Problems of River Bank Erosion along the *Ganga* in Murshidabad District of West Bengal," *Journal of Geography and Environment*, 1: 25–32.

———. 2002. *The Encroaching Ganga and Social Conflicts: The Case of West Bengal, India*. Habra: Department of Geography, Habra S. C. Mahavidyalaya (College). Available online at www.ibaradio.org/India/ganga/resources/ Rudra.pdf (accessed on February 17, 2006).

———. 2004. *Ganga-Bhangan Katha* [The story of bank erosion of the Ganga]. Kolkata: Mrittika.

———. 2008. *Banglar Nadikatha* [The story of the rivers of Bengal]. Kolkata: Sahitya Sansad.

Ruud, A. E. 1994. "Land and Power: The Marxist Conquest of Rural Bengal," *Modern Asian Studies*, 28(2): 357–380.

———. 1999. "From Untouchable to Communist: Wealth, Power and Status among Supporters of the Communist Party (Marxist) in Rural West Bengal," in B. Rogaly, B. Harriss-White, and S. Bose (eds.), *Sonar Bangla? Agricultural Growth and Agrarian Change in West Bengal and Bangladesh*. New Delhi: Sage Publications, pp. 253–78.

———. 2003. *The Poetics of Village Politics: The Making of West Bengal's Rural Communism*. New Delhi: Oxford University Press.

Saarinen, T. F. 1966. "Perception of the Drought Hazard on the Great Plains," Research Paper No. 106. Chicago: Department of Geography, University of Chicago.

Saarinen, T. F., D. Seamon, and J. L. Sell (eds.). 1984. "Environmental Perception and Behavior: An Inventory and Prospect," Research Paper No. 209. Chicago: Department of Geography, University of Chicago.

Saberwal, V., and M. Rangarajan. 2003. *Battles over Nature: Sciences and the Politics of Conservation*. Delhi: Permanent Black.

Saha, M. 1938. "The Problem of Indian Rivers," Presidential Address to Annual Meeting of the National Institute of Sciences, India, *Proceedings of National Institute of Sciences*, 4(23). Reprinted in 1993 in the *Collected Works of Meghnad Saha*. Calcutta University Press: Calcutta.

Saha, M., and K. Ray. 1942. "Planning for the Damodar River," Reprinted in *Science and Culture M. N. Saha Commemoration Volume*, 59(7–10), 1993: 75–96.

Saha, M. K. 2008. *Rahr Banglar Duranta Nadi Damodar* [in Bengali]. Srirampore: Laser Art.

Sahay, G. R. 2004. "Hierarchy, Difference and the Caste System: A Study of Rural Bihar," *Contributions to Indian Sociology*, 38(1–2): 113–136.

Salway, S., S. Rahman, and S. Jesmin. 2003. "A Profile of Women's Work Participation among the Urban Poor of Dhaka," *World Development*, 31(5): 881–901.

Samad, S. 1998. "State of Minorities of Bangladesh: From Secular to Islamic Hegemony," Report on the *Regional Consultation on Minority Rights in South Asia*, South Asian Forum for Human Rights, Kathmandu, August 20–22.

———. 2004. *State of Minorities in Bangladesh: From Secular to Islamic Hegemony*. Available online at http://mukto-mona.net/Articles/saleem/secular_to_islamic.htm (accessed on September, 2012).

Samaddar, R. 1999. *The Marginal Nation: Transborder Migration from Bangladesh to West Bengal*. New Delhi: Vedam Books.

Samanta, G. 2002. "Rural-urban Interaction: A Case Study of Burdwan Town and Surrounding Rural Areas," PhD thesis. Burdwan: Department of Geography, The University of Burdwan.

Samanta, G., and K. Lahiri-Dutt. 2003. "Transport Network and Rural Development in Burdwan District, West Bengal," in B. C. Vaidya (ed.), *Geography of Transport Development in India*. New Delhi: Concept Publishing, pp. 423–431.

Sanyal, M. K., P. K. Biswas, and S. Bardhan. 1998. "Institutional Change and Output Growth in West Bengal Agriculture: End of Impasse," *Economic and Political Weekly*, 33(47/48): 1108–1117.

Sarker, M. H., I. Huque, and M. Alam. 2003. "Rivers, *Chars* and *Char* Dwellers of Bangladesh," *International Journal of River Basin Management*, 1(2): 61–80.

Saussier, G. 1998. *Living in the Fringe*. Paris: Figura Association.

Schjolden, A. 2003. "Are Vulnerability and Adaptability Two Sides of the Same Coin?" *IHDP Newsletter*, 4:12–14.

Scoones, I. 2009. "Livelihoods Perspectives and Rural Development," *Journal of Peasant Studies*, 36(1): 171–196.

Scott, J. 1998. *Seeing Like a State: How Certain Schemes to Improve the Human Condition Have Failed*. New Haven: Yale University Press.

———. 2009. *The Art of Not Being Governed: An Anarchist History of Upland Southeast Asia*. New Haven: Yale University Press.

Sen, A. 1990. "Co-operative Conflicts," in J. Tinker (ed.), *Persistent Inequalities*. Oxford and New York: Oxford University Press, pp. 123–149.

———. 2000. "Why Human Security?" Presentation at the International Symposium on Human Security, Tokyo, July 28.

Sengupta, D. N. 1951. *An Account of the River Problems of West Bengal*. Calcutta: General Printers and Publishers.

Shah, A. 1992. "Dynamics of Public Infrastructure, Industrial Productivity and Profitability," *Review of Economics and Statistics*, 74(1): 28–36.

Shahedullah, S. 1991. *Barddhaman Jelay Communist Andoloner Prasanga* [The context of communist movement in Burdwan]. Burdwan: Natun Chithi Publication.

Sherwill, W. S. 1858. *Report on the Rivers of Bengal and Papers of 1856, 1857, 1858 on the Damoodah Embankments etc.*, Selections from the Records of the Bengal Gov't's Selection No. 29. Calcutta: G. A. Savielle Printing and Publishing and India Office Library, IOR/V/23/97, No 29A 1858. Available online at http://www.nationalarchives.gov.uk/a2a/records.aspx?cat=059-iorv_7&cid=1-1-3-48#1-1-3-48 (accessed on July 13, 2011).

Shu, J., and L. Hawthorne. 1996. "Asian Student Migration to Australia," *International Migration*, 34(1): 65–95.

Siddiqui, T. 2001. *Transcending Boundaries: Labor Migration of Women from Bangladesh.* Dhaka: University Press.

———. 2003. "Migration as a Livelihood Strategy of the Poor: The Bangladesh Case," Paper presented at the "Conference on Migration, Development and Pro-Poor Policy Choices in Asia," Dhaka, June 22–24.

Simon, H. A. 1957. *Administrative Behaviour*, 2nd ed. New York: MacMillan.

Singh, D. P. 1998. "Female Migration in India," *Indian Journal of Social Work*, 59(3): 728–742.

Singh, I. B. 2007. "The Ganga River," in Avijit Gupta (ed.), *Large Rivers: Geomorphology and Management.* Chichester: John Wiley & Sons, pp. 347–372.

Skaria, A. 1999. *Hybrid Histories: Forests, Frontiers and Wilderness in Western India*, New Delhi: Oxford University Press.

Slovic, P. (ed.). 2000. *The Perception of Risk.* London: Earthscan.

———. (ed.). 2010. *The Feeling of Risk: New Perspectives on Risk Perception.* London: Earthscan.

Smit, B., and J. Wandel. 2006. "Adaptation, Adaptive Capacity and Vulnerability," *Global Environmental Change*, 16: 282–292.

Smit, K., C. B. Barrett, and P. W. Box. 2000. "Participatory Risk Mapping for Targeting Research and Assistance: With an Example from East African Pastoralists," *World Development*, 28: 1945–1959.

Smith, H. A. 2000. "Facing Environmental Security," *Journal of Military and Strategic Studies*, Winter 2000/Spring 2001, pp. 36–49.

Smith, J. B., S. Huq, S. Lenhart, L. J. Mata, I. Nemešová, and S. Toure, eds. 1996. *Vulnerability and Adaptation to Climate Change: Interim Results from the US Country Studies Program.* Norwell, MA: Environmental Science and Technology Library, Kluwer Academic Publishers.

Sonnenfeld, J. 1967. "Environmental Perception and Adaptation Levels in the Arctic," in D. Lowenthal (ed.), *Environmental Perception and Behavior.* Chicago: University of Chicago Press, pp. 42–59.

Stokes, E. 1959. *The English Utilitarians in India.* Oxford: Oxford University Press.

Sundari, S., and M. K. Rukmani. 1998. "Costs and Benefits of Female Labor Migration," *Indian Journal of Social Work*, 59(3): 766–790.

Swamy, A. V. 2011. "Land and Law in Colonial India," in D. Ma and L. van Zanden (eds.), *Law and Long-Term Economic Change: A Eurasian Perspective.* Stanford: Stanford University Press, pp. 138–157.

Swift, J. 1989. "Why Are Rural Poor Vulnerable to Famine?" *IDS Bulletin*, 20(2): 8–15.

Swyngedouw, E. 1999. "Modernity and Hybridity: Nature, Regeneracioneisma, and the Production of the Spanish Waterscapes: 1890–1930," *Annals of the Association of American Geographers*, 89: 443–465.

Talwar-Oldenburg, V. 2010. *Dowry Murder: Reinvestigating a Cultural Whodunnit.* New Delhi: Penguin.

Tandon, S. K., and R. Sinha. 2007. "Geology of Large River Systems," in Avijit Gupta (ed.), *Large Rivers: Geomorphology and Management.* Chichester: John Wiley & Sons, pp. 7–28.

Terrell, J. E., P. H. John, S. Barut, N. Cellinese, A. Curet, T. Denham, C. M. Kusimba, K. Latinis, R. Oka, J. Palka, K. O. Pope, P. R. Williams, H. Haines, and J. Staller. 2003. "Domesticated Landscapes: The Subsistence Ecology of Plant and Animal Domestication," *Journal of Archaeological Method and Theory*, 10(4): 323–368.

Thackeray, S. W. 1889. *The Land and the Community in Three Books*. New York: D. Appleton.

Thompson, J. 2007. "Modern Britain and the New Imperial History," *History Compass*, 5(2): 455–462.

Toulmin, C., K. Brock, G. Carswell, K. A. Toufique, and M. Greeley. 2000. "Diversification of Livelihoods: Evidence from Mali, Ethiopia and Bangladesh," Mimeograph. Sussex: IDS, University of Sussex.

Tuan, Yi-Fu. 1974. *Topophilia: A Study of Environmental Perceptions, Attitudes and Values*. Englewood Cliffs, NJ: Prentice Hall.

Turner, N. J., I. J. Davidson-Hunt, and M. O'Flaherty. 2003. "Living on the Edge: Ecological and Cultural Edges as Sources of Diversity for Social-ecological Resilience," *Human Ecology*, 31(3): 439–461.

Umitsu, M. 1993. "Late Quaternary Sedimentary Environments and Landforms in the Ganges Delta," *Sedimentary Geology*, 84: 1041–1047.

United Nations. 1996. *Food Security for All, Food Security for Rural Women*. Geneva: International Steering Committee on Economic Advancement of Rural Women.

United Nations Development Programme [UNDP]. 1995. *Human Development Report*. New York: Oxford University Press.

———. 2004. *Reducing Disaster Risk a Challenge for Development*. New York: Bureau for Crisis Prevention and Recovery.

Urdal, H. 2005. "People vs Malthus: Population Pressure, Environmental Degradation, and Armed Conflict Revisited," *Journal of Peace Research*, 42(4): 417–434.

Valdivia, C., and J. Gilles. 2001. "Gender and Resource Management: Households and Groups, Strategies and Transitions," *Agriculture and Human Values*, 18(1): 5–9.

van Schendel, W. 1991. *Three Deltas: Accumulation and Poverty in Rural Burma, Bengal and South India*, Indo-Dutch Studies on Development Alternatives, vol. 8. New Delhi: Sage Publications.

———. 2002. "Stateless in South Asia: The Making of the India-Bangladesh Enclaves," *Journal of Asian Studies*, 1: 115–147.

———. 2005. *The Bengal Borderland: Beyond State and Nation in South Asia*. London: Anthem Press.

van Schendel, W., and I. Abraham. 2005. *Illicit Flows and Criminal Things: States, Borders and Other Side of Globalisation*. Bloomington: Indiana University Press.

Vecchio, N., and K. C. Roy. 1998. Poverty, Female-headed Households, and Sustainable Economic Development. Westport: Greenwood.

Vickery, C. 1977. "The Time-poor: A New Look at Poverty," *Journal of Human Resources*, 12:27-48.

Webster, N. 1999. "Institutions, Actors and Strategies in West Bengal's Rural Development: A Study on Irrigation," in B. Rogaly, B. Harriss-White, and S. Bose (eds.), *Sonar Bangla? Agricultural Growth and Agrarian Change in West Bengal and Bangladesh*. New Delhi: Sage Publications, pp. 57–75.

Weir, J. K. 2009. *Murray River Country: Ecological Dialogues with Traditional Owners*. Canberra: Aboriginal Studies Press.

Whatmore, S. 2002. *Hybrid Geographies: Natures, Cultures, Spaces*. London: Sage Publications.

White, G. 1945. *Human Adjustments to Floods*. Chicago: University of Chicago Press.

Whitehead, A. 1984. "'I Am Hungry, Mum': The Politics of Domestic Budgeting," in K. Young, C. Wolkowitz, and R. McCullagh (eds.), *Of Marriage and the Market: Women's Subordination Internationally and Its Lessons*. London: Routledge, pp. 88–111.

———. 1990. "Food Crisis and Gender Conflict in the African Countryside," in H. Bernstein (ed.), *The Food Question*. New York: Monthly Review Press, and London: Earthscan, pp. 54–68.

Whitehead, J. 2010. "John Locke and the Governance of India's Landscape: The Category of Wasteland in Colonial Revenue and Forest Legislation," *Economic and Political Weekly*, 45(50): 83–93.

Willcocks, W. 1930. *Lectures on the Ancient System of Irrigation in Bengal and Its Application to Modern Problems*. Calcutta: University of Calcutta.

Williams, M. 2003. "Words, Images, Enemies: Securitization and International Politics," *International Studies Quarterly*, 47: 511–531.

Wisner, B. 2003. "Sustainable Suffering? Reflections on Development and Disaster Vulnerability in the Post-Johannesburg World," *Regional Development Dialogue*, 24(1): 135–148.

Wohl, E. 2011. *A World of Rivers: Environmental Change on Ten of the World's Great Rivers*. Chicago: University of Chicago Press.

World Bank. 2000. *World Development Report*. Washington, DC: World Bank.

———. 2001. *Engendering Development: Through Gender Equality in Rights, Resources, and Voice*. Oxford: Oxford University Press.

Worster, D. 1990. "Seeing beyond Culture," *Journal of American History*, 76: 1142–1147.

Yaro, J. A. 2002. "The Poor Peasant: One Label, Different Lives: The Dynamics of Rural Livelihood Strategies in the Gia-Kajelo Community, Northern Ghana," *Norwegian Journal of Geography*, 56: 10–20.

Yeoh, B. S. A., S. Huang, and J. Gonzalez. 1999. "Migrant Female Domestic Workers: Debating the Economic, Social and Political Impacts in Singapore," *International Migration Review*, 33: 114–136.

Zaman, M. Q. 1989. "The Social and Political Context of Adjustment to Riverbank Erosion Hazard and Population Resettlement in Bangladesh," *Human Organization*, 48(3): 196–205.

Zimmerer, K. S. 2000. "The Reworking of Conservation Geographies: Non-equilibrium Landscapes and Nature-Society Hybrids," *Annals of the Association of American Geographers*, 90(2): 356–369.

———. 2007. "Cultural Ecology (and Political Ecology) in the 'Environmental Borderlands': Exploring the Expanded Connectivities within Geography," *Progress in Human Geography*, 31(2): 227–244.

Zucker, P. 1961. "Ruins: An Aesthetic Hybrid," *Journal of Aesthetics and Art Criticism*, 20(2): 119–130.

Index